Who's Who in George Eliot

By the same author

WHO'S WHO IN SHAW

Who's Who
in George Eliot

PHYLLIS HARTNOLL

TAPLINGER PUBLISHING COMPANY
NEW YORK

First published in the United States in 1977 by
TAPLINGER PUBLISHING CO., INC.
New York, New York

Library of Congress Catalog Card Number: 76–39621
ISBN 0–8008–8273–3

Contents

Foreword   *page* vii

Who's Who   1

Animals   168

The Characters—Book by Book   172

Contents

Foreword

Ladies and gentlemen, in the blue corner—George Eliot.

Now, hands up all those who groaned. Well, not exactly groaned. George Eliot does not make you groan. But I confess that when I sit down confronted with a solid little book entitled *Who's Who in George Eliot* I do notice a peculiar kind of noise in my mind. It is a sort of inward cerebral groan, self-pitying, yet a little hopeful, extreme, yet suspicious—the noise one used to reserve, in one's regenerate days, for front-bench attendance in chapel, right under the red eye of the evangelist. If George Eliot—a serious woman, a sensitive novelist, excellent when she writes of what she has loved to the point of understanding—if George Eliot can inspire this sort of initial reaction in one reader, it is perhaps time to wonder what has gone wrong.

It seems to me that the surface merits of George Eliot's novels—excellently displayed in Phyllis Hartnoll's alphabet of her characters—are not what make them readable nowadays. Her contemporaries enjoyed her for her pathos, her exceptional sense of the purifying effect of human trials and tribulations. *Adam Bede*, though, to take just one example, can be read at levels deeper than its pleasant descriptions of rural scenery (and that of the Poysers' farm is especially well done), and deeper indeed than its study of the decay of Hetty Sorrel and the elevation of Adam through the person of the Methodist preacher Dinah Morris. There are scenes and moments in this novel, as in several other works by George Eliot, where we seem about to be given some tremendous revelation—such as that a human being may spend the whole of the first half of his or her life, or longer, in pursuit or enactment of a 'personality' which he or she then discovers is not really his or hers. . . . This makes the job of compiling brief guides to this novelist's 'characters' exceptionally tricky. But it seems to me that Phyllis Hartnoll has done an exceptionally tricky job exceptionally well.

Perhaps it is at those moments when the implications of that realisation of the limitations of 'character' or 'personality' begin to flood into the authorial consciousness that George Eliot's prose rises to its highest level. For such a sensible novelist, she deals in crises to an alarming and exciting degree. I am reminded of a sentence of Simone Weil's, which could stand as epigraph to any of George Eliot's major works:

Love is not consolation, it is light.

ROBERT NYE

A

ABBOTT, COUSIN: Mrs. Glegg's elderly unmarried cousin. She and her sisters are afraid he will die without making a will in their favour, and Mrs. Pullet is particularly worried in case he dies before she has had time to wear her new bonnet. *The Mill on the Floss*

ABEL: Mr. Bulstrode's bailiff at Stone Court, where he is particularly successful with the lambs. He accepts the unexpected arrival of Raffles with equanimity, thinking he must be a poor relation of Mr. Bulstrode's and that 'the master' is very good to bother with him. *Middlemarch*

ABEL, MRS.: Housekeeper at Stone Court. She helps her husband to nurse Raffles, sitting up with him at night. She is convinced brandy will do him good, and persuades Bulstrode to let her administer some, not knowing the doctor has forbidden it, whereupon Raffles dies. *Middlemarch*

ACCIAJOLI, DIANORA: The bride of young Albizzi. Romola's cousin attends the wedding, and considers it a shabby affair, as it is the first to be held under the influence of Savonarola, with no splendour, no feasting, no jewels, and long sermons. *Romola*

ADAM, MRS.: Landlady of the lodgings which Mrs. Meyrick prepares for Mirah and her brother. *Daniel Deronda*

ALBANI, MAESTRO: Lady Cheverel's singing-master in Milan. He recommends Sarti to her as a music-copyist, which leads to her adoption of Sarti's daughter Caterina. *Scenes of Clerical Life II: Mr. Gilfil's Love-Story*

ALCHARISI: *see* Halm-Eberstein, The Princess Leonora

ALEXANDER VI, POPE: The 'Borgia' Pope, father of Cesare and Lucrezia Borgia. His worldliness and profligacy caused him to be attacked by Savonarola, whom he excommunicated, and he was partly responsible for the invasion of Italy by Charles VIII of France. *Romola*

ALICE: Lucy Deane's maid. She goes with Lucy when she pays a secret visit to Maggie Tulliver after her disgrace. *The Mill on the Floss*

The Countess Czerlaski's maid, a handsome, self-assured young woman who eventually marries the Countess's half-brother Mr. Bridmain. *Scenes of Clerical Life I: The Rev. Amos Barton*

ALICK: Mr. Poyser's head shepherd, ruddy-faced, broad-shouldered, rather bad-tempered, but honest and hard-working. He seldom goes to church—'I gotten summat else to think on'—but honours Sunday with a clean smock-frock. *Adam Bede*

ALLEN, SISTER: A Methodist worker in Snowfield, whom Dinah Morris decides to go and help instead of staying with her Aunt Poyser. *Adam Bede*

ANGUS: A manservant who accompanies the Grandcourts on their Mediterranean yachting trip. They put in at Genoa for repairs, and Angus goes to hire the small sailing-vessel in which Grandcourt is drowned. *Daniel Deronda*

ANN: Mrs. Raynor's little maid-servant, aged twelve. *Scenes of Clerical Life III: Janet's Repentance*

ANTELLA, LAMBERTO DELL': One of Piero de' Medici's men, banished from Florence with his master. He is captured carrying secret despatches, which incriminate a number of outstanding Florentines, including Romola's godfather, Bernardo del Nero, in a plot to bring back the Medici to Florence. *Romola*

ANTONIO, LUCA: A relation by marriage of Monna Brigida, who invites her to the wedding of Dianora Acciajoli. *Romola*

ARMSTRONG, MR.: A wealthy client of the lawyer, Dempster, who engages him for a lawsuit which promises to be both exciting and lucrative. But Dempster, being drunk, handles the business badly, which annoys Armstrong, who does Dempster a lot of harm by his complaints. *Scenes of Clerical Life III: Janet's Repentance*

ARROWPOINT, CATHERINE: The only child and heiress of the wealthy owners of Quetcham Hall. Good-natured but not very good-looking, she realises that most of her suitors only want her money, and refuses them all. Being extremely musical, she is provided by her parents with a resident music-master, Herr Klesmer, a composer who is on the verge of being recognised as a genius. She falls in love with him, but because of his pride is practically forced to propose herself. Overcoming her parents' resistance, they marry and are extremely happy together. They are among the first patrons in London of Daniel Deronda's protegée Mirah Lapiroth. *Daniel Deronda*

ARROWPOINT, MR.: The son of one of Nelson's admirals. An ineffectual gentleman, he marries an heiress and allows her to do as she pleases. He is upset when his only child wishes to marry her music-master and threatens to disinherit her, but relents and attends her wedding. *Daniel Deronda*

ARROWPOINT, MRS.: The only child of a merchant named Cuttler, who left her a large fortune. Squat, with coarse features and a high, parrot-like voice, she is extremely eccentric and has leanings towards literature, which are ridiculed by Gwendolen Harleth. She hopes her daughter Catherine will marry Grandcourt so that her quarter of a million pounds' inheritance will 'fall into the right hands', and is outraged when Catherine becomes engaged to her German music-master. But she is eventually reconciled to the marriage, particularly in view of the husband's growing reputation as a composer, and allows the newly-weds to spend their first Christmas at Quetcham Hall. *Daniel Deronda*

ASKERN, MR. The surgeon who is called in to attend to Tom Tulliver's foot after he has cut it with Poulter's sword. *The Mill on the Floss*

ASSHER, BEATRICE: The only child of Lady Assher, and the destined bride of Sir Christopher Cheverel's nephew and heir, Captain Wybrow. She comes to stay with the Cheverels, and is quietly condescending to the little Italian girl, Tina, who has been adopted by them, until she notices that Wybrow is paying rather too much attention to her. She is not re-assured by his denial of anything serious between them. After

Wybrow's death she blames Tina for causing, by her jealousy, the heart attack which killed him. *Scenes of Clerical Life II: Mr. Gilfil's Love-Story*

ASSHER, LADY: An elderly widow, with ill-defined features and heavy *embonpoint*. In her youth she was much admired by Sir Christopher Cheverel, and is delighted that his nephew should marry her daughter Beatrice. She is a great chatterbox, and goes 'dribbling on like a leaky shower-bath' until Sir Christopher decides it is better not to meet one's first love again after a lapse of forty years. *Scenes of Clerical Life II: Mr. Gilfil's Love-Story*

ASSHER, SIR JOHN: The father of Beatrice, a big man with a beaky nose, very particular about his shirts, but careless over the upkeep of his house and grounds, preferring to offer his friends good food and good wine and a game of whist every night. He died shortly before the Asshers' visit to Cheverel Manor, thus enabling his daughter to appear looking regal in deep mourning. *Scenes of Clerical Life II: Mr. Gilfil's Love-Story*

B

BACCIO: A young Florentine artist who helps to design the new Carnival decorations according to the ideas of Savonarola, much to the disgust of the old artist Piero di Cosimo. *Romola*

BACON, MISS: The miller's daughter, known as 'the beauty of Treddleston'; but she was not as lovely as Hetty Sorrel. *Adam Bede*

BAGSHAWE, THE REV. MR.: An elderly clergyman who had the misfortune to have as one of his curates a showy, talkative fellow called Sargent, who caused a small scandal through an indiscreet flirtation. *Scenes of Clerical Life I: The Rev. Amos Barton*

BAGSTER: A candidate in the Middlemarch elections. In the opinion of the town clerk Hawley he comes 'from heaven knows where, but [is] dead against ministers and an experienced Parliamentary man.' He withdraws after the failure of Brooke's electioneering speech. *Middlemarch*

BAIRD, THE REV. MR.: A cross-eyed clergyman who 'in later life gained considerable celebrity in London as an original writer and lecturer;' but in Amos Barton's time he used to preach in a little church something like a barn, with three rich farmers and their servants, fifteen labourers, and a due proportion of women and children as congregation. *Scenes of Clerical Life I: The Rev. Amos Barton*

BAKER, WILL: Father of the boy who goes to the house of the schoolmaster Bartle Massey every morning, and helps him clean up; Bartle won't have a woman near him. Massey is sure Will Baker's hulking bull-terrier is the father of his bitch Vixen's puppies. *Adam Bede*

BALE, KESTER: One of Mr. Poyser's farmhands. He could turn his hand to everything and do it well, but his special job was making beehive ricks. On Sunday mornings he would put on his best clothes and walk round the rickyards, admiring his own handiwork. *Adam Bede*

BALLARD, MRS.: The proprietress of an excellent girls' school in Middlemarch. *Middlemarch*

BAMBRIDGE, MR.: A large, red-faced, blasphemous, and immoral horse-dealer, who is acceptable to his fellow-citizens in pubs but not in drawing-rooms. Fred Vincy owes him a lot of money, and finds it difficult to pay his debts. When Bambridge is at a distant horse-fair he meets Raffles in the last stages of D.T.s, and is told all the scandal about Bulstrode. On his return home he repeats it, and it is soon known all over the town. *Middlemarch*

BANKS, MR.: Sir Hugo Mallinger's bailiff. *Daniel Deronda*

Transome's bailiff, who has taken advantage of the general mismanagement of the estate to feather his own nest. *Felix Holt*

BARDI, BARDO DE': The seventy-year-old father of Romola, of a great Florentine family, but now blind and very poor. He is a scholar and a recluse, living alone with his daughter since the departure of his much-loved son to join the Dominican order. Being himself anti-clerical, he thinks of this as a betrayal of his ideals. When the young Greek, Tito Melema, is brought to see him, he takes an immediate liking to him and thinks he will fill his son's place and help him with his book. He is glad when Romola and Tito fall in love and marry, and thinks that Tito, being in high favour with the Medici, will further his dearest wish, which is to see his library and collection of antiques preserved in Florence as the Bardi Library, and not dispersed among other collections, or given to one of the monastic foundations. The fall of the Medici puts an end to this project, and Bardi dies shortly after, not knowing that Tito will sell his library to the French invaders. *Romola*

BARDI, DINO DE': *see* Luca, Fra

BARDI, ROMOLA DE': The daughter of the old blind scholar Bardo de' Bardi, who has been educated to assist her father in his classical researches. Tall, fair-haired, with beautiful features, she lives shut away from the world, and her one aim is to marry a classical scholar who can take her brother's place and be more helpful to her father than she can. When Tito Melema becomes her father's secretary, she is delighted, and soon finds herself in love with him. He seems to her ardent nature all that is most worthy to be loved—handsome, kind, honourable, and deeply affectionate. But her godfather, Bernardo del Nero, who does not like or trust Tito, insists that the young couple shall wait a year before they are married. In the meantime Romola, who, like her father, considers her brother has deserted his family in becoming a monk, hears that he is dying, and goes to visit him. At his bedside she meets Savonarola, whom she has previously despised as a purveyor of monkish superstition and who is destined to have such an influence on her life in spite of the anti-clerical bias implanted in her by her father. Her brother reveals that he has had a terrifying vision of Romola's unhappiness in marriage, and begs her to remain single. After his death, Savonarola gives her the dead monk's crucifix, and she begins to feel the power of his personality. But she marries Tito, and for some time is blissfully happy. As a wedding gift Tito has given her a painted chest in which he locks away the crucifix, and with it, he says, all the misery her brother has caused her. But Tito causes her far more misery when, shortly after her father's death, he sells his library and all its contents to the French. She decides to leave him, and sets out on a journey to Rome, but is turned back by Savonarola, who convinces her that her place is with her husband during the time of trial which Florence is about to undergo. When famine and pestilence break out, Romola works untiringly among the sufferers, and among those she succours is Tito's adoptive father, Baldassarre Calvo, whom he has refused to recognise. Baldassarre eventually reveals to her his identity and Tito's betrayal of him, and he also tells her of the existence of Tito's mistress Tessa, and their two children. When in addition to all this Romola realises that Tito has betrayed the Medici conspirators, including her godfather, whom she sees executed in the public square, she loses the faith which Savonarola had inspired in her and decides once again to leave her hateful husband. She flees from Florence by night, reaches the coast, and buys a small boat in which she drifts away, waking to find herself near a village decimated by plague. When she has done all she can for the survivors, she returns to Florence, and hearing Tito is dead, she collects Tessa and the children and goes to live with them in the house of her elderly cousin Monna Brigida. She watches Savonarola's trial and execution from an upper window, and realises his greatness while deploring his human weaknesses. But out of gratitude for his help when she was in trouble she keeps a portrait of him in her house and hangs wreaths on it every year on the anniversary of his death. *Romola*

BARNES, JOHN: A Methodist preacher whom Seth Bede goes to see, remaining so long in argument with him about 'the state of perfection' that he is late home and is plaintively reproached by his widowed mother. *Adam Bede*

BARONE, SER FRANCESCO DI SER: *see* Ceccone, Ser

BARTOLOMMEO, FRA: A young Florentine painter—Buccio della Porta—who, inspired by Savonarola, painted a Christ Child on the wall of the monk's cell, and later became a Dominican monk. He then burned all his early work, but in later life took to painting again and executed a fine portrait of Savonarola. He was a pupil, with Piero di Cosimo, of the great artist Rosselli. *Romola*

BARTON, THE REV. AMOS: Curate of Shepperton Church, at a stipend of £80 a year on which to support a wife and six children. He is not very popular with his parishioners, who look on him as 'a confounded methodistical meddlesome chap' because of the reforms he tries to introduce. They think he would have done better to become a cabinet-maker like his father. Well-meaning and zealous, he is nevertheless dim and ineffectual, 'a good man in the wrong place.' Being very susceptible to flattery, he is completely hoodwinked by the Countess Czerlaski, and allows her to lodge in his house after her brother's marriage. This leads to scandal in the village, in spite of his obvious innocence. It also precipitates the decline in health of his overworked wife, who dies in childbirth. This disaster is followed by another when Mr. Carpe, the vicar, glad of the excuse given him by village gossip, dismisses Barton from his curacy in order to occupy it himself for a time before turning it over to his brother-in-law. *Scenes of Clerical Life I: The Rev. Amos Barton*

BARTON, CHUBBY, PATTY, AND SOPHY: The three daughters of Amos Barton, Patty, the eldest, is nine when her mother dies, a grave silent child who never marries, but remains with her father until his death. Sophy and Chubby, the latter her father's favourite, both marry. *Scenes of Clerical Life I: The Rev. Amos Barton*

BARTON, DICKEY, FRED, AND WALTER: The three sons of Amos Barton. Fred, the eldest, a rather dull child, becomes a bank clerk; Dickey—really Richard—a shy, stocky little chap who adores his pretty mamma, is made a great pet of by Mrs. Hackit, a local farmer's wife, and grows up to be six feet tall, with 'a broad chest, spectacles, masses of shaggy brown hair, red cheeks, and bright blue eyes.' He becomes a successful engineer; Walter, the year-old baby, eventually goes to sea. *Scenes of Clerical Life I: The Rev. Amos Barton*

BARTON, MRS. MILLY (AMELIA): The lovely, ladylike, hardworking wife of Amos Barton. Perpetually short of money, she spends her time making and mending, teaching her children, and pacifying angry tradesmen. For a time her aunt Miss Jackson lives with them and helps with the household expenses, but the maladroit Amos quarrels with her, and she leaves. When the Countess Czerlaski foists herself upon the Barton household, Milly accepts her quietly and works even harder so that the guest shall lack nothing. This imposes too great

8

.a strain on her, and when her seventh child is born prematurely and dies, she too dies at the age of 35. *Scenes of Clerical Life I: The Rev. Amos Barton*

BASS, TRAPPING: A poacher who has shot a gamekeeper. Mr. Brooke lets him off with a caution, much to the disgust of Sir James Chettam, who thinks he should have been dealt with severely. *Middlemarch*

BATES, MR.: Sir Christopher Cheverel's gardener, a sturdy Yorkshireman 'like a Bacchus in a blue apron', but though rubicund, very sober. He thinks his master mad to adopt an Italian child, but becomes very fond of 'Miss Tiny' as he calls her, while she calls him 'Uncle Bates' and knits him a blue-and-white striped muffler. He is with Sir Christopher when they find Wybrow's body in the Rookery, and after Tina disappears Bates gets ready to drag the lake, in the middle of which stands his cottage. He attends Tina's wedding to Mr. Gilfil, and thinks he could have provided much better flowers. *Scenes of Clerical Life II: Mr. Gilfil's Love-Story*

BATT & COWLEY: The lawyers who handle Bycliffe's case against the Durfey-Transomes. When he dies they drop it, but take it up again when told by Johnson of Esther Lyon's claim to the Transome estate, and win it. *Felix Holt*

BAZLEY: Lord Brackenshaw's agent, who handles the letting of all his property. *Daniel Deronda*

BEALE, MOLLY: A belligerent old virago, who indulges in a long-standing feud with her neighbour Dame Ricketts. *Scenes of Clerical Life III: Janet's Repentance*

BECK, MRS.: An elderly woman who lets lodgings. Her front parlour is occupied by the idle but agreeable Mr. Bowyer. *Middlemarch*

BECKY: Dorcas's servant after her marriage to Knott, the coachman. *Scenes of Clerical Life II: Mr. Gilfil's Love-Story*

BEDE, ADAM: A young carpenter in the employment of Jonathan Burge, who hopes he will marry his daughter Mary and take over the business. But Adam, who supports his drunken father and work-worn mother, with the help of his younger brother Seth, has no thoughts of marriage, though he is in love with Mrs. Poyser's niece Hetty Sorrel. Tall, with jet-black hair and an expression of good-humoured intelligence, Adam is well thought of by everyone, and has been brought up on terms of close friendship with Arthur Donnithorne, grandson and heir of the local landowner. When he discovers that Arthur and Hetty are lovers, he knocks Arthur down and then insists on his writing a letter to Hetty, saying they must not meet again, as marriage between them is impossible. In despair Hetty turns to Adam, whose father has recently died, and agrees to marry him, but runs away before the wedding day. Adam intends to go in search of her, but is stopped by Mr. Irwine, a local clergyman who has befriended him, and told that she is to be tried for the murder of her newborn baby. Believing her innocent, Adam takes a lodging near the prison to await the outcome, in company with Bartle Massey, the village schoolmaster. After Hetty has been persuaded by her cousin Dinah Morris to confess her crime, Adam has a final interview with her on the morning she is to be hanged, which was to have been their wedding day. When he hears that her sentence has been changed from hanging to transportation, he returns home, and he and the Poysers make arrangements to leave the neighbourhood. But Arthur pleads so strongly with Adam for them to stay and look after the estate while he goes abroad that they agree. It is not long before Adam realises that he is in love with Dinah, and he eventually marries her, buying Burge's timberyard, and settling there with his mother, brother, wife and two young children, Adam and Lisbeth. *Adam Bede*

BEDE, LISBETH: The mother of Adam and Seth, 'an anxious, spare, yet vigorous old woman', fond of her sons but fretting them by constant querulous complaining. She dislikes Hetty Sorrel, and is upset when Adam gets engaged to her, refusing to live elsewhere with Seth and thus forcing Adam to enlarge the old cottage so as to hold them all. After Hetty's crime and conviction she becomes easier to live with and in spite of her aversion to Methodists gets very fond of Dinah Morris, who was a great help to her when her husband was drowned. She finally plucks up the courage to tell Adam that Dinah is in love with him and that he would do well to marry her, and when he does she attends the wedding with Seth, in a new gown and bonnet, leaving the church afterwards on the arm of the village schoolmaster Bartle Massey. She has nothing left to complain of, and lives happily with her children and grandchildren in Burge's old house, which Adam buys, together with the timberyard. *Adam Bede*

BEDE, SETH: The younger brother of Adam Bede, who is also a carpenter working for Jonathan Burge. A gentler, less intelligent, but more thoughtful man than his brother, he has become a Methodist, and is in love with Mrs. Poyser's niece, Dinah Morris, also a Methodist, and a woman preacher. She refuses to marry him, on the grounds that her religious vocation impels her to remain single, but she later marries Adam. Seth accepts the situation with resignation, and remains a bachelor, becoming a kind uncle to Adam's children. *Adam Bede*

BEDE, THIAS (MATTHIAS): The father of Adam and Seth, a handsome man, and a good carpenter, younger than his wife Lisbeth. He trains his sons well in his own trade, but in later life takes to drink and causes them a great deal of trouble. He has promised to make a coffin for Bob Tholer, but although Adam puts everything ready for him before going to work in the morning, Thias forgets all about it, and makes for a pub, The Waggon Overthrown. On his way home late at night he is too drunk to keep his footing on the narrow plank-bridge over the Willow brook near his cottage, and is found drowned by his two sons, who are out looking for him. *Adam Bede*

BEEVOR, MRS.: A friend of the Dowager Lady Chettam, who upset her friends and family by marrying again less than a year after her first husband died. She was severely punished, however, as Captain Beevor 'dragged her about by the hair and held up loaded pistols at her.' *Middlemarch*

BELLAMY, MR. AND MRS.: Sir Christopher Cheverel's butler and housekeeper, the latter a 'natty little person, in snowy cap and apron'. *Scenes of Clerical Life II: Mr. Gilfil's Love-Story*

BEN: A worker at Dorlcote Mill who is threatened with dismissal when Tulliver goes bankrupt. *The Mill on the Floss*

BENEDETTO: The Jewish baby, sole survivor of three families dead of the plague, who is rescued by Romola. She has him christened and arranges for him to be cared for by one of the village women she has nursed back to health. *Romola*

BENEVIENI, GIROLAMO: A young Florentine poet who is a fervent admirer of Savonarola. *Romola*

BERTA, MONNA: A Florentine widow who comes under the influence of Savonarola and reproaches Romola's cousin Monna Brigida for her fine clothes, jewels, and false hair. *Romola*

BEST, MRS.: The housekeeper at Donnithorne Chase, at daggers drawn with the lady's maid, Mrs. Pomfret. *Adam Bede*

BETHELL: One of the outdoor servants at Donnithorne Chase, who would have been sent by the Squire to pick up a weekly supply of dairy products if Mrs. Poyser had agreed to supply the household with them; but she refuses, saying she doesn't choose to have 'gentlefolks' servants' corrupting her dairy-maids. *Adam Bede*

BETTY: Dairymaid at Mrs. Poyser's. *Adam Bede*

Mrs. Patten's dairymaid, who is suspected of being sly, and frying the best bacon for the shepherd's dinner. *Scenes of Clerical Life I: The Rev. Amos Barton*

Janet Dempster's cook, who is very fond of warm beer, and sympathizes with her mistress's drinking under stress. Old Mrs. Dempster has very little faith in her abilities, and when she is first engaged is annoyed because Janet goes out and leaves Betty to prepare the dinner 'to which gentlemen are coming'. *Scenes of Clerical Life III: Janet's Repentance*

BINCOME: A neighbour of Mr. Tulliver's, who objects when Bincome sells his farm and land to a newcomer, Pivart, who takes measures for irrigation which Tulliver thinks will affect his water-power. *The Mill on the Floss*

BLARNEY, LORD: A friend of the Countess Czerlaski's, to whom she promises to write asking him to offer the next vacant living in his gift to poor Amos Barton. But she has no intention of doing so. *Scenes of Clerical Life I: The Rev. Amos Barton*

BLICK, DR.: The medical practitioner to whom Dr. Kimble's patients will probably go when Kimble dies, as he has no son to succeed him, and they will be unwilling to entrust themselves to a newcomer. *Silas Marner*

BLOUGH, LORD: A nobleman in the north of England who has recently had a model kitchen installed in his country seat. Mr. Vandernoodt has unfortunately seen it, and bores everyone at the Abbey by describing it in detail. *Daniel Deronda*

BODKIN, BROTHER: A chapel-goer who works at Pendrell's bank. Although a valuable and hard-working employee, he is dismissed after Pendrell's decision, in the face of the rising tide of Dissent, to employ only Churchmen. *Felix Holt*

BOND, MISS: A thin and somewhat acidulated spinster, who deplores Amos Barton's addiction to 'the things of the flesh' as exemplified by supper with a parishioner and a glass, or even two, of brandy-and-water. *Scenes of Clerical Life 1: The Rev. Amos Barton*

BOND, MR.: Churchwarden at Shepperton, with Mr. Hackit. They both deplore Mr. Barton's plans for rebuilding the church, and his habit of meddling with business, which, in common with all parsons, he does not understand. *Scenes of Clerical Life I: The Rev. Amos Barton*

BOND, MRS.: Wife of the Shepperton churchwarden. She is very kind to Milly Barton when she is ill, and takes the older children home with her. She is especially fond of Dickey, the second boy. *Scenes of Clerical Life I: The Rev. Amos Barton*

BOND, TOMMY: A small boy in Shepperton who has just graduated from petticoats to corduroy trousers, and is therefore emboldened to stop Mr. Gilfil from stepping on his spinning top. This delights the vicar, who nicknames the boy 'little Corduroys' and keeps him supplied with sugar-plums. *Scenes of Clerical Life II: Mr Gilfil's Love-Story*

BONI: Owner of the druggist's shop in which Monna Brigida tries to take refuge during the Carnival while Romola is rescuing Tessa from the somewhat over-zealous followers of Savonarola, intent on stripping her of her necklace. *Romola*

BONSI, DOMENICO: A learned doctor of law and one of the four Florentine noblemen who sign the peace treaty with Charles VIII of France. *Romola*

BOWYER, MR.: An idle, middle-aged man who lodges in Mrs. Beck's front parlour. Fat and shabby, he has no visible means of subsistence, and is always hoping people will invite him to a meal, which he pays for by singing comic songs and doing conjuring tricks. He is suspected of being the ventriloquist who ruined Mr. Brooke's election speech. Mary Garth is afraid Fred Vincy may grow up to be like him. *Middlemarch*

BRACCIO, SER: A guest at Romola's betrothal party. *Romola*

BRACKENSHAW, LADY BEATRICE AND LADY MARIA: The well-brought-up daughters of Lord Brackenshaw, who are held up to Gwendolen Harleth as patterns of propriety. *Daniel Deronda*

BRACKENSHAW, LORD AND LADY: Neighbours of the Gascoignes. They are very good to Mrs. Gascoigne's widowed sister, Fanny Davilow, letting her have Offendene at a low rent, and inviting her and her eldest daughter Gwendolen Harleth to their parties. It is at the Archery Meeting at Brackenshaw Park that Gwendolen first meets her future husband Grandcourt, and after her marriage it is there that she first wears the Grandcourt diamonds which Lydia Glasher, Grandcourt's mistress, sent her on her wedding day. *Middlemarch*

BRADY: The saddler to whom Dawes took Dempster's trace to be mended. It was his dilatoriness that led indirectly to the accident in which Dempster met his death. *Scenes of Clerical Life III: Janet's Repentance*

BRAND, DR.: The medical practitioner who attends the Barton family, and is with the mother when she dies. *Scenes of Clerical Life I: The Rev. Amos Barton*

BRATTI: *see* Ferravecchi, Bratti

BRECON, YOUNG: A Cambridge man known to Sir Hugo Mallinger, 'a superior expensive kind of idiot. . .who got a Double First, and has been learning to knit braces ever since.' He cites him as a warning to Daniel not to overwork. *Daniel Deronda*

BRENDALL, HARRY: The young man who would have inherited Mrs. Arrowpoint's name and fortune if she had carried out her threat to disinherit her daughter Catherine on her marriage to Herr Klesmer. *Daniel Deronda*

BRENT: Sir Maximus Debarry's head gardener. *Felix Holt*

BRETTON, MRS.: An elderly lady who dies just when Rosamond Vincy is marrying Lydgate. Rosamond wants her house, and Lydgate takes it, though it is too big for them, and too expensive, the rent being £90 a year. *Middlemarch*

BREWITT: A blacksmith who thinks his trade the finest in the world, and complains to the Rev. Gascoigne that his apprentice has no mind to it—'and yet ... what would a young fellow have if he doesn't like the blacksmithing?' *Daniel Deronda*

BRICK, MRS.: A tough, wrinkled old woman, very partial to snuff, who is an inhabitant of Shepperton workhouse. *Scenes of Clerical Life I: The Rev. Amos Barton*

BRIDGET: The Irwines' maid-servant. *Adam Bede*

BRIDMAIN, EDMUND: A thick-set, not unattractive man, who 'by unimpeached integrity and industry had attained a partnership in a silk manufactory and retired in his forties with a moderate fortune'—£500 a year. He is half-brother to the Countess Czerlaski, and shares a house with her until he suddenly marries her lady's maid. *Scenes of Clerical Life I: The Rev. Amos Barton*

BRIGGS: The Chettams' coachman. *Middlemarch*

BRIGIDA, MONNA: A short, stout, black-eyed woman, nearing fifty, elaborately dressed and wearing a quantity of jewels. She has very little sympathy with the austerities preached by Savonarola, though she is at one moment frightened into discarding some of her false hair and fripperies. A first cousin of Romola's mother, she took care of Romola after her mother's death, and there is a deep and enduring affection between them. When Romola is widowed, she, with her husband's mistress Tessa and their two children, all take refuge in Monna Brigida's house and remain with her until her death. *Romola*

BRIMSTONE: A poacher turned brick-maker, who is converted to Methodism and goes to night-school so that he can learn to read the Bible. *Adam Bede*

BRINDLE, MIKE (MICHAEL BRINCEY): One of the miners at Sproxton whom Felix Holt hopes to educate a little, together with his small son. He is one of the witnesses at Felix's trial, and speaks up boldly in his favour. *Felix Holt*

BRINLEY, MRS.: The wife of a poor carpenter with whom Janet Dempster occasionally drinks tea, much to the scandal of her genteel friends. *Scenes of Clerical Life III: Janet's Repentance*

BRITTON, LUKE: The tenant of one of Squire Donnithorne's farms. He sits at the top of the tenants' table at the heir's coming-of-age party, and opens the tenants' ball with Kate Irwine, his wife dancing with Captain Donnithorne's friend, Mr. Gawaine. Britton's son wants to marry Poyser's niece Hetty Sorrel, but Poyser discourages his advances because his father is such a poor farmer—land foul, ditches not drained, stock poorly chosen, hedges badly kept—and he is afraid the son may turn out to be as bad. *Adam Bede*

BROOKE, ARTHUR: The bachelor uncle of Dorothea and Celia. 'Of acquiescent temper and miscellaneous opinions', he has a grasshopper mind, darting from one subject to another, but without any very firm views on anything. He dabbled in most things in his youth, and now 'collects documents'. He hopes his elder niece, Dorothea, will marry his neighbour Sir James Chettam, whose land marches with his, and so join the two estates together, and is very surprised when she gets engaged to the prematurely-old recluse and clergyman Casaubon. He is not very much in favour of the match, but sees no reason for opposing it, especially as he is very busy preparing to stand for Parliament with the help of Casaubon's cousin Will Ladislaw. His family and friends are against the idea of his entering politics, thinking he will not make a good showing as a candidate, and waspish Mrs. Cadwallader says she hopes he will stand as a Whig; then the Tory candidate will certainly be elected. But he goes on obstinately with his plans, buying a local newspaper, the *Pioneer*, to advance his cause, and making some much-needed repairs to his farms to counteract the prevalent—and correct—idea that he is a bad landlord. When Casaubon dies and leaves a will which indicates by its codicil that he believes Dorothea and Ladislaw intend to marry after his death, Brooke is furious, but refuses to send Ladislaw away, as that would seem to lend credence to the scandal. After he has failed, as anticipated, to make a good electioneering speech, he gives up politics in disgust and goes abroad. On his return he finds Dorothea determined to marry Ladislaw, in spite of her husband's will, and has to console himself with the fact that his younger niece Celia has married Sir James Chettam, and that their first child is called after him. *Middlemarch*

BROOKE, CELIA (KITTY): The younger sister of Dorothea. She is practical and even-tempered, and with a good deal of worldly wisdom and common sense tries to dissuade her sister from some of her more fanciful philanthropic schemes. She dislikes Mr. Casaubon, and is horrified when Dorothea agrees to marry him, declining an invitation to accompany her on her honeymoon. While this is taking place in Italy, Celia, much to everyone's satisfaction, marries her sister's former suitor, Sir James Chettam, and settles down to a happy and fruitful existence, marred only by a temporary estrangement from Dorothea after the latter's second marriage, to Ladislaw, and removal to London. The breach is healed when Dorothea is very ill following the birth of her first child and Celia insists on going to stay with her. *Middlemarch*

BROOKE, DOROTHEA (DODO): The beautiful, passionate, strong-minded, and highly intelligent orphan niece of Mr. Brooke, with whom she and her sister Celia make their home once they have completed their education abroad. She has vague but intense aspirations after a life of devotion to some great cause, and seems to have found her ideal in the dry, scholarly clergyman Edward Casaubon. He is writing an immense philosophical and religious tome, and she longs to help him, even going so far as to learn Latin, Greek, and Hebrew for the purpose. She sees nothing of his selfishness and cold-hearted nature, and against the advice of her family and friends, marries him in a state of passionate self-delusion. She has a rude awakening, and is dismayed when her husband leaves her alone all day on their honeymoon so that he can work in the Vatican Library. Lonely and disillusioned, realising already that her husband's erudition is only pedantry, and that his great work will never be written, she meets again his attractive young cousin Will Ladislaw, who falls in love with her. She is unaware of this, and is surprised when, on their return home, Casaubon refuses to allow the young man to come and stay with them. They have an argument about it—their first—and soon after Casaubon has a heart attack. Full of contrition, she tries again to help her husband in his work, and is dismayed when her uncle invites Ladislaw to stay with him, and makes him editor of the *Pioneer*. She is even more dismayed when she realises that Ladislaw's grandmother, who was Casaubon's sister, was disinherited by her father for marrying against his wishes, and that her husband has benefited considerably through it. She foolishly suggests to Casaubon that he should make Ladislaw an allowance and leave him half his estate. He refuses angrily, and makes a will disinheriting Dorothea if after his death she should marry Ladislaw. Shortly afterwards he dies and his will causes a scandal. Dorothea's distress over it is intensified when the mischief-making Mrs. Cadwallader tells her that Ladislaw is suspected of being in love with the wife of Mr. Lydgate, and she with him. Dorothea refuses to believe this, but when she visits the Lydgates' house unexpectedly and finds Will and Rosamond together in close proximity to each other, she thinks it must be true. After the revelation of Mr. Bulstrode's misdeeds, in which Lydgate is implicated, Dorothea goes to comfort his wife, who confesses to her that Ladislaw has no interest in her, and is in love with Dorothea herself. When Dorothea and Ladislaw next meet, all misunderstandings are swept away, and in spite of universal disapproval, they marry and move to London, where they have two children and lead useful and interesting lives. *Middlemarch*

BROOKS: An elderly under-gardener at Cheverel Manor, who has the reversion of the head gardener Bates's old muffler when Tina knits him a new one. *Scenes of Clerical Life II: Mr. Gilfil's Love-Story*

BRUMBY, DICK: A boyhood acquaintance of Bob Jakin's, whom Bob got tired of 'leathering' because it never had any effect. *The Mill on the Floss*

BRUMLEY: A litigant whose suit was lost by Lawyer Wakem, thus encouraging Mr. Tulliver to think that he will win his own suit against Wakem's client Pivart. *The Mill on the Floss*

BRYCE: A hunting man to whom Dunsey Cass sells his brother Godfrey's horse. Owing to Dunsey's bad horsemanship, it is killed in the hunting-field before its new owner has taken possession of it. *Silas Marner*

BUCHAN: A saddler who, being a Scot, much enjoys the philosophical discussions which take place at the Hand and Banner in Holborn, to which Daniel Deronda is taken by Mordecai. *Daniel Deronda*

BUCKS, MRS.: A lady with a cork leg, much admired by Bob Jakin for her astuteness in business matters. *The Mill on the Floss*

BUDD, MR.. A leatherworker with a small factory. In spite of his openly scandalous life, he is elected churchwarden, through Dempster's efforts, and becomes his ally in his unscrupulous fight against the reforms instituted by the Rev. Edgar Tryan, threatening to dismiss any of his employees if they attend Tryan's lectures. *Scenes of Clerical Life III: Janet's Repentance*

BUGLE: Fanny Davilow's lady's maid. *Daniel Deronda*

BULSTRODE, ELLEN AND KATE: Daughters of a Middlemarch banker, dull and rather pious young girls, very unlike their brilliant cousin Rosamond Vincy. When their father is disgraced they are sent away to boarding school. *Middlemarch*

BULSTRODE, MRS. (HARRIET): The wife of the Middlemarch banker Nicholas Bulstrode. Before her marriage she was a Vincy, belonging to an old and well-respected local family. A narrow-minded but kindly woman, she is a great help to her husband in his Church and philanthropic work, and deplores the worldly attitude of her sister-in-law and many of her friends. When her husband's past history becomes known and he is censured by his business associates, she realises there is something wrong, but cannot discover what it is, until her brother Walter tells her the whole story. After an initial period of revulsion against Bulstrode for his wrongdoing, her loyalty enables her to comfort and support him without reproaches and with dignity in shared disgrace. He was luckier than he deserved when he married her. *Middlemarch*

BULSTRODE, NICHOLAS: A complex and contradictory personality, a hypocrite who can deceive himself, firmly believing that when he does what best suits his own purposes he is doing the will of God. An orphan educated at a charity school, he is shrewd and intelligent, and makes his way in business through his own efforts. He attends chapel, and is regarded as an excellent preacher and leader in prayer. He thinks of becoming a missionary, but is tempted by an offer from a pawnbroker, Dunkirk, the richest man in the congregation, who offers to take him into his own business. He accepts and becomes Dunkirk's 'confidential accountant'. He soon discovers that the ostensible pawnbroker is really a high-class receiver of stolen goods, but consoles himself with the thought that money made in this questionable way can be used to save souls. After the death of Dunkirk, and of his only son, Bulstrode decides to marry his wealthy widow. But before she will agree, she wants to trace her only daughter Sarah, who ran away from home on discovering her father's occupation. With the help of a dissolute ruffian, John Raffles, Bulstrode traces her. She is married and has a young son, Will Ladislaw. Fearing her return will prevent his marriage, Bulstrode bribes Raffles to go to America, tells Mrs. Dunkirk her daughter is dead, and marries her. When she dies, he finds himself in possession of a sizeable fortune, with which he removes to Middlemarch and establishes a successful banking business. He becomes an outstanding Churchman, one of the leading citizens of the town, marries Harriet Vincy, endows a new hospital, and is generally considered a solid, prosperous, though unlikeable, citizen. After thirty years Raffles turns up again and blackmails him. He does all he can to escape, and thinks he has finally got clear when Raffles, who is in the last stages of D.T.s, meets a Middlemarch horse dealer at a distant fair, and tells him the whole story. It is soon known to all Bulstrode's acquaintances, and when Raffles dies at Stone Court, where Bulstrode has allowed him, ostensibly as a 'poor relation', to take refuge, the local gossips accuse Bulstrode of murder. His subsequent disgrace involves the local doctor, Lydgate, who had recently borrowed £1,000 from Bulstrode. This is interpreted as a bribe, and both families are forced to leave the town and settle elsewhere. *Middlemarch*

BULT, MR.: A politician of good family, who expects to receive a peerage, and needs money to keep it up. He comes to

Quetcham with the Arrowpoints' tacit approval, hoping to capture their daughter Catherine and her large fortune. Unfortunately he gets into an argument with Klesmer, and offends him by saying that he obviously has too much talent in argument to be 'merely a musician'. This precipitates an understanding between Catherine and Klesmer, and Bult loses the heiress. *Daniel Deronda*

BUNCH: A sheep-stealer who is to be hanged. Mr. Brooke, as a humane liberalist, goes to London to try and get him reprieved, but it proves impossible. *Middlemarch*

BUNNEY, MASTER: The old gardener at Lowick Manor *Middlemarch*

BURGE, JONATHAN: The employer of Adam and Seth Bede. He wants Adam to marry his daughter Mary and take over the business, but when he realises this is not feasible, he takes Adam into partnership and retires, leaving him in sole charge. *Adam Bede*

BURGE, MARY: A sallow-faced girl, with hair as lank as a hank of cotton. She is in love with Adam Bede, but realises she cannot compete with the lovely Hetty Sorrel. After Hetty's disgrace Mary allows herself to hope, but is again disappointed, and is content to act as bridesmaid at the wedding of Adam and Dinah Morris. *Adam Bede*

BUTTON, PEGGY: An elderly chapel-goer living at Sproxton, in whose cottage the Rev. Rufus Lyon holds a prayer meeting for the local miners every Wednesday evening, while on Saturdays Felix Holt tries, not very successfully, to educate them politically. *Felix Holt*

BUTTS, SALLY: A poor washerwoman who is befriended by the philanthropist Mr. Jerome because she has had to sell her mangle and cannot get work. *Scenes of Clerical Life III: Janet's Repentance*

BYCLIFFE, MAURICE CHRISTIAN: A young man who is heir to Transome Court, a large estate in the Midlands, if and when he can prove that the last descendant of the original owner has died. While serving in the Hanoverian army, he is taken prisoner by the French, and in spite of the opposition of her family, marries a French girl, Annette Ledru. Receiving further evidence in support of his claim to Transome Court, he decides to escape to England, and exchanges identities with a fellow prisoner, Henry Scaddon. Unknown to Bycliffe, Scaddon is wanted by the police for robbery and forgery, and through the machinations of the Transomes' lawyer, Matthew Jermyn, Bycliffe, who is unable to prove his identity once he arrives in England, is arrested as Scaddon, and dies in prison. *Felix Holt*

BYGATE, MR.: The Donnithornes' lawyer. *Adam Bede*

BYLES, LUKE: One of Dempster's cronies, who is collecting signatures against the Rev. Edgar Tryan's proposal to give evening lectures. He is only in favour of education for the lower orders if it is Church and not Chapel. After being insulted by Dempster, who is drunk, he prophesies correctly that if he goes on driving like a madman when he is in that state he will get pitched out of his two-wheeled gig and land on his head. *Scenes of Clerical Life III: Janet's Repentance*

C

CADWALLADER, MRS. ELINOR: The wife of the rector of Tipton, a bright-eyed, sharp-tongued, malicious lady, who makes amusingly sarcastic remarks about most of her neighbours, but is very kind to them when they are in trouble. Although of good family and quite well off, she dresses shabbily, drives a hard bargain with the farmers' wives over chickens and dairy produce, and pleads poverty as an excuse for not doing things that are distasteful to her. She is very fond of Mr. Brooke's two young nieces, and when Dorothea refuses to marry Sir James Chettam in favour of Mr. Casaubon, whom Mrs. Cadwallader dislikes intensely, she encourages a match between the rejected suitor and Dorothea's younger sister Celia. But her patience is sorely tried by Dorothea's second marriage to Will Ladislaw, and she tries to prevent it by repeating to Dorothea the gossip about Ladislaw's interest in Mr. Lydgate's wife. *Middlemarch*

CADWALLADER, THE REV. HUMPHREY: The rector of Tipton; an amiable gentleman, 'with full lips and a sweet smile; plain and rough in his exterior, but with that solid imperturbable ease and good-humour which is infectious'. Although he performs his clerical duties satisfactorily, he is really happier fishing, or working with a lathe in his workshop, or enjoying the company of his four little girls. Though conscious of being his well-born wife's social inferior, he nevertheless acts as a restraining influence on her, often forcing her to moderate or forgo her witty comments on those around her. *Middlemarch*

CALCONDILA, DEMETRIO: A learned Greek who settles in Florence and occupies the Chair of Greek at the university there. He helps in the education of Romola, and when he decides to move to Milan, Romola's husband Tito Melema is put forward as his successor. *Romola*

CALIBUT, MR.: A successful business man, praised by Mr. Nolan, who once worked with him in a City warehouse, as a good Tory because he encourages trade, and 'trade makes property . . . and property is Conservative'. *Felix Holt*

CALLUM: Caleb Garth's clerk. When Fred Vincy has to have a job in order to marry Mary Garth, it is agreed that Callum shall teach him the business and then be dismissed, Garth paying Fred £80 a year out of the saving thus effected. *Middlemarch*

CALVO, BALDASSARRE: A kind-hearted Italian who rescues the child Tito Melema from a life of poverty and brings him up as his own son, giving him an excellent education and taking him on extensive tours of Europe and the Near East. On a voyage to Venice the ship in which they are sailing is attacked by pirates. Tito escapes with his life and a hidden store of precious stones, together with an onyx ring given him by Baldassarre, but Baldassarre is sold into slavery in Turkey. He smuggles out a message to Tito, telling him to sell the jewels and come and ransom him, but when nothing happens he believes the message has gone astray. Turned adrift after a disabling illness, he is picked up by French troops and brought as a prisoner to Florence, where Tito, now a well-to-do and important person, sees him but refuses to recognize him, fearing to jeopardize his future. Baldassarre swears to be revenged, and secretly follows Tito everywhere, waiting for an opportunity of denouncing him. But he is hampered by the bodily and mental weakness resulting from his years as a slave. He discovers that Tito is married to Romola, and also has a mistress, Tessa, and while lodging in a barn belonging to the latter, attempts to knife Tito, who is wearing a coat of chain mail. Maddened by his failure, Baldassarre suddenly appears at a dinner, given by Bernardo Rucellai, where Tito is an important guest, but becomes confused and cannot tell a coherent story, or even prove his identity. Tito explains that he is a former servant of his late father, known as Jacopo di Nola, and that he harbours a grievance against Tito, who got him dismissed for theft. Rucellai thereupon sends him to prison, where he remains until the plague decimates Florence. Turned out to die he is rescued by Romola, and eventually tells her his story. She believes him, and he thinks she will help him to gain his revenge. To further his own cause, he tells her of the existence of Tessa and arranges a meeting between the two women. But horrified by Tito's treachery, Romola leaves Florence. Baldassarre is now penniless, but rather than resort to begging, he waits on the river bank in the hopes that scraps will be washed down. However, it is Tito, escaping from the rioters, who is cast up on the bank. In an access of fury Baldassarre strangles him and falls dead on his body. *Romola*

CAMBINI, ANDREA: A friend of Francesco Valori's, and a devoted follower of Savonarola. He is discussing the Medicean conspiracy with Fra Salvestro Maruffi when Romola comes to San Marco for her interview with Savonarola. *Romola*

CAPARRA, NICCOLO: A Florentine blacksmith, from whom Tito Melema, knowing that the vengeful Baldassarre may try to stab him, buys a fine coat of chain mail. *Romola*

CAPPONI, PIERO: A Florentine of good family, who is delighted when the Medici are driven out, and hopes this means better times for the city. In 1494 he stands firm for the liberties of Florence and forces Charles VIII of France to sign a reasonable peace treaty. Told of this by Tito Melema, who witnessed the incident, the crowds outside give him a great ovation. He is killed in a riot two years later and given a civic funeral. *Romola*

CARP, DR.: An eminent scholar who has mortally offended

Mr. Casaubon by writing an unfavourable review of one of his 'little pamphlets'. *Middlemarch*

CARPE, THE REV. MR.: The incumbent of Shepperton, who pays Amos Barton £80 out of the stipend of £115 to act as his resident curate. After hearing the gossip about Barton and the Countess Czerlaski he decides to dismiss Barton, which he does soon after the latter's wife Milly has died, and give the position to his brother-in-law. *Scenes of Clerical Life I: The Rev. Amos Barton*

CARR, MR.: An acquaintance of the hypochondriacal Mrs. Pullet, who 'lost the use of his limbs and was drawn about in a bath chair'. She is afraid her brother-in-law, Mr. Tulliver, after his stroke, will meet the same fate. *The Mill on the Floss*

CARROLL: The Irwines' butler. *Adam Bede*

CARTER, MRS.: Mr. Brooke's excellent cook. Mrs. Cadwallader sends her young cook to her to learn how to make pastry. *Middlemarch*

CASAUBON, DOROTHEA: *see* Brooke, Dorothea

CASAUBON, THE REV. EDWARD: A pedantic, dried-up stick of a clergyman, a bachelor of forty-five living alone at Lowick Manor. He is engaged on researches into comparative religions intended to form the basis of a 'Key to All Mythologies', but does not realise that most of his sources are already out of date, superseded by recent works, mainly in German. He meets and admires Dorothea Brooke, who thinks him a great philosopher and ardently desires to help him in his work. He decides that she would make a pleasant companion for his declining years, and marries her, only to make her desperately unhappy. Apart from despising her scholarly abilities—she learns Greek, Latin and Hebrew in order to assist in his work—he resents her independence of mind, and also becomes jealous of her friendship with his young cousin, Will Ladislaw, the grandson of his disinherited Aunt Julia. Before he dies of a heart attack about a year after his marriage, he adds a cruel codicil to his will leaving all his property away from Dorothea if she marries Ladislaw. He also tries unsuccessfully to make her promise that she will devote the rest of her life to finishing his *magnum opus*. *Middlemarch*

CASS, BOB: Squire Cass's youngest and favourite son. At the New Year's Eve ball he dances a very good hornpipe, and his father says the boy is just such a one as he was at that age. *Silas Marner*

CASS, DUNSTAN (DUNSEY): The second son of old Cass, an idle, profligate, and spiteful young fellow 'who seemed to enjoy his drink the more when other people went dry'. He blackmails his elder brother over the matter of his secret marriage, and has to be constantly bribed to keep quiet. Having killed his brother's fine hunter Wildfire, he walks home, but stops at Silas Marner's cottage on the edge of the quarry and steals his life's savings. When he fails to return home, no one connects him with the robbery, thinking he has run away, as he did once before, to escape the wrath of his father and family. Sixteen years later the quarry is drained, and his skeleton is found, with the money beside it. *Silas Marner*

CASS, GODFREY: The eldest son of Squire Cass, a good-natured but weak-willed young man who since his mother's death has fallen under the evil influence of his younger brother Dunsey. With much physical courage and great strength he unites moral cowardice and a natural irresolution which lead him into serious trouble. He is in love with Nancy Lammeter, but seduces a local prostitute called Molly Farren, and in a fit of remorse falls into a trap set by Dunsey and marries her, thus laying himself open to blackmail. When Silas Marner brings Eppie to the New Year's Eve ball, Godfrey recognises the baby as his, but does not acknowledge her, and hurries away to make sure that Silas was right in saying the mother is dead. Freed from this burden, he marries Nancy. But it is not until sixteen years later, when Dunsey's body is found, that he summons up the courage to confess to her that Eppie, who has been brought up by Silas, is his daughter. As they have no children they decide to ask Eppie to come and live with them, but she refuses, and all Godfrey can do for her is to pay for her wedding to Aaron Winthrop. *Silas Marner*

CASS, SQUIRE: The owner of a large property which he mismanages badly, and is always threatening to leave away from his unsatisfactory eldest son, Godfrey. A tall, stout man, with a hard glance but a slack and feeble mouth, he is of good family, but since his wife's death has become slovenly, and keeps his four sons at home in idleness. *Silas Marner*

CASSON, MR.: Landlord of the Donnithorne Arms, who appears to consist principally of two spheres, a sleek, ruddy head and a rotund body. He was formerly the Donnithornes' butler, and rather despises the village people, particularly Adam Bede, whom he thinks spoilt—'a little too lifted-up and peppery like'—by the notice taken of him by the Squire and Parson. *Adam Bede*

CECCA: A Florentine architect and engineer, who before the coming of Savonarola prepared very fine floats and effects for the Carnival processions. *Romola*

CECCO: A rough, ragged, Florentine workman, who is ready to snatch the bread Romola is carrying to the hospital, but nevertheless is kind-hearted enough to help her rescue and shelter old Baldassarre. *Romola*

CECCONE, SER (SER FRANCESCO DI SER BARONE): A bitter, ungrateful, scheming Florentine notary, who hates Tito Melema because he believes, not without cause, that Tito has taken his place and prevented him from getting work. Although an adherent of the Medici party, he betrays Tito to Dolfo Spini, thereby precipitating his death. Ceccone was employed to take down Savonarola's confessions under torture, and was later believed to have invented or falsified many of the recantations contained in the document. *Romola*

CEI, FRANCESCO: A sharp-tongued Florentine poet who resents his own incapacity and hates everyone, particularly Savonarola. He distrusts Tito Melema 'because he is always smiling', and helps to inflame Dolfo Spini against him. *Romola*

CENNINI, BERNARDO: The first man to set up a printing press in Florence. *Romola*

CENNINI, DOMENICO: A goldsmith and moneylender, elder son of the Cennini who was the first Florentine printer. Though not a follower of Savonarola, he believes in his integrity and thinks that if it came to a struggle with the Papacy, Florence would back him up. But he deplores the execution of Bernardo del Nero and his associates, which he thinks Savonarola could have prevented. *Romola*

CENNINI, PIETRO: The second son of the Florentine printer Bernardo Cennini, with whom he works. He is the scholar of the family and is glad to employ Tito Melema as a proofreader when he turns up penniless and in need of work. Like his elder brother, he thinks Savonarola sincere but misguided. *Romola*

CHAD'S BESS: *see* Cranage, Bessy

CHARISI, DANIEL: The grandfather of Daniel Deronda. A strict Jew, he believed in the resurgence of Israel as a nation, and after his marriage to an English Jewess of Portuguese descent named Morteira, he hoped for a son to carry on his work. But his only daughter had no sympathy with his ideals, and longed only to escape and become an opera singer. He forced her to marry her cousin Ephraim, in the hope that she would produce a grandson for him, but died before the child was born, leaving to his friend Joseph Kalonymos a chest full of precious manuscripts in trust for his descendants. *Daniel Deronda*

CHARISI, EPHRAIM: The father of Daniel Deronda. A gentle, affectionate man, he married his first cousin, Leonora, thus offering her a chance to escape from the tyranny of her father, and putting no obstacles in the way of her operatic career. He died when his son Daniel was about two years old, leaving him a large fortune in trust. *Daniel Deronda*

CHARLES VIII OF FRANCE: The son of Louis XI, he invades Italy, and is hailed by Savonarola as the heavenly avenger who is to cleanse Florence of her sins. He signs a treaty with the city, and then marches on through Italy and captures Naples, much to the annoyance of its Suzerain, Pope Alexander. *Romola*

CHERRY, MRS.: A young lady's maid employed at Treby Manor, who is having a flirtation with the butler, Scales. When they find Philip Debarry's man Christian asleep under a tree in the park one Sunday afternoon, Scales, who dislikes him, plays a silly practical joke on him, cutting off one of his coat-tails and throwing it into a thicket, not knowing that it contains the proofs of Esther Lyon's right to the Transome estates. When it is later established that the coat pocket also contained valuable papers belonging to Philip, Cherry urges Scales to confess 'for fear of the constables and hanging'. *Felix Holt*

CHESTER: A young gardener at Donnithorne Chase. *Adam Bede*

CHETTAM, LADY: A mild-mannered but obstinate dowager, rather slow in the uptake, who attributes her robust health to home-made bitters and constant medical attendance. When her only son Sir James seems likely to marry Dorothea Brooke, she protests gently, as she has no love for that very strong-minded and idealistic young lady, and does all she can to encourage his eventual marriage to Dorothea's younger sister Celia. *Middlemarch*

CHETTAM, SIR JAMES: A local landowner whose estates march with those of Mr. Brooke of Tipton. For this reason a marriage between him and one of Mr. Brooke's nieces seems highly desirable, and he eventually marries the younger, Celia, who makes him an excellent wife. But he was first in love with the elder, Dorothea, and had a shock when she preferred to marry Mr. Casaubon. As her brother-in-law he continues to take an interest in her welfare, and is very much against her second marriage to Will Ladislaw, partly because he does not like the man, but also, as Mr. Cadwallader points out to him, because he wants Dorothea to leave her property to his eldest son. After the marriage he will not let his wife have anything to do with her sister, until Celia insists on going up to London to see Dorothea after the birth of her first child. *Middlemarch*

CHEVEREL, LADY (HENRIETTA): The handsome, stately, accomplished wife of Sir Christopher Cheverel. She has a fine singing voice, and during a holiday in Italy engages as a music-copyist the ailing father of a small child, Caterina Sarti. When the father dies Lady Cheverel persuades her husband to let her bring the child back to England, where she becomes the pet of the whole household. *Scenes of Clerical Life II: Mr. Gilfil's Love-Story*

CHEVEREL, SIR CHRISTOPHER: A splendid old gentleman, owner of Cheverel Manor, whose heir is his nephew Captain Anthony Wybrow. A voyage in Italy with his wife fires him with enthusiasm for everything Italian, and he imports Italian workmen to turn his old manor-house into a marble palace with frescoed ceilings. He also agrees to give a home to a small Italian girl, Caterina Sarti, whom his wife has befriended. He becomes very fond of the 'little black-eyed monkey', and when she is eighteen plans to marry her to his ward, the Rev. Maynard Gilfil, who is acting as his chaplain while waiting for a living to fall vacant. At the same time he plans an alliance for his nephew with the daughter of one of his old friends. In ignorance of Caterina's passionate and jealous attachment to Wybrow, who has flirted outrageously with her, he thinks everything is progressing according to plan when he is shattered by the sudden death from heart failure of his young heir. In his distress he remembers his eldest sister, with whom he had quarrelled, and regretting that he had not shown her any sympathy when she lost one of her sons, he makes the surviving son his heir. He also realises for the first time that Caterina loved Wybrow, and he is thankful when she agrees to marry Gilfil. *Scenes of Clerical Life II: Mr. Gilfil's Love-Story*

CHICHELY, MR.: The Middlemarch coroner, a middle-aged bachelor, with an air of conscious superiority, who is highly respected for his skill in coursing, his main pastime. He greatly admires Rosamond Vincy, and thinks she should never have married Mr. Lydgate, whom he dislikes. But he is glad to be able to clear Lydgate of any suspicions in connection with the death of John Raffles. *Middlemarch*

CHOWNE, MR.: A dairy farmer who buys a shorthorn cow from Mr. Poyser, for no better reason than that his wife likes shorthorns. *Adam Bede*

CHOYCE: Mr. Poyser's neighbour, who wants some of the Poyser land for dairying. *Adam Bede*

CHRISTIAN, MAURICE (HENRY SCADDON): A plausible rogue, who by twenty-five has run through the money left him by his father. He then tries to defraud his creditors, and forges the signature of his uncle, who had intended to make him his heir. Sought by the police, he becomes a soldier and goes to France, where he is captured, but finds himself about to be repatriated in an exchange of prisoners. To avoid this, he changes identities with a friendly fellow-prisoner, Maurice Christian Bycliffe, who has urgent reasons for wanting to get to England, and receives from him a watch, a locket, and some papers, to be returned when next they meet. Bycliffe, arrested in England by mistake for Scaddon, dies in prison, and

Scaddon decides to start a new life as Maurice Christian, after he has been reported drowned in a bid for freedom. He becomes a courier, does well, and in due course turns up at Treby Manor as Philip Debarry's factotum. He sees Esther Lyon, notes her resemblance to Bycliffe, puts together odd items of gossip about her, and eventually realises that she is Bycliffe's daughter. A chance encounter with Jermyn's London attorney, Johnson, leads to the discovery that she is heiress to the Transomes' estate, and as a key witness Christian is able to help prove her claim. He is rewarded with £1,000 and disappears again to the Continent. *Felix Holt*

CHUBB, MR. (WILLIAM): The landlord of the Sugar Loaf, a public-house in Sproxton where the better sort of miners gather. 'He was thin and sallow, and never. . .the worse (or the better) for liquor.' He helps Johnson to trick the miners—who have no votes—into shouting for Transome instead of Garstin on election day, but is careful himself to vote for Garstin, from whom he rents his pub, appearing at the poll 'so festooned in blue rosettes that he looked (at a sufficient distance) like a very large gentianella.' *Felix Holt*

CIONI, SER: A Florentine notary, who is openly opposed to the Medici, and thinks the arrival of French troops will be good for the city, though he urges the Florentines to hold their own and stand up for their rights. *Romola*

CLEMENT, SIR JAMES: Liberal candidate for North Loamshire, dismissed by Jermyn as 'a poor baronet. . .who cannot be expected to be liberal in that wider sense which commands majorities.' He has no chance of being elected and retires before polling day. *Felix Holt*

CLEMMENS: The 'very respectable solicitor' in Brassing who drew up Peter Featherstone's last will. *Middlemarch*

CLEVES, THE REV. MARTIN: A rough-featured and unclerical-looking clergyman who is much loved by his parishioners because he preaches sermons that the wheelwright and the blacksmith can understand, comforts them in their troubles, and is yet a scholar and a gentleman. Among the local clergy he is the only one to disbelieve the scandal about Amos Barton and the Countess, saying that Amos is 'a right-minded man who has the knack of doing himself injustice by his manner.'

He conducts Milly Barton's funeral, collects £30 for the family, and sends it to Amos with a kind letter, adding £10 from his own scanty stipend. *Scenes of Clerical Life I: The Rev. Amos Barton*

CLIFF, MR.: A London tailor, mad about horses, who bought a house in Raveloe and built enormous stables there, settling down with the intention of making his only son into a country gentleman. But the boy died, and his father turned crazy, going out to the stables at midnight, shouting and cracking his whip. After his death his ghost was said to haunt the stables, and no one would go near them. *Silas Marner*

CLINTOCK, YOUNG: Son of an archdeacon, and a great lover of croquet. He begs Gwendolen Harleth, with whom he is in love, to play with him instead of joining in the archery at Lord Brackenshaw's, and should have danced a quadrille with her after dinner, but is called away by his father, thus leaving Gwendolen to be partnered by her future husband, Grandcourt. *Daniel Deronda*

CLINTUP, MR.: A diffident though distinguished nurseryman who causes a sensation at the Larchers' sale by buying a steel fender for six shillings on the grounds that the auctioneer had made a good joke about it which he looks forward to retelling. *Middlemarch*

COHEN, ADDY: The wife of the Jewish pawnbroker who Daniel Deronda thinks is Mirah's brother. Lively and unrefined, 'a sort of paroquet in a bright blue dress, with coral necklace and earrings, her hair set up in a huge bush', she is full of curiosity about the relations between Daniel and her lodger Mordecai. *Daniel Deronda*

COHEN, ADELAIDE REBEKAH: The daughter of Ezra Cohen, a black-eyed, black-haired beauty of about four years old, very proud of her gold earrings and her braided amber Sabbath frock. *Daniel Deronda*

COHEN, EUGENIE ESTHER: The Cohens' baby, named after the French Empress, whom the parents once saw at the Crystal Palace. *Daniel Deronda*

COHEN, EZRA: A young Jew who keeps a rather superior pawnshop-cum-jeweller's off Holborn. Daniel Deronda, who is trying to find the mother and brother of Mirah Lapidoth (originally Cohen), thinks Ezra may be her brother, and cultivates his acquaintance. In the process he becomes very fond of the whole family, and remains friendly with them even after Mirah's brother turns out to be their lodger, Mordecai. They attend Mirah's wedding to Daniel, at which Ezra makes an excellent and well-received speech. *Daniel Deronda*

COHEN, EZRA MORDECAI: *see* Mordecai

COHEN, JACOB ALEXANDER: The six-year-old son of Ezra, and a pupil of the scholarly Mordecai, who lodges with his parents. Mordecai hopes he may become a poet or philosopher, but he is only a sharp-witted youngster who is evidently a good business man in the making. *Daniel Deronda*

COHEN, MRS.: An elderly, good-natured Jewess who lives with her son and his family, and helps them with their pawnbroking and jewellery business. When Daniel Deronda learns she had a daughter who is never mentioned, he thinks she may be the mother of Mirah. *Daniel Deronda*

COHEN, SARA: The mother of Mordecai and Mirah. After years of unhappiness her husband disappeared, taking with him his young daughter, and the heart-broken mother, left dependent on her son, died four years later, still praying and hoping for her daughter's return. *Daniel Deronda*

COOK, PHIB: A washerwoman who left her washtub to join in the rioting over Tryan's lectures 'in soap-suds, a bonnet-poke, and general dampness'. *Scenes of Clerical Life III: Janet's Repentance*

COOPER, TIMOTHY: A wiry old farm-labourer, who lives alone in a remote cottage and keeps his life savings in an old stocking. He thinks everything, including the railways, is bad for the working man, but refuses to join in the attack on the railway surveyors. *Middlemarch*

CORSINI, LUCA: A Florentine scholar who is an enthusiastic follower of Savonarola. He prepares a Latin oration to greet Charles VIII of France on his arrival in Florence, but is prevented from delivering it by a heavy shower of rain. *Romola*

COSIMO, PIERO DI: A Florentine painter, who took his name from that of his master, Cosimo Rosselli. A strange, outlandish figure, with a short, trimmed beard, an old felt hat, and a threadbare mantle, he startles Tito Melema on their first meeting by asking him to pose as the traitor Sinon. He has divined the weakness and self-love behind the young Greek's handsome and attractive countenance. He is present when Tito repudiates his benefactor Baldassarre, and makes a drawing of the old man which helps in his identification when his dead body is brought back to Florence with Tito's. *Romola*

COULTER, ANN: A young woman who, according to village gossip, had an idiot child because she offended the local witch by refusing to wear one of her charms round her neck. *Silas Marner*

COX: Squire Cass's bailiff. He tells the Squire that his tenant Fowler has not paid his rent and must be turned out of his farm, not knowing that Fowler has paid the money to Godfrey Cass, who gave it to his brother Dunsey to stop him revealing the truth about Godfrey's secret marriage. *Silas Marner*

CRABBE, MR.: A gossipy glazier, who 'gathered much news and groped among it dimly'. He frequents the Tankard Inn, where he sets on foot the rumour that Bulstrode has somehow contrived the death of John Raffles, 'a gentleman so fresh and rosy, it was a wonder he should die so suddenly.' *Middlemarch*

CRACKENTHORP, THE REV. MR.: The rector of Raveloe, a merry-eyed, small-featured, grey-haired man with his chin propped by an ample many-creased white neckcloth. He tells Silas Marner that his money has been stolen because he thought too much of it and did not go to church—but at Christmas he gives him some pigs' pettitoes for a treat. His wife is a nervous little woman who fidgets all the time with her lace and ribbons, making subdued noises, very much like a guinea-pig that twitches its nose. *Silas Marner*

CRAGSTONE, LADY: An elderly acquaintance of Lady Mallinger's, who takes a dislike to her because she gambles and sets a bad example to young ladies like Gwendolen Harleth. *Daniel Deronda*

CRAIG, MR.: The Scottish head gardener at Donnithorne Chase.

He admires Hetty Sorrel and after careful consideration decides he would like to marry her. But neither Hetty nor her Aunt Poyser encourages his suit, for, as the latter says, he is like 'a cock as thinks the sun's rose on purpose to hear him crow'. *Adam Bede*

CRAKE, SIR JOHN: The local master of harriers, whom Tom Tulliver much admires. Tom is delighted to learn that though Sir John learned Latin as a boy, he has forgotten it, and resolves to do the same. *The Mill on the Floss*

CRAMP, MRS.: The Bartons' charwoman, who comes in intermittently and is a great help to Nanny. *Scenes of Clerical Life I: The Rev. Amos Barton*

CRANAGE, BEN (WIRY BEN): A carpenter, known as Wiry Ben, who works with Adam and Seth Bede at Burge's timberyard. During Captain Donnithorne's coming-of-age celebrations he imbibes a little too freely and decides to dance a hornpipe. *Adam Bede*

CRANAGE, BESSY: The daughter of Chad Cranage the blacksmith, a buxom wench known as Chad's Bess. Being naturally flighty, she sometimes wonders what pious young women like Dinah Morris get out of life; but she is sufficiently stirred by Dinah's preaching on the green to burst into tears and give up wearing the earrings she is so proud of. At the coming-of-age celebrations for Captain Donnithorne she wins a race, but is bitterly disappointed at receiving a length of dark material instead of the red cloak she coveted, and gives the stuff away to her cousin Mrs. Salt. She attends Dinah's wedding 'in her neatest cap and apron'. *Adam Bede*

CRANAGE, CHAD: The Hayslope blacksmith, who wears a leather apron and skull-cap. He is so afraid of being converted by Dinah that he hurries back from her sermon to his anvil: 'Folks mun ha' horse-shoes, praichin' or no praichin'; the devil canna lay hould o' me for that!' He always washes his face on Sunday, which makes his little granddaughter cry because she does not recognise him. *Adam Bede*

CRANCH, MRS. (MARTHA): The needy sister of Peter Featherstone, who thinks she has more right to his money than the Vincys or the Garths, so installs her son Tom in his kitchen when he is dying. But Peter refuses to see him, and although

35

Martha is a widow with six children, he leaves her nothing, but he says in his will that she is to go to his funeral—unusual for woman at that time. *Middlemarch*

CRANE: An outdoor servant whom Mrs. Davilow is glad to be able to keep on at Offendene after her daughter marries Grandcourt. *Daniel Deronda*

CREDI, LORENZO DI: A Florentine artist who helps to design the new-style Carnival decorations under the influence of Savonarola, much to the indignation of such older artists as Piero di Cosimo. *Romola*

CREWE, THE REV. MR.: The perpetual curate at Milby, an elderly man with a brown Brutus wig, who delivers inaudible sermons on Sundays, and on weekdays imparts the rudiments of Latin to three pupils at the Grammar School. He is admired by his congregation for having scraped together a good deal of money out of keeping a school for young gentlemen, and his stingy housekeeping is thought of as a jest, not a real defect. His wife, who is very deaf, often gives away half her own scanty meal to a poor parishioner, and is cross at having to entertain the Bishop, saying she would rather be feeding all the hungry old couples in Milby than going to such trouble and expense for people who eat too much every day of their lives. *Scenes of Clerical Life III: Janet's Repentance*

CRICHLEY, THE REV. MR.: An elderly clergyman who is occupying the living intended by Sir Christopher Cheverel for his ward and chaplain, Maynard Gilfil. *Scenes of Clerical Life II: Mr. Gilfil's Love-Story*

CRINITO, PIETRO: A Florentine poet and scholar who is censured by Savonarola's followers for wasting his few coins on extravagant trifles. *Romola*

CRISTOFORO, FRA: Monna Brigida's confessor. When she tells him that Savonarola's sermons have almost persuaded her to give up her jewels and cosmetics, he tells her Savonarola is doing the devil's work, and she must not listen to him again. *Romola*

CROMLECH, LORD: A local landowner who, Dunsey Cass tells his brother Godfrey, would like to buy his horse Wildfire for

£120; but this is only another of Dunsey's unnecessary lies. *Silas Marner*

CRONACA: A Florentine architect who becomes a follower of Savonarola. He knows Romola's brother, Fra Luca, who has brought Tito the letter from Baldassarre asking for a ransom. Tito, thinking that Fra Luca knows something of his betrayal of Baldassarre, is frightened when he hears through Cronaca that Fra Luca has returned to Florence to die and on his death-bed imparted a secret to his sister. *Romola*

CROOP: A shoemaker, 'more Celtic than Jew', who much enjoys the political and philosophical discussions at the Hand and Banner in Holborn. *Daniel Deronda*

CROW, MR.: High constable at Treby Magna during the election. Having been warned that there may be trouble, he swears in a number of special constables. After suspending the poll because of rioting, Crow, who is not popular, makes the mistake of telling the mob that the soldiers are on their way, and is pelted with potatoes and turnips. *Felix Holt*

CROWDER, MR.: One of Sir Maximus Debarry's tenants, 'respectable, though much in arrear as to his rent'. Being a good listener and rather slow in the uptake, he is a welcome visitor to the steward's room, and during a discussion there reveals that he is the only man present old enough to remember the action which Bycliffe brought against the Transomes. He also says that the petitioner's name was Scaddon, which gives a nasty jolt to the real Henry Scaddon, present as Maurice Christian, factotum to Philip Debarry. *Felix Holt*

CROWSE, MR.: A young curate who, according to Mary Garth, has only one-tenth of Fred Vincy's cleverness; but then Fred is ten times lazier, and she cannot bear to think of him becoming like Crowse, with his 'empty gentility', if he persists in taking orders. 'What right have such men to represent Christianity—as if it were an institution for getting up idiots genteelly.' *Middlemarch*

CUFF, JACOB: A well-known ornament of the pothouse, who is suspected of having struck the first blow in the riot at Treby Magna on election day; he certainly frightened poor Goffe so much that he voted for the wrong candidate. *Felix Holt*

CUSHAT, MR. AND MRS.: Friends of Grandcourt's, whom Lush has invited on his behalf to stay at Diplow, and has to get rid of in a hurry when Grandcourt goes on the Continent in search of Gwendolen. *Daniel Deronda*

CZERLASKI, THE COUNTESS (CAROLINE): An undeniably beautiful young widow who, though born Caroline Bridmain and by profession a governess, married a Polish refugee who gave dancing lessons in London, and comports herself in all respects like a true Countess. Unfortunately this costs money, and she has only £60 a year. She is looking out for a second husband, and meanwhile lives with her wealthy half-brother, Edward Bridmain. When he marries her lady's maid, she rushes out of the house and takes refuge with Milly Barton, whose husband Amos is so dazzled by her captivating ways, and so susceptible to her flattery, that he unwittingly causes a scandal in the parish. The Countess is too comfortable in her new lodgings to wish to move, but when the Bartons' faithful Nanny flares up in defence of her overworked mistress and tells the Countess some home truths, she sweeps out in a fury leaving a tragic situation behind her. *Scenes of Clerical Life I: The Rev. Amos Barton*

D

DACEY, LADY: The unfortunate wife of a local landowner who is engaged in a lawsuit which, say the gossips, 'is fretting poor Lady Dacey to death'—added to which her eldest son 'has lost thousands upon thousands to the Prince of Wales, and they say my lady is going to pawn her jewels to pay for him'. Hetty Sorrel hopes that when she is married to Captain Donnithorne she will have a long silk gown with a sweeping train and feathers in her hair, like Lady Dacey, whom she has seen going in to dinner at Donnithorne Chase. *Adam Bede*

DAGGE, JOEL: A blacksmith's son who is following the hunt on foot when Primrose falls and throws Rex Gascoigne, whose shoulder is dislocated. Joel is able to put it back, having learned the trick of so doing from a bone-setter. *Daniel Deronda*

DAGGE, SALLY: The blacksmith's little daughter, who has twice had the misfortune to dislocate her shoulder and had it put right by her brother Joel. *Daniel Deronda*

DAGLEY, MR.: One of Mr. Brooke's tenant-farmers, who complains bitterly that there isn't a good gate on his land, and that he and his family have to live in their back kitchen and leave the rest of the dilapidated farmhouse to the rats. He has just returned from market, wearing a ragged coat and breeches and his milking-hat — a very old beaver flattened in front— when Brooke comes to complain that young Jacob Dagley has been caught poaching. Having had more to drink than usual while listening to inflammatory electioneering speeches, Dagley plucks up the courage to tell his landlord just what he thinks of his cheeseparing ways, much to the despair of his wife, a poor downtrodden creature who cannot even go to church because she has no Sunday clothes. Luckily Mr. Brooke is about to stand for Parliament, and has already been designated a bad landlord by his opponents, so Dagley does not, as he might have done, lose his farm, but actually obtains some much-needed repairs. *Middlemarch*

DALTON: The coachman at Donnithorne Chase, one of whose horses kicks and lames Captain Donnithorne's mare Meg. *Adam Bede*

DANE, WILLIAM: The young Silas Marner's close friend, a self-complacent youth, with narrow slanting eyes and compressed lips. He contrives to steal some money and throw the blame on Silas, whose fiancée then breaks off their engagement so that she can marry the crafty William. *Silas Marner*

DARLEIGH, SQUIRE: A close friend of the Dodson family, to whose parties the future Mrs. Tulliver and her three sisters were always invited. *The Mill on the Floss*

DAVID: One of Poyser's farm hands, a thin man with a bad squint. *Adam Bede*

Mr. Gilfil's man, who with his wife Martha makes up the whole of the old Vicar's staff. *Scenes of Clerical Life II: Mr. Gilfil's Love-Story*

39

DAVILOW, ALICE, BERTHA, FANNY AND ISABEL: The four daughters of Fanny Davilow by her second husband—Alice, a rather dull girl with no ear for music; Bertha, an empty-headed giggler; Fanny, round-shouldered and bad-mannered: Isabel, inquisitive and fretful—all this in the opinion of their brilliant elder half-sister Gwendolen Harleth, whom they much admire. She despises them all, and refuses to go out as a governess in case her pupils should resemble her half-sisters. *Daniel Deronda*

DAVILOW, MRS. (FANNY): The mother of Gwendolen Harleth by her first husband, and of four nondescript girls by her second, who treated her badly and died leaving her practically penniless. She is helped by her brother-in-law, the Rev. Henry Gascoigne, who finds a house for her near his rectory. A year later she and her sister lose their little incomes in a bank failure. The Davilows are preparing to move to a small cottage and earn what money they can when Gwendolen announces that she is going to marry the wealthy Mr. Grandcourt, whom she has previously rejected. Mrs. Davilow, who adores her daughter but has never pretended to understand or govern her, and knows nothing of Grandcourt's character, is delighted, and gratefully accepts an adequate allowance from him. It is not until after his death that she realises what Gwendolen has had to suffer. *Daniel Deronda*

DAWES: Dempster's man, who is so late bringing round the gig one morning that Dempster slashes at him with his whip, whereupon Dawes leaves him, and Dempster has to drive himself, which he does so badly that he is thrown out and fatally injured. *Scenes of Clerical Life III: Janet's Repentance*

DEANE, LUCY: The only child of Mrs. Tulliver's sister Susan. A neat, good-natured, well-behaved young girl, she is constantly being held up as an example to the harum-scarum Maggie Tulliver, who is nevertheless very fond of her. Unfortunately Maggie and Lucy's fiancé, Stephen Guest, fall in love and elope, though Maggie returns alone almost immediately. After an initial period of repulsion. Lucy forgives Maggie and visits her for the last time before going on holiday with the Misses Guest. Some years later Lucy and Stephen marry, much to the satisfaction of everyone, especially Stephen's sisters. *The Mill on the Floss*

DEANE, MR.: Mr. Tulliver's brother-in-law. He works for a local firm which thinks highly of him, and after old Tulliver's bankruptcy and stroke Tom Tulliver asks his uncle to help him get work. 'With that tendency to repress youthful hopes which stout and successful men of fifty find one of their easiest duties', Deane tells Tom frankly that he is no use to anyone, but relents sufficiently to give him a lowly start. Tom does well, and Deane's firm finally buys the old mill and puts Tom in as manager, shortly before the flood in which Tom is drowned. Deane has no liking for Maggie Tulliver, however, and after her abortive attempt to elope with his daughter Lucy's fiancé, firmly bars the door against her. *The Mill on the Floss*

DEANE, MRS. (SUSAN): The elder sister of Mrs. Tulliver, the thinnest and sallowest of the family, unaccountably the mother of the pretty child Lucy, who looks just like Mrs. Tulliver. She is apt to make rather bitter and sarcastic remarks, and Mrs. Tulliver objects to her presence at family councils because 'she's as jealous and having (i.e. miserly) as can be, and allays trying to make the worst o' my poor children to the aunts and uncles'. After Mrs. Deane's death Mrs. Tulliver, recently widowed and penniless, goes to live with her brother-in-law to look after him and Lucy. *The Mill on the Floss*

DEBARRY, THE REV. AUGUSTUS: 'A fine specimen of the old-fashioned aristocratic clergyman, preaching short sermons, understanding business, and acting liberally about his tithe'. He tolerated the few old Dissenters, but finds the upstart mining community a nuisance, and the political sermons of the Independent preachers as pernicious as alehouses. He is indignant when the Dissenting minister calls him 'a blind leader of the blind', and refuses to debate in public with Mr. Lyon, sending his curate instead. As a magistrate, he is active during the election-day rioting, reading the Riot Act and posting guards at the entrances of the wine vaults and brewery to prevent the rioters getting drunk. *Felix Holt*

DEBARRY, HARRIET AND SELINA: The daughters of Sir Maximus Debarry, quietly elegant in their dress and manners, but so badly educated that their father calls Selina an 'ignorant puss'. *Felix Holt*

DEBARRY, SIR MAXIMUS: Lord of the Manor of Treby Magna, who lives with his wife in a vast house, as big as a village, where money is no object and numberless servants live like fighting cocks. 'A gentleman of the right sort', he 'condescended to no mean enquiries' and only snarled in a subdued way when looking over the accounts, being willing to endure some personal inconvenience in order to maintain his hereditary establishment. His estate neighbours that of the Transomes, and he was in his youth an admirer of Mrs. Transome, 'a fine woman . . . we were all ready to fight for the sake of dancing with her'. He is one of the few who know that her second son Harold was fathered by the lawyer Jermyn, and although he cannot approve of Harold's Radical politics, he stands by him when trouble comes. His wife, 'a mountain of satin, lace, and exquisite muslin embroidery', cannot forgive Harold for standing against her Tory son, Philip, nor for his marriage to a Greek woman by whom he has a turbulent three-year-old son who bites his own grandmother! *Felix Holt*

DEBARRY, PHILIP: Son and heir of Sir Maximus Debarry, nephew of the Rev. Augustus Debarry. He has decided to stand for Parliament in the Tory interest when Harold Transome returns home and stands as a Radical. Philip has brought back with him from his travels on the Continent a 'useful fellow' called Maurice Christian, who acts as his secretary-courier. Christian was a prisoner-of-war with Esther Lyon's father, Maurice Bycliffe, and it is mainly the evidence he can produce which confirms Esther's right to the Transome estates. *Felix Holt*

DEMPSTER, JANET: The wife of the lawyer Robert Dempster, who calls her Gypsy when he is in a good humour, which happens less often as he gets older. The daughter of a widow named Raynor, Janet was a pretty, well-spoken girl with a sweet smile, spoilt by her mother, and well educated with a view to becoming a governess. Fifteen years with a drunken husband have aged and embittered her, and she has herself taken to drink; but she remains essentially kind-hearted, sitting up with sick neighbours and carrying food to the poor. On one of these visits she meets the Rev. Edgar Tryan, with whom her husband is at loggerheads, and in spite of herself is attracted to him. But she refuses to allow herself to think well of him, and helps her husband to draw up a satiric 'playbill' which ridicules his proposed course of lectures. Then her husband, in a drunken fury, turns her out of doors in her nightdress, and she is forced to take refuge with old Mrs. Pettifer. In her despair she sends for Tryan, who consoles and comforts her, and she has already made up her mind to return to her husband when she hears that he has been brought home unconscious after being thrown out of his gig. She nurses him devotedly till he dies, and grieves for his loss, remembering how much she loved him when they were first married. Going through his bureau at the request of the executor, she finds a bottle of brandy, and is tempted to drink herself into oblivion, but resists, helped by a visit to Tryan. Finding him in the last stages of consumption, she persuades him to move to a little house she has inherited, with Mrs. Pettifer to look after him, and when his death is imminent she and her mother, who has also become very fond of him, nurse him devotedly. Afterwards Janet returns to her own home, adopts a little girl, and lives quietly, occupied with charitable works, and always grateful to Tryan, who during his short ministry saved her from depravity and despair. *Scenes of Clerical Life III: Janet's Repentance*

DEMPSTER, MRS.: The mother of Lawyer Dempster, a little old lady, with a pale, unwrinkled face, white hair once blonde, a white cap and white shawl, who had once been very pretty. She dislikes her daughter-in-law Janet, and blames her for Dempster's drunkenness and bad behaviour, and also for not having any children. But it is a passive and silent dislike, which does not aggravate the domestic discord. She just sits eternally knitting through all the storms and reconciliations, and dies quietly, still believing that Dempster could have been as good to the right wife as he was to his mother. *Scenes of Clerical Life III: Janet's Repentance*

DEMPSTER, ROBERT: A lawyer at Milby, a tall and massive man addicted to snuff and strong drink. As an ambitious youngster he was very promising, and made a happy marriage with a local girl, Janet Raynor. But he has gradually turned into a bully and a drunkard, and caused his wife much unhappiness. He takes an intense dislike to the young clergyman, Edgar Tryan, and considers him a hypocrite, who does good works, 'which open the floodgates to all immorality', solely in order

to step into Mr. Crewe's shoes when the old man dies. Dempster becomes the hero of the mob when he succeeds in suppressing Tryan's intended course of lectures, and flushed with triumph, degenerates into a loudmouthed braggart, ignorant and quarrelsome. Then in a drunken rage he drives furiously about the countryside, flogging his horse, and is finally thrown out of his gig on to his head, dying shortly afterwards.
Scenes of Clerical Life III: Janet's Repentance

DENNER: Mrs. Transome's maid and housekeeper, the wife of the butler, Hickes, but always retaining her maiden name. A small, exquisitely neat and clean old woman, she has been with Mrs. Transome since she was 'the beautiful Miss Lingon', and knows all her secrets, including the details of her clandestine love-affair with the lawyer Jermyn, and was present at the birth of their illegitimate son, Harold; but never by word or glance did she reveal her knowledge. Mrs. Transome says 'she talks like a French infidel . . . a hard-headed godless little woman, but with a character to be reckoned on as you reckon on the qualities of iron'. She is afraid of nothing: 'Life is like a game of whist . . . I don't enjoy the game much, but I like to play my cards well and see what will be the end of it'. After the revelation of Mrs. Transome's unfaithfulness, Denner accompanies her abroad, and remains with her until Mrs. Transome returns to die at Treby Manor.
Felix Holt

DERONDA, DANIEL: A handsome, intelligent, distinguished-looking young man who has grown up under the guardianship of Sir Hugo Mallinger, whom he secretly believes to be his father. After a good academic education he is uncertain of his future, and travels abroad, where he sees and is attracted by Gwendolen Harleth. He meets her again later as the bride of his uncle's nephew and heir, Mr. Grandcourt, and realises her marriage was a mistake. Meanwhile he has rescued from suicide and placed in safety with his friend Hans Meyrick's mother a charming little Jewish girl, Mirah Lapidoth, who has come to London to escape a suitor forced on her by her dissolute father, and to look for her mother and brother. With great difficulty Daniel, who now begins to interest himself greatly in the Jews and their history, finds Mirah's brother, Ezra Cohen, known as Mordecai. Poor and consumptive, Mordecai lodges in the house of a young pawnbroker, and is kept by charity, and sustained by his vision of a future in which Israel will again be a great nation. Daniel brings the brother and sister together, and realises that he has fallen in love with Mirah, who, having been trained as a singer, is earning her living by giving music lessons. But she tells him she will only marry a Jew. At this point Daniel is told by Sir Hugo that his mother, whom he has so often wondered about, wishes to see him. He hurries to Genoa to meet her, expecting a great reconciliation, but finds her proud and cold, driven by illness but against her inclination to repair the wrong she has done him by cutting him out of her life so that she could continue her operatic career. She reveals to him that he is the grandson of a great Jewish patriot and philosopher, whose vision of a united Israel was similar to that of Mordecai. He is delighted, and wants to hurry back with his good news to Mirah, but is delayed by finding that Gwendolen and her husband are staying in the same hotel as himself. He then learns that Grandcourt has been drowned, and he stays to do all the necessary business and look after Gwendolen till her mother arrives. He knows that she loves him, and he has done all he can to help and encourage her during her unhappy marriage with Grandcourt, but he is not prepared to sacrifice his and Mirah's happiness to her. He returns to England, marries Mirah, and after the death of Mordecai takes her on a voyage of exploration to the Near East, intending to continue the work of his grandfather and Mordecai. *Daniel Deronda*

DIBBITTS: A little apothecary who profits by Lydgate's decision not to do his own dispensing. Dr. Toller says he is in luck, and will now be able to get rid of all his stale drugs. *Middlemarch*

DIBBS: One of Transome's farm-tenants. He is a staunch Tory, but when Harold Transome stands as a Radical he is quite prepared to vote for him, since 'it stands to reason a man should vote for his landlord'. *Felix Holt*

DICKISON, MR.: Landlord of the Marquis of Granby at Basset, a melancholy man with a 'pimpled face, looking as irrelevant to the daylight as a last night's guttered candle'. *The Mill on the Floss*

DILL, MR.: The Middlemarch barber, who collects and disseminates a good deal of gossip, not always accurate. *Middlemarch*

45

DINGALL: The Treddleston grocer, who gives such poor prices for butter that the farmers' wives think he is on the verge of bankruptcy, and are sorry for his wife, 'a sensible woman, of very good kin'. *Adam Bede*

DIX: A neighbour of Tulliver's. Also a mill owner, he has been engaged in litigation with Tulliver about the mill stream, and the matter is settled by arbitration. When Tulliver has a much more serious quarrel with another neighbour, Pivart, he begins to think quite kindly of Dix. *The Mill on the Floss*

DODSON: The maiden name of Mrs. Glegg, Mrs. Pullet, Mrs. Deane, and Mrs. Tulliver—Jane, Sophy, Susan and Bessy. Jane and Sophy, the two eldest, have no children. Susan, the third sister, has one girl, Lucy; and Bessy, the youngest Dodson girl, is the mother of Tom and Maggie Tulliver. A highly respectable family, much looked up to in the parish, then Dodsons have their own ways of doing such things as bleaching linen, making cowslip wine, bottling gooseberries, and curing hams, and no other way can be so good. Always ready to utter home truths to each other, the four women nevertheless agree in thinking that the weakest member of the family is to be preferred to a non-Dobson. *The Mill on the Floss*

DOLBY: The architect responsible for the rebuilding of Shepperton Church. *Scenes of Clerical Life I: The Rev. Amos Barton*

DOLLOP, MRS.: The landlady of the Tankard Inn in Middlemarch. She is firmly convinced that the new doctor, Lydgate, kills off his patients in order to use their bodies for 'cutting up', and is very much against the newfangled post mortems, maintaining that a good doctor should know what is the matter with a patient before he dies. She is quite ready to believe that Lydgate murdered Raffles at the instigation of Mr. Bulstrode, whom she always knew to be 'a wrong 'un' since the time he tried to buy her inn over her head; she thinks Will Ladislaw should have all Bulstrode's money, since it was rightly his mother's, and that he should not depend on Hawley, but get another lawyer, as 'there's always two sides, if no more; else who'd go to law?' *Middlemarch*

DOLLY: Burge's housekeeper, 'a clean old woman, in a dark-striped linen gown, a red kerchief, and a linen cap'. She is one of Lisbeth Bede's few friends, and helps to lay out her husband, Thias Bede, though she is too dim-sighted to be much use. *Adam Bede*

Mrs. Glegg's servant (once called Sally by mistake). *The Mill on the Floss*

DOMENICO, FRA: A devoted follower of Savonarola, who is prepared to walk into the fire to prove the truth of his doctrines. He is arrested and executed with Savonarola. *Romola*

DOMINIC: A man of Mediterranean origin from no country in particular, who serves Harold Transome as valet, secretary, and courier, and comes with him to England from Smyrna to help look after his young son, Harry. He once met Maurice Christian in Naples, and recognizes him, and so becomes involved in Esther Lyon's claim to the Transome estate. *Felix Holt*

DONNITHORNE, CAPTAIN ARTHUR: Grandson and heir of Squire Donnithorne, and beloved godson of Mrs. Irwine. He is popular with the villagers, and has been brought up on terms of close friendship with Adam Bede, whom he much admires. He is about to celebrate his majority, and everyone looks forward to the day when he will take his grandfather's place and right everyone's wrongs. But he is captivated by the beauty and innocence of Hetty Sorrel, and in spite of good resolutions and the certain knowledge that they can never marry, he seduces her, not knowing that Adam Bede is in love with her. When Adam learns of their clandestine meetings, he knocks Arthur down, and then forces him to write Hetty a letter, saying he was not serious in his intentions, and they must not meet again. Arthur then leaves for Windsor, where his regiment is stationed, and by the time Hetty arrives there to look for him, he is off in Ireland. Summoned from Ireland by the news of his grandfather's imminent death, he arrives in high fettle, only to be told that Hetty has been condemned to death for the murder of her—and his—child. With his whole life in ruins, he strains every nerve to get her a partial reprieve—transportation instead of hanging—and then settles up his affairs and goes abroad. Eight years later he is invalided home, hoping to recover his health in his native air, and to renew his friendship with Adam Bede, now happily married to Dinah Morris. *Adam Bede*

DONNITHORNE, LYDIA (LYDDY): The elderly, plain daughter of Squire Donnithorne, much envied by Hetty Sorrel for her command of such luxuries as scent on her handkerchief. But she really leads an unhappy, restricted life, taking no interest in anything much beyond her fat pug Fido, and when Arthur returns home after his grandfather's death she is the only person in the house who does not know about Hetty Sorrel. She later makes her home in Bath. *Adam Bede*

DONNITHORNE, SQUIRE: Owner of Donnithorne Chase, a mean, selfish man, now over eighty, who lets his estate run to seed for want of a little expenditure. *Adam Bede*

DORCAS: A maid at Cheverley Court when Tina Sarti is brought there from Italy. She looks after the child, until her marriage to Daniel Knott the coachman, and is much loved by her. When Tina runs away after Wybrow's death she takes refuge with Dorcas and Daniel. *Scenes of Clerical Life II: Mr. Gilfil's Love-Story*

DOVER, MR.: A silversmith from whom Lydgate buys plate and jewellery before his marriage. When his bill for £360 remains unpaid, Dover accepts a bill of sale on the furniture, and is about to take possession when Lydgate comes home with the £1,000 lent him by Bulstrode and pays off the debt. *Middlemarch*

DOVIZI, BERNARDO: Later Cardinal da Bibbiena. He comes to Florence with the Cardinal Giovanni de' Medici, and gets to know Tito Melema, whom he insists on taking with him as confidential adviser on an embassy to Rome. *Romola*

DOVIZI, PIERO: Known as Piero da Bibbiena, he is employed by Piero de' Medici. His enemies call him a 'sharp-muzzled' fellow, a weasel who slips through holes for his master. *Romola*

DOW: A printer in Treby Magna, originally a Tory; but being pushed out of favour by a newcomer, Quorlen, he becomes a Whig. *Felix Holt*

DOWLAS, MR: The Raveloe farrier, a cross-grained, argumentative fellow, who never goes to church, considering himself exempt, since he almost belongs to the medical profession and is likely to be needed suddenly for delicate cows. But he agrees that Silas brought a blessing on himself when he adopted an orphan child. *Silas Marner*

DOWNES, BILL: A young stone-cutter who goes to Bartle Massey's evening classes, and has great difficulty in learning to read. *Adam Bede*

DOWNES, KIT: One of Mr. Brooke's poor tenants. Dorothea tries to get her uncle to do something for him, pointing out that he lives with a wife and seven children in a house with only one sitting-room and a bedroom hardly bigger than a table. *Middlemarch*

DREDGE: A miner at Sproxton, who is all in favour of elections because they mean free beer. He gives his wife a black eye for daring to attend a chapel meeting at Peggy Button's, and egged on by Johnson, Transome's agent, he is in the thick of the election-day rioting. He ends up in jail, being later sentenced to a year's imprisonment with hard labour. *Felix Holt*

DRUMLOW, THE REV. MR.: The clergyman who married young Lammeter and Miss Osgood. Being a little confused, what with old age and taking a little something to keep out the cold, he said: 'Wilt thou have this woman to be thy wedded husband?'; but no one noticed, except Macey, the parish clerk. Later Macey was worried in case the couple were not properly married, but Drumlow explained to him that it is signing the register that makes a marriage legal. *Silas Marner*

DUKE, THE REV. ARCHIBALD: A very small man with a sallow, puffy face, dyspeptic and evangelical. He thinks the success of *The Pickwick Papers* is a strong proof of original sin, and is very upset by the scandal over the Rev. Amos Barton and the Countess Czerlaski—such a bad example for the parish! *Scenes of Clerical Life I: The Rev. Amos Barton*

DUMMILOW, JOB: An old villager who is very glad of a flannel jacket, given him by the rector's sisters, the Miss Irwines. *Adam Bede*

DUNCAN, ARCHIE: A mean-spirited young man who, when Sarah Dunkirk refused to marry him, taunted her with being the daughter, not of a pawnbroker, as she thought, but of a very successful receiver of stolen goods. This made Sarah decide to run away from home and go on the stage. *Middlemarch*

DUNKIRK, SARAH: The daughter of an elderly pawnbroker who, unknown to his family, is a high-class receiver of stolen goods. When she discovers this, Sarah runs away from home and goes on the stage. She marries the son of the Rev. Edward Casaubon's disinherited aunt Julia Ladislaw, and is the mother of Will. When her mother, Mrs. Dunkirk, loses both her husband and her only son, she promises to marry her husband's partner, Mr. Bulstrode, but he must first see if he can trace her daughter. He does so, when Will is about five years old, but, afraid of losing the Dunkirk money, he suppresses the fact, telling the mother that Sarah is dead and has left no children. *Middlemarch*

DUNN, MARY: The daughter of an excellent draper who lost the custom of several wealthy Church ladies because he attended the Rev. Edgar Tryan's lectures, of which they disapproved. Mary is a plain child with long lanky hair, always out of curl, who, much to the indignation of her headmistress Miss Townley, is prepared for confirmation by Mr. Tryan, and as a result is ostracised by her fellow pupils. She thinks she could have won back their friendship with an unlimited supply of plum cake, but unfortunately her mother thinks plum cake unwholesome. *Scenes of Clerical Life III: Janet's Repentance*

DURFEY: The family who bought the Transome estate, adopting the name, and from Durfey-Transome becoming, in a couple of generations, Transome only. *Felix Holt*
    See also Transome, Durfey

DYMOCK & HALLIWELL: Harold Transome's lawyers, who handle all the business relating to Esther Lyon's claim to his estate. *Felix Holt*

E

ELY, PARSON: A dark-haired, distinguished-looking clergyman, who disapproves of Amos Barton's extempore 'cottage preaching' on Sunday evenings: 'It does as much harm as good to give a too familiar aspect to religious teaching.' He despises Barton, but does not show it, being careful never to offend anyone. *Scenes of Clerical Life I: The Rev. Amos Barton*

EPPIE (HEPHZIBAH): The child of Godfrey Cass by a sluttish woman named Molly Farren whom he has married secretly and refused to acknowledge. To revenge herself, Molly plans to turn up with Eppie at the Casses' New Year's Eve Ball, but is caught in a snowstorm and dies on the way. Eppie is rescued by Silas Marner, who adopts her and brings her up, everyone being ignorant of her parentage. At eighteen she is a lovely girl, with rippling auburn hair and charmingly shy manners. When Godfrey Cass finally decides to tell her that he is her father and would like her to come and live with him and his wife, she indignantly refuses, and says that Silas is all the father she needs. She marries Aaron Winthrop, a young gardener whose mother helped Silas to care for her when she was a baby. *Silas Marner*

F

FANTONI, GIAN: A Florentine in whose house Romola takes refuge when she is held up by the mob on her way to find Baldassarre. *Romola*

FAREBROTHER, THE REV. CAMDEN: A handsome but rather eccentric little clergyman, in threadbare black, who knows he is in the wrong profession, and consoles himself by going fishing and studying natural history. He is an excellent whist and billiards player, and likes to win, which rather scandalizes some of his parishioners. He has never married, as he has to keep his widowed mother and her sister, Miss Noble, as well as his unmarried sister Winifred, but he is in love with Mary Garth, and thinks it rather ironical that Fred Vincy should choose to make a confidant of him and ask him to plead his cause with Mary, which he does to such good effect that they marry. Farebrother is rather 'Whiggish' in politics, and is the only man in Middlemarch whom Mr. Lydgate really likes. They have long discussions together, and Lydgate is instrumental in getting Dorothea to give Farebrother the living left vacant by her husband's death. This eases Farebrother's burdens considerably, and he is grateful, refusing to believe the scandal about Lydgate taking a bribe from Bulstrode in connection with the death of Raffles, and accepting his assurance that he is innocent, though he quite believes Bulstrode to be a rascal. He reserves judgement on Dorothea's second marriage, saying she has the right to do as she likes. *Middlemarch*

FAREBROTHER, MRS.: The mother of the Rev. Camden Farebrother, white-haired, befrilled and kerchiefed with dainty cleanliness, upright, quick-eyed, and still under seventy. She admires but tyrannises over her son, and takes very little notice of her rather dim daughter. But she is fond of Mary Garth, whom she looks forward to welcoming as a daughter-in-law, and is disappointed when Mary decides to marry Frend Vincy, whose sister Rosamond she has never liked because snobbish Rosamond has never taken any notice of Mrs. Farebrother's timid little sister, Miss Noble. *Middlemarch*

FAREBROTHER, WINIFRED: Sister of the Rev. Camden Farebrother, for whom she keeps house, together with her mother and Aunt Henrietta. She is not ill-looking, but 'nipped and subdued as spinsters are apt to be'. She very much wishes her brother would marry Mary Garth and bring some young life into the house. *Middlemarch*

FARQUHAR, ARABELLA AND JULIA: The snobbish daughters of the local squire. They despise Amos Barton, who tells his wife that Arabella is setting her cap at Parson Ely, but won't get him. Both girls are kind to Amos after Milly's death, and undertake to give Sophy and Fred lessons twice a week. *Scenes of Clerical Life I: The Rev. Amos Barton*

FARQUHAR, MR. AND MRS.: A worthy couple who invite the Bartons to dinner, where Mrs. Farquhar in her 'gros de Naples' does not look as elegant as Milly Barton in her 'old frayed black'. The couple talk mostly about Mr. Bridmain and the Countess, and are convinced they are not brother and sister. But they are kind to the Bartons when Milly is ill, and after her death Mrs. Farquhar takes care of the two youngest children—Chubby and Walter. *Scenes of Clerical Life I: The Rev. Amos Barton*

FARREN, MOLLY: A drunken slut by whom Godfrey Cass has had a child and foolishly married in secret. Infuriated by his refusal to acknowledge her, she sets off for his father's house with the child in her arms, intending to make a nasty scene at the Casses' New Year's Eve ball. But on the way she succumbs to the combined effects of cold and opium, and dies under a furze-bush. Her daughter is found and brought up by Silas Marner. *Silas Marner*

FAWKES, BESSIE: A poor village woman with a large family of small children, whom good Dolly Winthrop nurses during her last illness. *Silas Marner*

FAWKS, BILL: A rough character, remembered by Bob Jakin as the only person, other than Tom Tulliver, who ever gave him anything—'He gen me the terrier pup istid o' drowndin' it, an' I had to jaw him a good un afore he'd give it me.' *The Mill on the Floss*

FEATHERSTONE, JONAH: Brother of Peter Featherstone. Hoping to be remembered in his will, he installs himself in the kitchen when Peter is dying, but receives nothing. He is careful not to offend Rigg, Peter's illegitimate son, who inherits all his property, in case he can get something out of him later on, and is disappointed when Rigg sells up and leaves the district. *Middlemarch*

FEATHERSTONE, PETER: A wealthy old man who has been married twice, and has no children. The relations of both wives hope therefore to inherit his money, though his favourite appears to be his nephew Fred Vincy; but on the other hand his niece Mary Garth lives with him and runs his house. His own brothers and sisters feel that they have more right to what he leaves, being 'kin', than those related only by marriage, and when he is dying they descend on the house to establish their rights. In the end, Featherstone having failed to get Mary to burn his most recent will, everything is divided between his illegitimate son Joshua Rigg and a charitable bequest for the building of almshouses for old men. Peter had enjoyed the thought of his uncouth son living in Stone Court among the other landowners of the district, but had not foreseen that he would sell the house and land to Peter's bitterest enemy, Mr. Bulstrode, and be seen no more. *Middlemarch*

FEATHERSTONE, SAMUEL: *see* Featherstone, Solomon

FEATHERSTONE, SOLOMON: Brother of the wealthy and irascible Peter Featherstone. He is well off, but sees no reason why he should not inherit some of Peter's money, and does all he can to make trouble between his brother and any other person whom he seems likely to favour in his will, particularly young Fred Vincy, Peter's nephew by marriage. Solomon is delighted when the eventual heir, Joshua Rigg, sells Stone Court instead of living in it 'to trouble his neighbours', and says it serves his brother right for leaving property away from the family. Solomon, who is once called Samuel by mistake, is an overseer of roads, and does all he can to hinder the men who are planning the new railway in order to get more money for land belonging to him which they need. *Middlemarch*

FELLOWES, THE REV. MR.: A man of imposing appearance, with a mellifluous voice and the readiest of tongues, popular everywhere except in his own parish, where he cultivates his own glebe and keeps up running feuds with at least half a dozen parishioners. He dislikes Barton because 'he is not a gentleman', and is very ready to pass on scandal about him; but he is not really malicious, only thoughtless and rather a busybody. *Scenes of Clerical Life I: The Rev. Amos Barton*

FENN, JULIET: A plain girl, 'underhung, and with receding brow resembling that of the more intelligent fishes'. She was as 'middling as market day', but an excellent archer, winning the gold arrow at the Brackenshaw Archery Meeting. She went with her father to the Christmas party at the Abbey, and Gwendolen, though newly married, is annoyed because Daniel Deronda pays her too much attention. *Daniel Deronda*

FENN, MR.: The member for West Orchards 'in the cider interest'. He is invited with his two daughters to the Abbey to meet Gwendolen on her first visit there as the bride of the heir, Mr. Grandcourt. *Daniel Deronda*

FERRAVECCHI, BRATTI: A 'grey-haired, broad-shouldered man of the type which, in Tuscan phrase, is moulded with the fist and polished with the pickaxe'. A pedlar and owner of a small bric-à-brac shop in the street from which he takes his name, he finds Tito Melema asleep in the street in Florence after he has been shipwrecked, and befriends him. It is through him that Tito sells to a Genoese traveller the onyx ring by which Baldassarre tracks him down, and later Bratti sells to Baldassarre the knife with which he tries to kill Tito. Bratti also brings together Tito and Tessa, discovers where Tito has hidden Tessa and her children, and is instrumental, after Tito's death, in leading Romola to their lodgings outside the city. *Romola*

FILMORE, MR.: Assistant to the surgeon at Treby Magna, and a close friend of the Debarry's butler Scales. He admires Maurice Christian because he is such a fine card player: 'I wish I could play *écarté* as he does; it's beautiful to see him . . . he'll empty a man's pocket in no time.' *Felix Holt*

The Rev. Theodore Sherlock's tutor at Oxford, who said of him that he might become a first-rate man if his diffidence didn't do him injustice. *Felix Holt*

FIRNISS, MISS: The proprietress of a boarding school where Maggie Tulliver and her cousin Lucy Deane go when they are thirteen. One of Mr. Riley's daughters, left penniless by her father's sudden death, becomes an under-teacher there. Miss Firniss was very willing to engage Maggie in a similar capacity after her father's bankruptcy and death, but was forced to withdraw her offer when Maggie ran away with Stephen Guest. *The Mill on the Floss*

FITCHETT, MR.: An old man who lives in the Shepperton workhouse. He was formerly a footman with the Oldinport family, and has retained something of the jaunty demeanour with which he used to usher in her Ladyship's morning visitors. *Scenes of Clerical Life I: The Rev. Amos Barton*

FITCHETT, MRS.: The lodge-keeper at Tipton Grange. She remarks on the cheeseparing ways of the Rector's wife, Mrs. Cadwallader, who offers her a pair of tumbler-pigeons in exchange for a couple of her laying hens. *Middlemarch*

FITZADAM, MR. AND MRS.: Members of the house-party assembled to greet Grandcourt and his bride at Monk's Topping. They belong 'to the Worcestershire branch' of the family. *Daniel Deronda*

FLAVELL: A Methodist preacher, in shabby black gaiters, who is out for a walk with his wife when a hare crosses his path.

He cannot resist killing and pocketing it, and finds himself up before the magistrates for poaching. His defence is that he thought the Lord had sent him a good dinner and he had a right to it. Mr. Brooke, and Dorothea, rather sympathize with him, to the scandal of their land-owning neighbours. *Middlemarch*

FLETCHER: Hawley's clerk, who confides far too much of his master's business to Dill, the barber, whence it percolates through the town. *Middlemarch*

FODGE, POLL (MARY HIGGINS): 'A one-eyed woman with a scarred and seamy face, the most notorious rebel in the workhouse' at Shepperton. She defends her unsavoury son from the master, Mr. Spratt, who wants to punish him for behaving badly in prayers, and complains to Barton, the workhouse chaplain, that Spratt eats roast goose while the paupers have nothing but greasy broth. *Scenes of Clerical Life I: The Rev. Amos Barton*

FORD: An old villager in Foxholm—'a true Staffordshire patriarch'—who remembers watching the wedding of Tina Sarti and Mr. Gilfil, and thinking that Lady Cheverel, in her blue-and-white silk, looked just like Queen Charlotte. *Scenes of Clerical Life II: Mr. Gilfil's Love-Story*

FORD, HIRAM: A local carrier who is assured by Solomon Featherstone that the trains will take away his trade. He therefore gets together a group of haymakers, who attack the railway surveyors with pitchforks. *Middlemarch*

FOWLER: One of Squire Cass's tenants, who, according to the agent, Cox, owes over £100 in rent. Cass is about to turn Fowler out of the farm when he discovers that the money has been paid to his eldest son Godfrey and handed on to Godfrey's brother Dunsey to stop him telling the Squire of Godfrey's secret marriage. *Silas Marner*

FRANCESCO: An Italian painter whom Sir Christopher Cheverel brought back to England to decorate his drawing-room. 'He has the knack of sleeping as he stands with his brushes in his hands.' *Scenes of Clerical Life II: Mr. Gilfil's Love-Story*

FRASER, MR.: A young Scotsman who acted as secretary to

Sir Hugo Mallinger and tutor to the young Daniel Deronda. It was a chance remark of his that led Daniel to believe that he was Sir Hugo's illegitimate son. *Daniel Deronda*

FREKE, THE REV. MR.: A local clergyman who has a passion for rebuilding. *Middlemarch*

FRENCH, MRS.: Sir Hugo Mallinger's elderly housekeeper. *Daniel Deronda*

FRIPP, DAME: An old woman who has a remarkable way with leeches, and is always called in by Mr. Pilgrim to apply them to his patients. *Scenes of Clerical Life II: Mr. Gilfil's Love-Story*

FURLEY: A small business man who holds a mortgage on Tulliver's mill and land. It is the shock of learning that Furley has sold the mortgage to his mortal enemy, Lawyer Wakem, that brings on Tulliver's stroke. *The Mill on the Floss*

FURNESS, THE REV. MR.: A young cleric who was unsuccessful at Cambridge, and wrote some very poor poems. His sermons are equally awful. *Scenes of Clerical Life I: The Rev. Amos Barton*

G

GADDI, FRANCESCO: One of the Florentine notables who greets Charles VIII of France at the gates of the city. As he speaks a little French, he is pushed forward in an emergency to say a few words of welcome, but delegates the task to Tito Melema. *Romola*

GADSBY: An acquaintance of Riley's, who tells him that the Rev. Walter Stelling is an excellent classical scholar, and would be a good tutor for Tom Tulliver. *The Mill on the Floss*

GADSBY, MRS.: A yeomanry captain's wife, formerly a kitchen-maid, and still behaving like one. She goes hunting, and Mr. Gascoigne warns Gwendolen not to do the same, since 'no lady of good position follows the Wessex hunt'. *Daniel Deronda*

GAMBIT, MR.: A local practitioner who looks after the members of the Benefit Club which meets at Mrs. Dollop's inn, the Tankard. He is especially esteemed as an *accoucheur*, and is so employed by the fertile Mrs. Maumsey, who has great faith in his drugs—'the pink mixture, not the brown'. He has had very little education and has had to make his own way, which tends to make him scornful of such newly-qualified doctors as Lydgate, whom he thinks a hypocrite because he says he has no faith in medicines and does not do his own dispensing. *Middlemarch*

GARDNER, MARIA: A young lady who, in spite of a stutter, is thought by some to be the prettiest girl in Miss Townley's school, especially when her lovely dark-brown ringlets have been oiled and twisted with special care because she is being confirmed. *Scenes of Clerical Life III: Janet's Repentance*

GARNETT: An acquaintance of Mr. Tulliver's, who evidently reared his son to his own business and was ousted by him before the old man was ready to go. Tulliver has no intention of being treated like that by his own son, and decides to educate him 'an' put him to a business, as he may make a nest for himself an' not want to push me out o' mine.' *The Mill on the Floss*

GARRATT: One of the maids at Sir James Chettam's, who looks after Celia's baby while the nurse has her lunch. *Middlemarch*

GARSTIN, PETER: The Tory candidate for North Loamshire, who joins forces with Philip Debarry to keep out Harold Transome—'a thin miserly fellow who keeps his pockets buttoned'. As the harsh manager of the local coal-mining company, he is an easy target for the rabble-rousing tactics of the Radical agent, Johnson. *Felix Holt*

GARTH, ALFRED: The younger son of Caleb Garth, who at fifteen is just the right age to be apprenticed to Mr. Hanmer as an engineer. His mother has saved up £92 for this purpose, but Caleb lends the money to Fred Vincy, for whom he has backed a bill that Fred cannot meet. Alfred's sister Mary offers to go and teach in a girls' school so as to pay for his apprenticeship, but luckily she does not have to, as her father unexpectedly lands a double job—as agent for Sir James Chettam and for Mr. Brooke. *Middlemarch*

GARTH, BEN: The youngest of the Garths' four boys, who is taught at home by his mother while she does the cooking. *Middlemarch*

GARTH, CALEB: The brother-in-law of Peter Featherstone, whose first wife was Garth's sister. He is an able, but rather inarticulate man, self-taught, with very high standards from which he will not depart. He refuses to work for Bulstrode when he discovers from Raffles what a rascal the old man is, and he insists always on giving good value for money when he takes on a job. He once had a flourishing building business, in addition to being a land agent and valuer, but went bankrupt through being too trustful. With great difficulty, and very much helped by his wife, a former teacher, he has cleared himself of debt, paying everyone in full. But he foolishly backs a bill for young Fred Vincy, simply because he likes the lad, and has to meet it, which takes all the family's savings. This makes him chary of accepting Fred as a suitor to his daughter Mary, as he knows Fred hopes to inherit his old uncle's money, and will therefore never do any work. But when Fred has been disinherited in favour of the uncle's illegitimate son, and has to find work, Caleb relents, takes him on as his own assistant, teaches him the job, and finally settles the young married couple in Stone Court, which they farm successfully, first as tenants, later as owners. *Middlemarch*

GARTH, CHRISTY: The eldest son of Caleb Garth, and the bookish one of the family, much to his father's disappointment but his mother's joy. He is being educated in Scotland, where he pays his university fees by giving private lessons, and hopes to become a tutor and lecturer. *Middlemarch*

GARTH, JIM: Caleb's youngest son, who thinks girls' schools must be terrible, with no games worth playing, and the prospect of walking in a crocodile. He sympathizes with his sister Mary when she doesn't want to go and teach in one. *Middlemarch*

GARTH, LETTY: The youngest Garth child, who is being taught at home by her mother with her brother Ben. She is much quicker than he is, but easily distracted—'a most inconvenient child, who listens to everything'. *Middlemarch*

GARTH, MARY: Caleb Garth's eldest daughter, who goes to Stone Court to nurse her old uncle Peter Featherstone. She is in love with Fred Vincy, but will not marry him, because he lives in expectation of inheriting his uncle's fortune, and will not work. Just before Peter Featherstone dies he asks Mary, who is sitting up with him, to burn his last will, by which Fred gets nothing. She refuses, and the will stands. Mary's father, and the local clergyman, Farebrother, an elderly man who is in love with her, tell her she has acted rightly, but she is sorry to have done Fred out of the £10,000 he was left in the previous will. But she still cannot bring herself to marry him, especially when he says that his Oxford education has left him no option, being penniless, but to become a clergyman. She thinks, quite rightly, that he is totally unsuited for the Church, and it is not until her father has taken Fred on as his assistant, and Fred has proved that he can work and earn enough to keep her, that she agrees to marry him and settle down at Stone Court, where she lives happily with Fred and, eventually, three sons. *Middlemarch*

GARTH, MRS. SUSAN: The wife of Caleb Garth, a former schoolteacher. A curly-haired, square-faced, handsome woman, and an independent thinker. She loves her husband, and understands his sensitive and unbusinesslike nature even when his kindness to undeserving people makes her angry. But 'she had that rare sense which discerns what is unalterable and submits to it without murmuring'. She is sorry when Mary marries Fred, as she thinks the Rev. Camden Farebrother would have made her a better husband. *Middlemarch*

GASCOIGNE, ANNA: The eldest child of Gwendolen Harleth's uncle, who hopes that the two girls will be friends when Gwendolen comes to live near them. But Gwendolen thinks Anna gauche and uninteresting, and Anna thinks Gwendolen shallow and cold-hearted, particularly after she has first made Rex, Anna's favourite brother, fall in love with her, and then repulsed him cruelly. Anna is so angry at the misery Gwendolen has caused that she is very unwilling to be a bridesmaid at her wedding to Grandcourt. Later, on a visit to London, she meets Mirah Lapidoth at the house of Rex's friend Hans Meyrick, and leads her to believe that Daniel Deronda, with whom Mirah is in love, is himself in love with Gwendolen. *Daniel Deronda*

GASCOIGNE, EDWY, LOTTA AND WARHAM: The three younger

children at Pennicote Rectory. Warham, the second son, is being sent to India, and is too busy studying for his examinations for the Indian Civil Service to dance attendance on his attractive cousin Gwendolen Harleth; Lotta, who is very unlike her sister Anna, being boisterous and self-centred, is delighted when Edwy is brought home from school to share her lessons after the family's financial losses. *Daniel Deronda*

GASCOIGNE, THE REV. HENRY: The Rector of Pennicote, whose wife Nancy is the sister of Fanny Davilow. When Fanny is widowed for the second time, Gascoigne very kindly takes a house for her near his, and is prepared to do all he can for her five daughters, particularly his favourite, Gwendolen Harleth. He was originally Captain Gaskin, 'having taken orders and a diphthong shortly before his marriage'. Handsome, and not outwardly clerical in looks or manner, he runs his parish well, and is tolerant and kindly. He blames himself for not having foreseen that his eldest son Rex would fall in love with Gwendolen, but feels she has treated him badly, and does all he can to help Rex recover from his infatuation. Although he has heard rumours that Grandcourt, who wishes to marry Gwendolen, has had a shady past, he thinks they are exaggerated, and is glad to help the marriage on, particularly when her mother, as well as his own wife, loses all the money left her by her parents. After Grandcourt's death Gascoigne accompanies Mrs. Davilow to Genoa to fetch Gwendolen home, and again does all he can to help her. *Daniel Deronda*

GASCOIGNE, MRS. (NANCY): Sister to Fanny Davilow. Slight and dark, with an alert expression, she is an excellent parson's wife, and devoted to her children. She does not like her niece Gwendolen Harleth, and in spite of the misery it causes to her son Rex, she is glad Gwendolen is not in love with him. She is all in favour of her marriage to Grandcourt, and not at all sympathetic when it turns out badly. *Daniel Deronda*

GASCOIGNE, REX: The eldest son of the Rev. Henry Gascoigne, a fine, open-hearted youth, with a bright, happy nature and no vices. He falls deeply in love with his handsome, vivacious cousin Gwendolen Harleth, and takes her out hunting in defiance of his father's prohibition. He is thrown, and quite badly hurt. Gwendolen shows no concern over his accident, and when he proposes to her, turns him down with peremptory coldness. In despair, he decides to emigrate, but his father persuades him to finish his time at Cambridge, and he finally settles in London, reading law, and enjoying the company of the three Meyrick girls, whose brother Hans, also a Cambridge man, coached him for his scholarship to university. *Daniel Deronda*

GAWAINE, MR.: A progressive landlord, whose sweeping reforms are not popular among his tenantry. He is a friend of Captain Donnithorne, who rides over to see him instead of keeping his appointment with Hetty Sorrel, but cannot resist returning just in time to catch her as she goes home through the wood. *Adam Bede*

GEDGE, MR.: Landlord of the Royal Oak at Shepperton. He has a poor opinion of his customers, and thinks he will find more congenial company elsewhere. But when he migrates to the Saracen's Head in the nearby market town he finds the people there just the same. 'A poor lot, sir, big and little, and them as comes for a go o' gin are no better than them as comes for a pint o' twopenny—a poor lot.' *Adam Bede*

GELL: A young man who works for Tom Tulliver's uncle, Mr. Deane. He is constantly being held up as an example to poor Tom, who later surpasses him, much to his uncle's surprise and pleasure. *The Mill on the Floss*

GHITA, MONNA: The mother of Tessa, a stout, brawny woman, who sends Tito Melema packing when she finds him flirting with her daughter. When she is ill her husband sends for the quack doctor Tacco, but she dies before he arrives. *Romola*

GIBBS: Grandcourt's valet, who goes with him on his yachting trip in the Mediterranean, and helps with all the necessary business after he has been drowned at Genoa. *Daniel Deronda*

GIBBS, JOHN: One of Tulliver's waggoners, who died of 'th' inflammation'. *The Mill on the Floss*

GIBBS, MISS (JANET): The niece of Mrs. Patten, a single lady of about fifty, who has refused the most ineligible offers out of devotion to her aged aunt, and expects a substantial legacy in return. *Scenes of Clerical Life I: The Rev. Amos Barton*

GIDEON: A maker of optical instruments, a red-haired, generous-featured Jew, whom Deronda meets at the discussion group in the Hand and Banner. Gideon thinks, unlike Mordecai, that Jews should in time merge with the race they live among, and says he would not mind if his children married Christians. *Daniel Deronda*

GILES: An unsuccessful candidate in a Parliamentary election, who was reputed to have paid out £10,000 in bribes, and failed because it was not enough. *Middlemarch*

GILFIL, THE REV. MAYNARD: The clergyman who held the living of Shepperton before Amos Barton. To the older parishioners he was the pattern of perfection, and is always being compared to Barton, to the detriment of the latter. *Scenes of Clerical Life I: The Rev. Amos Barton*

Although many of his parishioners in his later life think Gilfil is a bachelor, he was for a short time married to a young Italian girl, Caterina Sarti, an orphan befriended in Naples by Lady Cheverel and brought back to England as a small child. Gilfil, who was the ward of Sir Christopher Cheverel and acted as chaplain to the family, fell in love with her, and the Cheverels intended that they should marry, but Tina, as she is called, fell in love with Sir Christopher's nephew and heir, Captain Wybrow. In spite of Gilfil's remonstrances, Wybrow amuses himself by flirting with her outrageously until the day comes when he has to tell her he is getting married. In the ensuing turmoil Wybrow dies of a heart attack and Tina, who feels she is responsible for his death, runs away. Gilfil follows her, takes her to the house of his married sister, and when she has recovered a little from her traumatic experience—she intended to murder Wybrow—persuades her to marry him. They settle at Shepperton, where less than a year later she dies in childbirth. *Scenes of Clerical Life II: Mr. Gilfil's Love-Story*

GILLS: A stone-cutter at Sproxton, who is anxious that the free beer and higher wages which he thinks will result from the Reform Bill should not be confined to his neighbours the miners. *Felix Holt*

GIRDLE, MRS.: The miller's wife at Pennicote. She attends the wedding of Gwendolen Harleth and Grandcourt, and comments unfavourably on the bridegroom. She also tells her daughter that gentlemen, like Squire Pelton, are as cruel to their wives as working men are. *Daniel Deronda*

GIROLAMO, FRA: *see* Savonarola, Fra Girolamo

GIULIANO, FRA: A Franciscan who is paired with the Dominican Fra Domenico when arrangements are made for an ordeal by fire in Florence in order to prove or disprove the truth of Savonarola's doctrines. *Romola*

GLASHER, MRS. LYDIA: The wife of Colonel Glasher, a brutal Irishman whom she left after five years of marriage to become the mistress of Mr. Grandcourt. She has a boy and three girls by him, and when her husband dies she hopes that Grandcourt will marry her and make the boy, Henleigh, his heir. But Grandcourt is already tired of her, and wants to marry Gwendolen Harleth. To prevent this Lydia, helped by Grandcourt's hanger-on, Lush, arranges to meet Gwendolen secretly, and extracts a promise from her that she will not marry Grandcourt and so stand in the boy's way. When the marriage is finally decided upon, and Grandcourt asks Lydia to return his mother's diamonds, which he gave her in the early days of his infatuation, she refuses, but arranges for them to be delivered to Gwendolen on the evening after her wedding, together with a cruel letter, cursing her for breaking her promise and prophesying that her marriage will be unhappy. *Daniel Deronda*

GLEGG, MR.: The husband of Mrs. Tulliver's eldest sister Jane, 'a kind-looking, white-haired old gentleman', very unlike his shrewish wife. A retired woolstapler, he is a keen gardener, doing the work of two ordinary gardeners among his fruit and vegetables; though well-off, he is rather mean, and when his brother-in-law is sold up he decides not to give him money, but to pass on to him some of his old flannel waistcoats, and also to buy Mrs. Tulliver a pound or two of best black tea now and again. But he is shrewd enough to invest money in Tom Tulliver's successful business venture. Being fond of his niece Lucy Deane, whom he much prefers to the tomboy Maggie Tulliver, he believes Maggie guilty over the affair with Stephen Guest, and quarrels with his wife about it, since she, to everyone's surprise, thinks Maggie innocent and is prepared to be reconciled to her. *The Mill on the Floss*

GLEGG, MRS. (JANE): The eldest of the four Dodson sisters. A handsome but censorious woman, she is disliked by most of her relatives, having an unhappy knack of telling them home truths. When Maggie Tulliver disappears, she clings to the belief that she is drowned rather than disgraced, but on her return Mrs. Glegg is the only member of the family to stand up for her, much to Maggie's surprise and heartfelt gratitude. *The Mill on the Floss*

GOBY, MR.: A 'whittaw' or saddler, who goes to Poyser's farm to mend the harness, and when it rains entertains the farm-hands in the barn with all the latest gossip from town. *Adam Bede*

GOBY, MRS.: 'As respectable a woman as any in Parley Street, who had money in trust before her marriage'. Her great friend, Mrs. Dollop, of the Tankard Inn, is scandalized when Lydgate wants to do a post mortem on her—an unheard-of thing at that time—and says he should have known what was the matter with her before she died. *Middlemarch*

GODWIN: The surgeon who treats Captain Donnithorne's wounded arm, and makes him keep it in a sling longer than Donnithorne thinks necessary. *Adam Bede*

GOFFE, MR.: The tenant of Rabbit's End, one of Transome's farms. A poor, spiritless creature, with a wife and five children, he is always complaining that he doesn't know which-a-way to turn, and his view of the election is that it is no worse than sheep-rot. But he is so intimidated by the rioters on his way to the poll that he inadvertently votes for the Tory candidate instead of for his landlord Transome, a Radical. *Felix Holt*

GOGOFF, MR. AND MRS.: A rather tiresome couple whom Grand-court met in Paris and invited to Diplow. He afterwards regretted it, and referred to Mrs. Gogoff as 'a giantess . . . who spoils the look of the room.' *Daniel Deronda*

GOODRICH, MR.: Tom Tulliver's drawing-master, who makes him do rustic bridges, brooks, and ruins while his father thinks he is learning surveying and the drawing out of plans and maps. *The Mill on the Floss*

GOODWIN: A wood-inlayer, well-built, open-faced, pleasant-voiced. Though not a Jew, he goes to the meetings at the

Hand and Banner and much enjoys the discussions with Mordecai. *Daniel Deronda*

GORE, MR.: Tulliver's lawyer, who does not dare to tell him outright that Wakem holds the mortgage on the mill, so writes instead the letter which is presumed to be the cause of Tulliver's stroke. *The Mill on the Floss*

GORO: A wool-beater in Florence, who thinks that the death of Lorenzo de' Medici is not the worst evil that can befall Florence. The arrival of French troops is a far worse disaster, since it hinders trade. *Romola*

GOTTLIB, MR.: A London banker, much respected in the city and an acquaintance of Mr. Girlome's. When there was a run on the bank in 1816 'a gentleman came in with bags of gold and said "Tell Mr. Gottlib there's plenty more where that came from". And it stopped the run, it did indeed'. *Felix Holt*

GRANDCOURT, HENLEIGH MALLINGER: The nephew and heir of Sir Hugo Mallinger. He is also the possible heir, through his mother, of a baronetcy and a peerage, and at thirty-five is considered a good matrimonial catch, in spite of some dubious stories about his early life. He has in fact a mistress, Lydia Glasher, the errant wife of Colonel Glasher, who has had four children by him. Deciding to settle down, he rents Diplow Hall and entertains lavishly. At first, since he is known to be financially embarrassed, it is thought that he will marry Catherine Arrowpoint for her money, but he meets Gwendolen Harleth, and is attracted by her beauty, and also by her imperious, passionate, and unschooled temperament. A cruel man, who has always enjoyed unlimited power over his dependents, he thinks it would be amusing to tame her. His plans almost go awry when she learns of the existence of Lydia, but poverty finally leads her to accept him. The marriage is a disaster from the beginning, though Grandcourt much enjoys his conflicts with Gwendolen, which he invariably wins. She does not know that he is aware of her meeting with Lydia, and as a result despises her for having married him in full knowledge of his past. But her ignorance of this makes her easier to manage, since she is terrified that he will find out. Matters come to a head when Grandcourt decides Gwendolen is showing far too much interest in Daniel

Deronda. To separate them he takes Gwendolen on his yacht round the Mediterranean, but they have to put in at Genoa for repairs. By coincidence Deronda is also in Genoa, and although Grandcourt realises that they have most probably met by accident, he is determined to keep them apart, and so arranges to take his wife out in a small sailing boat. It overturns, and Grandcourt is drowned. In his will he has left everything to his illegitimate son, except for a paltry £2,000 a year to Gwendolen, and—the crowning insult—the house occupied by Mrs. Glasher and the children. *Daniel Deronda*

GRAVES, MISS: A teacher at the school where Gwendolen Harleth was educated. When offered a similar position after the loss of her mother's money, Gwendolen remembers Miss Graves, and decides to marry Grandcourt instead. *Daniel Deronda*

GRAY, MRS.: The milliner who made Mrs. Pullet's new bonnet, 'with a full crown'. *The Mill on the Floss*

GRIFFIN: Beatrice Assher's lady's maid, who has a good deal to put up with, as Beatrice is so very particular about her clothes. She is under notice to leave when Captain Wybrow dies, and in the ensuing confusion she takes to her bed and is no use to anyone. *Scenes of Clerical Life II: Mr. Gilfil's Love-Story*

GRIFFIN, MR. AND MRS.: An elderly couple who are told by their vicar, Tyke, that they will have no more free coal if they go and hear Mr. Farebrother preach. *Middlemarch*

GRINSELL, LORD: A nobleman who, according to the Dowager Lady Chettam, took it very much to heart when one of his daughters married again less than a year after her first husband died. *Middlemarch*

GRUBY, MR.: A grocer who supplies snuff to Dempster. Dempster takes so much of it that it spills down his coat and the cat sneezes whenever she comes near him. *Scenes of Clerical Life III: Janet's Repentance*

GUCCIO: A Florentine who goes with his friend Oddo the dyer, hoping to help drive out Piero de' Medici, only to find that he has already left the city. *Romola*

GUEST, THE MISSES: Stephen Guest's sisters, the younger being Laura. They dislike Maggie Tulliver, being subconsciously aware that her innate simplicity shows up their airs and affectations. Lucy Deane they rather look down on, but they are prepared to tolerate her as a sister-in-law, and after Stephen's elopement, which they blame entirely on Maggie, they take Lucy to Scarborough, still hoping Stephen will return and marry her, which he eventually does. *The Mill on the Floss*

GUEST, STEPHEN: A selfish, but very attractive young man, son of the head of the firm which employs Lucy Deane's father. Stephen is flattered by Lucy's artless admiration, and is prepared to marry her until he meets her cousin Maggie Tulliver. He is completely captivated by her, and she too finds herself unwillingly attracted to him. They fight against the bond which seems to unite them, and at one moment have the courage to part. Stephen does not want to fall in love with Maggie; he finds her too unusual and disturbing, and he knows that Lucy will make him a far more suitable wife. But her involuntary hold over him strengthens with absence, and when by a fortuitous chain of circumstances they find themselves alone on a river picnic, Stephen rows so far that they cannot return home before dark. They spend the night on the deck of a Dutch barge, and next day Stephen tries to persuade Maggie to elope with him. But she is horrified at what has happened, and insists on going straight home, alone, while Stephen, realising far more clearly than Maggie the interpretation that will be put on their escapade, takes refuge in Holland. Some years after the death of Maggie Tulliver, Stephen, mainly owing to the efforts of his sisters, finally marries Lucy. *The Mill on the Floss*

GUICCIARDINI, PIERO: One of the outstanding men of Florence, strongly opposed to the death sentence passed on Bernardo del Nero and his companions for conspiring to bring back the Medici, and also against the sentence passed on Savonarola. *Romola*

GUNN, THE MISSES: The two daughters of a wine merchant, who are invited to the Casses' New Year's Eve ball. They arrive dressed most unsuitably in the height of fashion, with very tight skirts, high waists, and low necks, and think the company very countrified and ignorant. *Silas Marner*

GYPSIES: When Maggie Tulliver as a small child runs away from home, she meets a band of gypsies in a lane near Dunlow Common. She has so often been told she looks like a gypsy, with her dark hair and eyes, that she thinks it might be romantic to live with them, but is quickly undeceived by their rough ways and coarse bullying, and is very glad when they decide to take her home in the hope of a reward. On the way they meet Maggie's father, who gives them five shillings. *The Mill on the Floss*

H

HACKBUTT, MR. AND MRS.: A rich tanner and his wife, who dislike Mr. Bulstrode, and are glad when he is discredited in the eyes of the town. Mr. Hackbutt, who also disapproves of Bulstrode's son-in-law Lydgate because he does not do his dispensing—'a doctor should be responsible for the quality of the drugs given to his patients'—is one of the group that forces Bulstrode to resign. Mrs. Hackbutt, whose daughter Fanny has lessons from Mary Garth's mother, is sorry for Mrs. Bulstrode, but thinks she was always rather 'showy' and is now being punished. She also thinks she should leave her husband, which Mrs. Bulstrode refuses to do. When Ned Plympton marries Sophy Toller, and Rosamond Lydgate sabotages her husband's plan to let their expensive house to the young couple, the Hackbutts let them one they own next door to themselves, and put it in order for them. *Middlemarch*

HACKIT, MR. AND MRS.: A shrewd, substantial couple who have a farm in the parish of Shepperton. Mr. Hackit is a church-warden, and though he does not object to Amos Barton personally, he has no opinion of his business capacity—'his education has unfitted him for it'. Mrs. Hackit, who has a chronic liver complaint, and has long been a patient of Mr. Pilgrim, quite likes Barton 'for all he's not overburthened i'th' upper storey', and is very fond of his wife Milly, sending her delicacies when she is ill, and telling Barton that he ought to send the Countess packing. After Milly's death she helps look after the children, and always takes a special interest in Dickey, who spends his holidays on the farm. *Scenes of Clerical Life I: The Rev. Amos Barton*

When the Hackits first come to their farm, Mr. Gilfil is vicar of Shepperton. Hackit, who considers Squire Oldinport, from whom he rents his farm, a bad landlord, is delighted when he comes off worst in an argument with Gilfil; and Mrs. Hackit, who has been much struck by his sermon on honesty just after her grocer has given her short weight, is very upset by his death, and gives old Dame Fripp a length of crape to wear round her little coal-scuttle bonnet at his funeral, as a token of respect. *Scenes of Clerical Life II: Mr. Gilfil's Love-Story*

HALM-EBERSTEIN, THE PRINCESS LEONORA: The mother of Daniel Deronda. The daughter of an orthodox Jew, Daniel Charisi, who, like Mordecai, was fired by the vision of a united Jewry, she grew up in rebellion against the discipline imposed on her. When her father, hoping for a grandson to carry on his work, arranged for her to marry her cousin, Ephraim Charisi, she agreed because she knew that through marriage she could escape from her father and fulfil her destiny as an opera-singer. As Alcharisi, she became internationally famous, and when her husband died, leaving her with a son of about two years old, she disembarrassed herself of the child, and ensured his escape from what she regarded as the tyranny of a Jewish background, by confiding him to the care of Sir Hugo Mallinger, one of her most ardent admirers, to be brought up as 'an English gentleman', settling on him the fortune left by his father. When her powers began to wane, she married a Russian prince, by whom she had five children. Now, stricken by a mortal illness and with only a year to live, she is troubled by pangs of conscience and feels she has robbed both her father and her son of something they might have cherished. On an impulse she arranges to meet Daniel at Genoa, and reveals the secret of his parentage. But she feels no affection for him, and in spite of his wish to remain with her and be acknowledged as her son, she refuses to let her husband know of his existence, and leaves Genoa without seeing him again. *Daniel Deronda*

HARDY, JIM: A poor coal-carrier who loses his horse, and is succoured by the benevolent Mr. Jerome. *Scenes of Clerical Life III: Janet's Repentance*

HARFAGER, CLARA: A young lady whose friends 'don't know what to do with her'. Mrs. Cadwallader would like her to marry Mr. Lydgate, instead of Rosamond Vincy, as 'she would be an asset to our society', which Rosamond, being a tradesman's daughter, cannot be. *Middlemarch*

HARLETH, GWENDOLEN: The beautiful, high-spirited, and badly spoiled daughter of Fanny Davilow by her first marriage. She intensely dislikes her step-father and the four plain daughters her mother has borne him, and is thankful when he dies and the family settles near the Gascoignes, Mrs. Gascoigne being her mother's sister. She foresees a period of intense and gratifying social success, terminating in a brilliant marriage, for she is sure she is marked out for some particular destiny, and is impatient both of her mother's undemanding affection and her uncle's sensibly restraining hand. Romantic but conventional, she wants her life to be exceptional, but does not know how to make it so, and is mortified by any failure on her part to live up to her ideals, as when the musician Klesmer shows plainly that he considers her musically inadequate. She is quite willing to flirt with her cousin Rex Gascoigne, but contemptuously refuses his offer of marriage. She is, however, flattered by the attentions of the older and more sophisticated Henleigh Grandcourt, and is on the verge of becoming engaged to him when she meets Lydia Glasher, who tells her that she is Grandcourt's mistress and has four children by him. This repels Gwendolen, and she promises Lydia that she will not marry Grandcourt, chiefly in order that Lydia may herself persuade him into marriage and so legitimize their young son. Gwendolen hurriedly accepts an invitation from her friends the von Langens and goes abroad with them, thus breaking off her relationship with Grandcourt. But the sudden loss of all her mother's money, and the realization that she will have to go out as a governess, undermines her resolution. She breaks her promise, and allows herself to marry Grandcourt, believing that as his wife she will be able to manage him as easily as she has hitherto managed all her friends and relations. She has no inkling of his cruel, indeed sadistic, nature, nor does she know that he is aware of her meeting with his mistress, and despises her for marrying him under such conditions. Almost immediately after her wedding she receives from Lydia Glasher the family diamonds which Grandcourt had given her in the first flush of his infatuation, together with a letter castigating Gwendolen for breaking her solemn promise. The marriage which begins under such unhappy auspices goes from bad to worse, and Gwendolen finds herself broken and mastered by an egotism which exceeds her own in strength and ingenuity. She finds some comfort in the friendship and counsel of the young Daniel Deronda, whom she at first reveres as a wise and compassionate confidant, and then falls in love with. Her husband, who has watched the whole affair with quiet, sardonic amusement, decides the matter has gone far enough, and takes her on a Mediterranean cruise, in the course of which he is drowned at Genoa. Daniel Deronda, being in Genoa at the same time on his own affairs, does all he can to succour and console the young widow, who feels responsible for the death of her husband to the extent of confiding to Daniel that she deliberately held back the rope that might have saved him. Daniel rebukes her for such morbid thoughts, but in spite of his kindness she realises that she means nothing to him. Back in England she sends for him repeatedly for reassurance and advice, until at last he tells her that he is a Jew and that he is about to marry the Jewish singer Mirah Lapidoth, whom she has met and admired at London concerts. For a long time after his departure Gwendolen, who has been left only a small annuity in her husband's will and has settled with her mother and sisters near the Gascoignes, is seriously ill, but she recovers sufficiently to send Daniel a brave letter on his wedding day, saying she will strive to become the woman he wants her to be, and that 'it shall be better with me because I have known you'. *Daniel Deronda*

HARRY: A worker at Tulliver's mill. He forgot to feed Tom Tulliver's rabbits while he was away at school and they all died. *The Mill on the Floss*

HART, DR.: The Cheverels' doctor, who is sent for when Wybrow is found dead in the Rookery. He certifies that death was due to a long-established disease of the heart, accelerated by strong emotion. *Scenes of Clerical Life II: Mr. Gilfil's Love-Story*

HARTOPP, MRS. BESSIE: A buxom peasant woman, recently widowed, who has been ordered by Sir Christopher Cheverel's bailiff to quit her late husband's farm. She comes to remonstrate with Sir Christopher, not knowing that he plans to put her into a more convenient small-holding. *Scenes of Clerical Life II: Mr. Gilfil's Love-Story*

HAWKINS: A Radical, and a member of the Rev. Rufus Lyon's congregation, who is canvassed at the factory where he works by Harold Transome. He is annoyed with Lyon for arranging to debate with the curate, Sherlock, and agrees that 'Tories and clergymen . . . if they ever aped civility to Dissenters, would never do anything but laugh at them in their sleeves'. *Felix Holt*

HAWLEY, ARABELLA: A young lady in Middlemarch who went into a consumption and died after being crossed in love. Rosamond Vincy threatens to do the same if her father will not agree to her marrying Lydgate. *Middlemarch*

HAWLEY, FRANK: The town-clerk of Middlemarch, who also has a flourishing legal practice. He dislikes and distrusts Bulstrode, the banker, and extends his dislike to the new doctor, Lydgate, because he was appointed to the staff of the new hospital by Bulstrode. He is also antipathetic to Mr. Brooke, considers him a bad landlord, and disapproves of his action in buying the local paper and getting Ladislaw, who is staying with him, to write Radical articles in it supporting Brooke's parliamentary ambitions. He investigates several incidents connected with the activities of Bulstrode, Lydgate, and Brooke, but can find nothing illegal in any of them, though he is willing to believe that Lydgate was bribed by Bulstrode to keep quiet about his relationship with Raffles. He is spokesman for the committee which forces the resignation of Bulstrode from the Hospital Board. *Middlemarch*

HAXEY, JOB: The weaver who wove the material from which Mrs. Tulliver, who had spun the thread herself, made tablecloths in preparation for her wedding. *The Mill on the Floss*

HAYNES, MR.: A gentleman who is constantly frustrated in his desire to rent Offendene from Lord Brackenshaw by the fluctuating fortunes of Mrs. Davilow, who keeps taking and relinquishing it. He finally gives up and moves elsewhere. *Daniel Deronda*

HAZELOW, TOM: The cousin of Bill Downes, who sends Bill a letter which he cannot read. This decides Bill to go to night-school with the schoolmaster Bartle Massey in order to learn to read and write. *Adam Bede*

HERON, THE REV. ARTHUR: The brother-in-law of Mr Gilfil, whose wife Lucy goes to Dorcas's farm to take care of Tina Sarti after she has run away from the Cheverels, and later takes her back to Foxholm Parsonage until she marries Gilfil. The five-year-old Ozzie (Oswald) Heron becomes very attached to Tin-Tin, as he calls her, and does more than anyone to help her recover from her illness. He attends her wedding 'in a new velvet cap and tunic'. *Scenes of Clerical Life II: Mr. Gilfil's Love-Story*

HESTER: Housekeeper to the Cheverels' gardener, Bates, whom Mrs. Sharp the lady's maid hopes to replace by marrying Bates. *Scenes of Clerical Life II: Mr. Gilfil's Love-Story*

HIBBERT, MISS: An unfortunate young lady whose singing was considered 'small piping' compared with Tina's. *Scenes of Clerical Life II: Mr. Gilfil's Love-Story*

HICKES: The Transomes' butler. *Felix Holt*

HICKES, MRS.: *see* Denner

HICKS, DR.: A local doctor, replaced after his sudden death by young Lydgate. The Dowager Lady Chettam, who does not like her doctor to be well-connected, says of him 'He was coarse and butcher-like, but he knew my constitution'. *Middlemarch*

HIGGINS, MARY: *see* Fodge, Poll

HIGGINS, MRS.: A parishioner of Mr. Gilfil's, who was indignant because Mrs. Jennings appeared in church the Sunday after his funeral wearing coloured ribbons. She herself was very proud of the fact that from the time she married until her husband's death, she 'niver was out o' black two year to-gether!' *Scenes of Clerical Life II: Mr. Gilfil's Love-Story*

HOLDSWORTH, MICHAEL: A farmer who had a pair of oxen 'sweltered' (i.e. overcome by the heat) while he was ploughing on Good Friday—a warning to all his neighbours against sacrilege. *Adam Bede*

HOLLIS, LADY FLORA: A lively, middle-aged woman, who is invited by Grandcourt to Diplow, and is consumed with curiosity about his relationship with Gwendolen Harleth. When Gwendolen goes abroad before Grandcourt has had a chance to propose to her, Lady Flora pays a round of visits. She returns to tell Grandcourt at lunch that Gwendolen has gone to Leubronn, and the general opinion is that she has refused him. This is enough to break up the party and send Grandcourt off in pursuit of Gwendolen. *Daniel Deronda*

HOLT, FELIX: The son of a quack doctor, apprenticed to a country practitioner, where he learns enough to know that his father's remedies are useless, and may be dangerous. He therefore destroys them after his father's death, and supports himself and his mother by binding himself 'journeyman to Mr. Prowd the watchmaker' to learn the trade, and also by teaching a few ragged boys, mostly miners' sons. 'Shaggy-headed, large-eyed, strong-limbed, without waistcoat or cravat', he is a staunch Radical and a Dissenter, and attends the Rev. Rufus Lyon's chapel. He meets the minister's adopted daughter, Esther, on her return from an excellent school, and though he rails at her for her fashionable clothes and air of social superiority, he secretly falls in love with her. Felix gets caught up in the election-day riots, which he is trying to prevent, and is arrested and tried as one of the ring-leaders, and for manslaughter, since he was held responsible for the death of the constable, Tucker, whom in fact he was trying to save. In spite of the evidence given on his behalf by a number of prominent citizens, including Esther herself, he is sentenced to four years in prison. Some of the local gentry, realizing there has been a miscarriage of justice, secure his release, and he returns home to find that Esther, who has proved to be the heiress to the Transome estates, has become sadly disillusioned with high society after a visit to Transome Court. She discovers that she loves Felix, in spite of his uncouth ways and anti-clerical ideas, and prefers poverty and marriage with him to affluence and misery as the wife of Harold Transome. *Felix Holt*

HOLT, MR.: A north-country weaver who gave up his trade and moved to the Midlands as a purveyor of quack medicines which he made himself, notably 'Cathartic Lozenges', a 'Restorative Elixir' and a 'Cancer Cure'. Though totally uneducated, he was a fluent speaker, and 'there was many a one said it was as good as a dose of physic to hear him talk'. On his death he left a large stock of medicines which his widow hoped to sell, and so support herself and her son. *Felix Holt*

HOLT, MRS. (MARY): The mother of Felix, a respectable and vociferous widow whose maiden name was Wall. She is furious when her son insists on throwing away the quack medicines left by his father, and confides her troubles to Mr. Lyon, who considers her one of the trials he is called on to bear. But she is very kind to little Job Tudge, who is consumptive, and is finally brought to tolerate Esther Lyon as her son's wife, particularly after the birth of her grandson, 'who has a good deal more science than his father, but not much more money'. *Felix Holt*

HOOD, JEM: The bassoon-player in Shepperton Church choir, who is angry when the new curate, Amos Barton, replaces the old metrical psalm at a wedding by a new-fangled hymn. *Scenes of Clerical Life I: The Rev. Amos Barton*

HOPKINS: A meek-mannered linen-draper in Middlemarch, who much enjoys a gossip with the men because his customers are mostly women. He is the first person to whom Bambridge tells the scandalous story of Bulstrode and Raffles, and remarks that it was only the previous day that he had provided the funeral for Raffles, 'a very decent funeral' at which Bulstrode was the only mourner. *Middlemarch*

HORNER, THE REV. MR.: For a short time minister in charge of Salem Independent Chapel in Milby, dismissed because he was too much given to tippling and quarrelling with his wife. *Scenes of Clerical Life III: Janet's Repentance*

HORROCK, MR.: The local vet, with whom Fred Vincy goes to Houndsley Horse Fair; a silent man, with a permanently sceptical expression. *Middlemarch*

HUDSON: Gwendolen Harleth's lady's maid, engaged before

Gwendolen gets married and taken by her to Ryelands after the wedding. *Daniel Deronda*

HUTCHINS: One of Grandcourt's outdoor servants at Diplow. *Daniel Deronda*

HYNDMARSH, MR.: A grocer who buys the large stock of pickles and ketchup put up by Mrs. Tulliver before her husband's bankruptcy. *The Mill on the Floss*

I

IRWINE, THE REV. ADOLPHUS: 'Rector of Broxton, Vicar of Hayslope, and Vicar of Blythe, a pluralist at whom the severest Church-reformer would have found it difficult to look sour.' Elderly and unmarried, with powdered hair drawn backward and tied with a black ribbon, he keeps his mother, who calls him Dauphin and wishes he would marry, and two spinster sisters in 'ladylike ease' on an income of £700 a year. Although he disapproves of Methodism, he is intrigued by Dinah Morris's quiet dignity, and refuses to interfere with her preaching, telling the parish clerk, Joshua Rann, who tries to stir him up against her, that the thing will die a natural death before long, and anyhow she seems to have improved some of the villagers, notably Will Maskery, formerly a wife-beater and heavy drinker. Irwine is fond of both Captain Donnithorne and of Adam Bede, and when he hears that Hetty Sorrel, who is engaged to Adam, is to be tried for the murder of Donnithorne's child, his chief fear is that Adam will kill Donnithorne. He also reproaches himself for not having seen what was going on in his own parish, and goes to the trial in order to give evidence in Hetty's favour. He agrees, when Donnithorne leaves home in a self-imposed exile, to help oversee his estate if Adam and the Poysers, who are also thinking of quitting the neighbourhood, will stay and help him. He thus keeps everyone together, and after marrying Adam and Dinah, he has the pleasure of seeing Donnithorne return after a lapse of eight years. *Adam Bede*

IRWINE, ANNE: Younger sister of the Rev. Adolphus Irwine, and an invalid who gets little sympathy from her indomitable mother. The villagers, who seldom see her, pity her and often send up little offerings of eggs and chickens to the Vicarage. *Adam Bede*

IRWINE, KATE: Elder sister of the Rev. Adolphus Irwine, a 'thin, middle-aged lady', who spends most of her so-called leisure planning economies so that her 'splendid' mother, who considers her a poor thing and wonders how she came to have such a commonplace daughter, need not suffer from their straitened circumstances. *Adam Bede*

IRWINE, MRS.: The mother of the Rev. Adolphus Irwine, tall, erect, a brunette with intensely black eyes, still handsome in spite of her advanced age, and dressed in black with white cambric and a lace collar and some lovely pieces of jewellery. Resigned to comparative poverty since her husband's death, she despises her plain, useful daughters, and dotes on her only son. After old Squire Donnithorne's death she looks forward to the easing of her son's financial position under the new squire, her godson Captain Donnithorne, but is distressed when she hears of the captain's disastrous association with Hetty Sorrel. *Adam Bede*

J

JABEZ: The Transomes' footman. Harold Transome, when he returns home from abroad, considers him a 'dolt', and refuses to be waited on by him, preferring the ministrations of Hickes until the arrival of his own man, Dominic. *Felix Holt*

JACKSON, MISS: The aunt of Mrs. Barton, who lives with her after her marriage, so easing the financial burden on the young couple, who quickly acquire a large family. Unfortunately Amos Barton, not remarkable for tact, manages to quarrel with her after about eight years, and she leaves to live with another niece, whereupon the Bartons get heavily into debt. After Mrs. Barton's death her aunt returns to look after the children for some months. *Scenes of Clerical Life I: The Rev. Amos Barton*

JACOBS: A schoolmaster at the academy which Tom Tulliver attends for a couple of years—familiarly known as 'Old Goggles'. *The Mill on the Floss*

JACOPO: The village boy who helps Romola and the local priest to care for the survivors of the plague brought by the marooned Jews. *Romola*

JAKIN, BOB: A ragged, red headed, freckle-faced bird-scarer, who fascinates Tom Tulliver; he has a mongrel dog named Mumps, keeps a small snake in his hat, and makes a pet of a bat. Maggie Tulliver hates him because she is always left behind when he and Tom go off on adventures. When the Tullivers are in trouble, Bob, who has never forgotten that Tom once gave him a cherished pocket-knife with two blades, offers him the £9 he has been given as a reward for putting out a fire in a mill. Tom refuses gratefully, and Bob uses the money to go into trade, later inducing Tom to join him in sending goods abroad. He has always admired Maggie from afar, and when she returns after her enforced elopement with Stephen Guest, he is very happy to let her the rooms in his house formerly occupied by her brother, who has shut her out of the mill. When the flood comes, Bob saves one of his boats and Maggie, the other and they are both swept away. But Bob manages to survive, and is reunited with his family. *The Mill on the Floss*

JAKIN, MRS.: A large, fat woman who lives in a queer little round house down by the Floss, and owns a brindled dog that barks at Maggie and Tom. She is the mother of Tom's disreputable friend Bob, and after his marriage she lives with him and his wife. They run two pleasure boats, and also take in lodgers, one of whom is Tom, for a short time, and another Maggie. *The Mill on the Floss*

JAKIN, PRISSY: The wife of Bob Jakin, 'a tiny woman with the general physiognomy of a Dutch doll'. She knows of her husband's admiration for Maggie Tulliver, and is quite willing to call her first baby Maggie. When Maggie Tulliver, repudiated by her friends and family, takes refuge with the

Jakins, Prissy entrusts the baby to her, thinking it will bring her comfort. *The Mill on the Floss*

JAMES: A doctor's assistant, who secretly married the doctor's niece, and was forgiven when it was found out, because 'it was too late to do anything about it'. Hetty Sorrel hopes Captain Donnithorne will marry her secretly, with the same result. *Adam Bede*

JARRETT: The village carpenter, who is called in to make a stage at Offendene for the Christmas entertainment given there by Gwendolen Harleth and her friends. *Daniel Deronda*

JAY, BETTY: A poor villager who is glad to receive the scraps from the Casses' kitchen—the liquor, for instance, in which the hams were boiled for the New Year's Eve ball. *Silas Marner*

JEFFRIES: The man employed by Mrs. Davilow to look after the horses at Offendene. When she loses all her money, the horses are sold and Jeffries dismissed. *Daniel Deronda*

JENNING: A friend of young Clintock, the archdeacon's son, who has written a poem in four cantos, in the style of Pope, on croquet. His friends are urging him to publish it, and Clintock offers to let Gwendolen Harleth read it when he is trying to persuade her to take up croquet instead of archery. *Daniel Deronda*

JENNINGS, MRS.: A newcomer to Shepperton, town-bred, who shocks the neighbours by wearing salmon-coloured ribbons and a green shawl to church the Sunday after the Rev. Gilfil's funeral. *Scenes of Clerical Life II: Mr. Gilfil's Love-Story*

JERMYN, LOUISA: One of the three daughters of the lawyer Jermyn. She has lessons from Esther Lyon, and is surprised to find her so well educated and ladylike, as she had always believed Dissenters to be ignorant, vulgar people. Esther, for her part, considers Louisa 'vulgarity personified—with large feet, and the most odious scent on her handkerchief'. *Felix Holt*

JERMYN, MATTHEW: The Transomes' family lawyer. As a handsome young man he had a brief but passionate affair with Mrs. Transome, and is the father of her second son, Harold.

The secret was well kept, and everyone accepted Harold as old Transome's son. On the death of his dissolute elder brother, Harold returns from Turkey, where he has made a considerable fortune, as the acknowledged heir of the Transome estate, which Jermyn has been managing for many years. Harold suspects that the lawyer has done very well for himself out of the transaction, and an immediate antipathy is apparent between the father and son. Jermyn, who has been instrumental in blocking the claim of Maurice Bycliffe to the reversion of the estate, is betrayed by his London agent, Johnson, and when Bycliffe's daughter Esther is found to be the legal owner of Transome Court, Jermyn realises that his career is in jeopardy. He tries to stop Harold from bringing a suit against him for mismanagement and other misdemeanours by threatening to produce Esther to oust Harold; when Harold says he knows all about Esther and intends to marry her and so keep a hold on his property, Jermyn quarrels with him and rashly reveals in public the secret of his parentage. This precipitates the ruin of Jermyn himself, and he and his family leave the town, going to reside 'at a great distance; some said "abroad", that large home of ruined reputations.' *Felix Holt*

JEROME, MR. (THOMAS): A retired corn-factor, the richest and most benevolent member of the congregation of Salem Independent Chapel, who expresses his kindness towards his fellow-men by loans to the rich and sacks of potatoes to the poor. He had become a Dissenter by chance at fifteen, under the influence of Jacob Wright, but when he discovered the sterling worth of the Rev. Edgar Tryan, and his infamous persecution by Robert Dempster, he returned to the Church and became one of Tryan's kindest and most influential supporters. He is very good to Janet Dempster after her husband's death, and acts as pall bearer at Tryan's funeral. *Scenes of Clerical Life III: Janet's Repentance*

JEROME, MRS. (SUSAN): The buxom old-fashioned wife of Mr. Jerome, who presides over her handsome tea-table in a stiff grey silk gown and an elaborate lace cap fastened by a frill under the chin. She married Jerome in spite of his being Chapel, and is glad when he returns to the Church, because she has an innate respect for the cloth. She is delighted when Dempster is found to have left all his property to his wife unconditionally, and confides to Janet that she knows nothing of her own husband's will, but 'I should like to hev a thousand or two at my own disposial; it makes a widow a deal more looked on.' A placid woman, she is seldom ruffled, but does object to her husband letting Lizzie, their small grandchild, get her frock stained in the strawberry beds. *Scenes of Clerical Life III: Janet's Repentance*

JETSOME: A dissolute young man whom Wakem makes manager of Dorlcote Mill. He proves unequal to the task, and Wakem sells the mill to Guest & Co., Tom Tulliver being installed as manager when Jetsome is thrown from his horse while drunk. He was probably Wakem's illegitimate son. *The Mill on the Floss*

JOB: An old labourer who is envied by little Ben Garth because he doesn't have to bother about grammar. *Middlemarch*

A young man who is courting Janet Dempster's parlourmaid, Kitty. He is exceptionally lucky, for that period, in that he is allowed to visit Kitty, and Janet speaks most pleasantly to him when she finds him in the kitchen on Sunday evening. *Scenes of Clerical Life III: Janet's Repentance*

JOCOSA: *see* Merry, Miss

JODSON, MR.: An elderly gentleman who died, most conveniently, just as Mrs. Davilow wanted his house, which was only a mile along the lane from her brother-in-law's rectory. *Daniel Deronda*

JOHN: Head groom at Donnithorne Chase, who has to manage with raw lads, as the Squire won't pay decent wages. One of them is responsible for the laming of Captain Donnithorne's mare Meg. *Adam Bede*

Sir James Chettam's groom. *Middlemarch*

The Countess Czerlaski's groom, who also waits at table, smelling of the stables, and upsets the gravy-boat over Mrs. Barton's black frock. *Scenes of Clerical Life I: The Rev. Amos Barton*

JOHNS, THE REV. MR.: An evangelical clergyman who was responsible for the early training of Amos Barton. *Scenes of Clerical Life I: The Rev. Amos Barton*

JOHNSON: Mr. Brooke's gamekeeper, who catches the Methodist preacher Favell with a hare which has run across his path; he is rather shocked at such lawlessness in a minister, and by Mr. Brooke's leniency in letting the man off lightly. Johnson also finds young Jacob Dagley with a freshly-killed leveret, and is told to lock him up in an empty stable for an hour or two. *Middlemarch*

JOHNSON, JOHN: An attorney, one of lawyer Jermyn's agents. He is sent to stir up the miners against the Tory candidate on election day, which leads to rioting, and also gets Felix Holt arrested as 'a dangerous revolutionary'. He owes his present position to Jermyn, who thinks of him as 'a most serviceable subordinate'. But Johnson secretly hates Jermyn, and also Harold Transome, who was rude to him once, and he is delighted to be able to bring about the lawyer's downfall by revealing the shady transactions he has been engaged in over the reversion of the Transome estate. *Felix Holt*

JONAS: Mr. Brooke's manservant. *Middlemarch*

JONAS, MR. A dyer in Middlemarch, a good-natured fellow who is in the Tankard Inn when the landlady, Mrs. Dollop, says she is sure Raffles was murdered. He is in favour of digging the body up to get at the truth of the matter. *Middlemarch*

JORTIN: The owner of a mare which Dunsey Cass pretends he wants to buy as an excuse for selling Wildfire. *Silas Marner*

JOSEPH: Trumbull's assistant in the auction rooms. *Middlemarch*

JOYCE: 'An impetuous young farmer of superior information', who has no opinion of Radicals and trades-union men. He would like to see them all conscripted into the yeomanry. *Felix Holt*

JUDITH: Mrs. Poyser's sister. She took in her niece Dinah Morris when she was orphaned, and they both became ardent Methodists. Mrs. Poyser, who gives Dinah a home when Judith dies, says she is exactly like her aunt, in ways and to look at. *Adam Bede*

K

KALONYMOS, JOSEPH: A friend of Daniel Deronda's grandfather, Daniel Charisi, and like him a believer in the eventual re-emergence of the Jewish nation. He knew that Charisi's daughter Leonora had had a son, but she told him the child had died. He believed her, and knowing she had renounced her Jewish faith, he took from her the chest which her father had left for his grandchild, if it were a boy, and put it in safety. Twenty years later he sees Daniel in Frankfurt and recognises him by his likeness to his grandfather. He confronts Leonora and forces her to meet and acknowledge Daniel, and later gives him his grandfather's chest, full of precious old Jewish manuscripts. *Daniel Deronda*

KEATING: A member of the local hunt who tries to buy Godfrey Cass's horse Wildfire; he is outbid by Bryce. *Silas Marner*

KECK: The editor of the *Trumpet*. Although a good Tory, he is not liked by Sir James Chettam, who has a low opinion of newspaper men; and Mr. Brooke, whom he attacks for being a Radical, says he is 'an illiterate fellow'. Keck accuses Ladislaw, who is writing for the rival paper, the *Pioneer*, of being not only crack-brained and too glib, but a Polish spy into the bargain. *Middlemarch*

KELL, MRS.: Mr. Brooke's housekeeper, who knows Ladislaw from his having stayed in the house, and allows him, in Mr. Brooke's absence, to fetch some of his drawings from the library, where Dorothea finds him. *Middlemarch*

KEMP, BROTHER: A member of the Rev. Lyon's Dissenting congregation. Having a good bass voice, he is in favour of singing during the services. This annoys the grocer, Nuttwood, who says: 'I cannot but think it a snare when a professing Christian has a bass voice like Brother Kemp's. It makes him desire to be heard of men'. Kemp is so sure of Felix Holt's guilt over the election riot that he prays for him in chapel as 'a young Ishmaelite, whom we would fain see brought back from the lawless life of the desert'. *Felix Holt*

KENCH: The constable to whom Silas Marner goes to complain of the theft of his gold. *Silas Marner*

KENN, DR.: The rector of St. Ogg's, a plain, middle-aged man with a look indicative of grave, penetrating kindness. He runs his parish well, but does not approve of Church bazaars because he believes charity should be less ostentatious. However, he attends the one at which Maggie Tulliver is present and, struck by her evident unhappiness, speaks kindly to her. When she returns from her elopement with Stephen Guest, she sends for him to advise her, but his wife has just died, leaving him with a large family, and he cannot go. Later on, having read Stephen's letter exonerating Maggie, he believes in her innocence and tries to help her, to the extent of engaging her as governess for his small daughters. But the outraged ladies of his congregation force him to dismiss her, and he urges her to leave the town and get a situation elsewhere, with his help. *The Mill on the Floss*

KEZIA: A bad-tempered but essentially kind-hearted housemaid, who remains faithful to the Tullivers after the father's bankruptcy, scrubbing the floor of the parlour after the sale so that they can have their tea there. *The Mill on the Floss*

KIBBLE: The silversmith where Lydgate buys the plate for his new home, resisting the temptation to choose an expensive pattern in favour of something elegant but less costly. *Middlemarch*

KIMBLE, DR.: A country apothecary who married Squire Cass's sister, and is godfather to Godfrey Cass. Always volatile in sober business hours, he becomes intense and bitter over cards and brandy, and is annoyed when he is called away from his game on New Year's Eve to see Molly Farren, who is already dead. *Silas Marner*

KIMBLE, MRS.: Squire Cass's sister. As he has no wife, she acts as hostess for him at the New Year's Eve ball, a tall, stout lady, rather short of breath, in old-fashioned clothes, but kind and jolly. She regrets that she has no son to take over her husband's practice, but is very fond of her nephews, and is the only person who worries when Dunsey does not come home for Christmas. The one thing that really makes her angry is her husband's unfortunate habit of revoking when playing cards. *Silas Marner*

KIRKE, MISS: An elderly lady with a spinal complaint who resides in the parish of St. Ogg's. She needs a 'reader and companion', and the rector, Dr. Kenn, tries to persuade her to employ Maggie Tulliver after her return from her escapade with Stephen Guest; but Miss Kirke refuses on the grounds that Maggie's mind 'must be of a quality with which she, for her part, could not risk *any* contact.' *The Mill on the Floss*

KITTY: A young woman who spun most of Mrs. Poyser's linen. Though 'a rare girl to spin', she squinted, and 'the children couldn't abide her'. *Adam Bede*

The Transomes' maid-servant. *Felix Holt*

Janet Dempster's parlourmaid. When Dempster shuts Janet out of the house in her nightgown and she takes refuge with Mrs. Pettifer, the servants think she has gone to her mother's; but Kitty discovers that her clothes are still in the closet, and is convinced Dempster has murdered her and hidden the body. *Scenes of Clerical Life III: Janet's Repentance*

KLESMER, HERR JULIUS: A composer and musician of some repute, who later becomes very famous. He is engaged to reside at Quetcham Hall in order to give music lessons to Catherine Arrowpoint, who is extremely musical. He meets Gwendolen Harleth, and is amused by her musical pretensions, later advising her not to try and follow a musical or acting career, since he realises she has no talent and no idea of the hard work involved. On the other hand, he much admires the excellent singing of Mirah Lapidoth and does all he can to further her career. While he is with the Arrowpoints, he and Catherine fall in love, but he will not propose to her because she is an heiress, and he is only on the threshold of his career. But Catherine loves him enough to propose herself, and also to overcome the resistance of her parents. They marry and settle in London, and both are active in promoting the careers of young musicians like Mirah. *Daniel Deronda*

KNOTT, DANIEL: Coachman to Sir Christopher Cheverel. He marries the nursemaid Dorcas, and takes over a farm where Tina—who was fond of Dorcas as a child—takes refuge after the death of Wybrow. *Scenes of Clerical Life II: Mr Gilfil's Love-Story*

KNOWLES: A waggoner who drove up to the Donnithorne Arms just as the landlord Casson was having his 10.30 a.m.

pint, and with him sees the 'mysterious stranger on a bald-faced horse—a smart man in top boots—'who is negotiating for the lease of Chase Farm. This is Thurle, a farmer, who withdraws from the affair when Mrs. Poyser refuses to exchange some of her dairy land for corn land. *Adam Bede*

L

LABRON, LAWYER: Philip Debarry's political agent at the election. He is the brother-in-law of Salt, the wool-factor and one of those who object to Harold Transome as an 'upstart', his immediate forebears, the Durfeys, having bought their name and estate from the original Transomes. *Felix Holt*

LADBROOK, MRS. AND MISS: Guests at the Casses' New Year's Eve ball. Mrs. Ladbrook wears a skull cap and 'front', on which she places a turban; both she and her daughter admire the fashionable attire of the Misses Gunn, though admitting that they go perhaps 'too far', *Silas Marner*

LADISLAW, JULIA: The elder sister of Mr. Casaubon's mother. She ran away with a Pole, and was disinherited, all the father's money going to the younger sister. Because of this Mr. Casaubon feels it incumbent upon him to educate her grandson Will Ladislaw, though he has no liking for him personally. *Middlemarch*

LADISLAW, WILL: The young cousin of Mr. Casaubon, who is paying for his education. Though not handsome, he is attractive, an amusing companion, and a fluent speaker and writer. Casaubon, who dislikes him—the dislike is mutual—wants him to choose a profession, and says his indecision is 'part of his general inaccuracy and indisposition to thoroughness of all kinds', but agrees that he shall travel on the Continent for a year or two with a view to becoming an artist. When Ladislaw hears that Dorothea is to marry Casaubon, he thinks she must be a dull, unattractive creature, but on meeting her he changes his mind, and is deeply affected by the beauty of her voice, like that 'of a soul that had once lived in an Aeolian harp'. They meet again in Rome, where Ladislaw is indignant to find that Dorothea, who is on her honeymoon, is left alone all day while her husband works in the Vatican Library. Trying to brighten her life a little, he finds himself falling in love, and returns to England to settle near her as her uncle's secretary. This naturally intensifies Casaubon's dislike of him, and he forbids Dorothea to invite him to the house. He also adds a codicil to his will disinheriting Dorothea if after his death she marries him. Meanwhile Ladislaw has become a general favourite in local society, and is not averse to a light-hearted flirtation with Rosamond, who finds him a relief from her hard-working and sadly disillusioned husband Mr. Lydgate. Unfortunately Dorothea finds them together, and is also told by the scandalmongering Mrs. Cadwallader that they are having an affair, which she does not believe. After Casaubon's death Ladislaw, who does not know of the codicil, longs to ask Dorothea to marry him, but refrains, thinking she is too far removed from him socially and financially. He is about to leave the town when he meets John Raffles, and learns through him of the trick which Bulstrode played on his mother, depriving her of her rightful inheritance. But as this also reveals that he is, as Sir James Chettam unkindly puts it, 'the grandson of a thieving Jew pawnbroker' he feels it makes marriage with Dorothea still more impossible. In despair, he indignantly spurns Bulstrode's offer of an allowance in recompense of his past sufferings, and before leaving the town begs Dorothea for one last meeting. He now knows of the codicil, and thinks she is bound to honour it. But when they meet, their mutual passion proves too strong for them and they agree to marry, in spite of the consequences. They settle in London, where Ladislaw becomes a journalist and eventually a Member of Parliament; Dorothea, after an initial period of estrangement from her sister Celia, is reconciled to her, and their children grow up together, the husbands maintaining a position of armed neutrality for the sake of their wives. *Middlemarch*

LAKINS, THE: A poor family in Butcher's Lane in which Janet Dempster takes a charitable interest. *Scenes of Clerical Life III: Janet's Repentance*

LAMB, JONATHAN: The old parish clerk in Milby, who is cheered by Janet Dempster's sweet smile. *Scenes of Clerical Life III: Janet's Repentance*

LAMBERT: The druggist from whose upper window some of the ladies of Treby Magna listen to the electioneering speeches, *Felix Holt*

LAMMETER, MR.: A local land-owner, spare but healthy-looking, whose father came from the north, to settle in the Midlands, after his wife died. The son married the daughter of a local land-owning family, Miss Osgood, by whom he had two daughters. *Silas Marner*

LAMMETER, NANCY: The younger daughter of Mr. Lammeter. She marries the squire's son, Godfrey Cass, and loses her first baby, after which she has no more children. When Godfrey suggests that they should adopt Eppie, she refuses, not knowing that Eppie is his daughter by his first, secret marriage. But when Godfrey is finally driven by his conscience to acknowledge the 18-year-old girl, Nancy says she would have adopted her if she had known about her sooner. She tries to get Eppie to come and live with her, but Eppie indignantly refuses to leave Silas Marner, who has brought her up, and all Godfrey can do is to pay for her wedding feast at the Rainbow Inn. *Silas Marner*

LAMMETER, PRISCILLA: The elder daughter of Mr. Lammeter. She is as plain as her sister Nancy is pretty, but does not mind, being always ready to make a joke at her own expense. She has a poor opinion of men, and never marries, remaining at home to look after her widowed father until his death. She is rather strict in her opinions, and Nancy is glad that she does not have to know that Eppie is Godfrey's child. *Silas Marner*

LANDINO, CRISTOFORO: A Florentine who is rather contemptuous of pure scholarship, and thinks Bardo de' Bardi is 'one of those scholars who lie overthrown in their learning like Cavaliers in armour and then get angry because they are over-ridden'. *Romola*

LANDOR, BENJAMIN: A young lawyer in Milby who has to be content with the meagre leavings of the popular and unscrupulous Dempster. He is suggested by Mrs. Raynor as a suitable person to mediate between Dempster and his wife with a view to their separation. But Janet is determined to return to her husband. *Scenes of Clerical Life III: Janet's Repentance*

LANDOR, EUSTACE: The younger brother of Benjamin, tall and dark, and in his own estimation something of a swell, since he has recently acquired a diamond ring. *Scenes of Clerical Life III: Janet's Repentance*

LANDOR, MISS: The acknowledged belle of Milby, clad regally in purple and ermine, with a plume of discreet feathers. She has been 'finished' at a fashionable school, so speaks very bad French, but is nevertheless considered very clever and a considerable quiz. *Scenes of Clerical Life III: Janet's Repentance*

LANDOR, MR.: A banker and the first substantial citizen in Milby to be attracted by Mr. Tryan's preaching. He is outraged by Dempster's behaviour over Tryan's evening lectures, which Dempster succeeds in getting banned, and protects Tryan from the mob inflamed against him by Dempster's rhetoric and free beer. He is one of the pall-bearer's at Tryan's funeral. *Scenes of Clerical Life III: Janet's Repentance*

LANDOR, MRS.: The wife of an attorney, and one of the first people to believe and spread the rumour that Mr. Bridmain and the Countess Czerlaski are not brother and sister. *Scenes of Clerical Life I: The Rev. Amos Barton*

LANGEN, THE BARON AND BARONESS VON: Friends of Gwendolen Harleth's, with whom she goes abroad when she wants to escape from Grandcourt. *Daniel Deronda*

LAPIDOTH: A lapsed Jew, whose real name was Cohen. Married, with two children, he worked for some time in the London theatres, and then left for America unbeknown to his wife, taking with him his small daughter Mirah. For some years he exploited her as a child prodigy, and took her to Vienna with the idea of launching her as an opera-singer. But her voice proves unequal to the strain, and Lapidoth, who has taken to drink and is practically penniless, decides to sell her to the highest bidder. He takes her to Prague, and is preparing to hand her over to his wealthy friend, 'the Count', when she runs away. Drifting from one job to another, he makes his way to London, and finds Mirah there, reunited with her brother Ezra (*see* Mordecai) and making a modest living as a music-teacher and concert-singer, under the patronage of Daniel Deronda and his friends. Overcoming his repugnance to face his fanatical son, he tries to settle down with his children, but quickly becomes bored, steals a valuable ring which Daniel Deronda has left on the table, and is not heard of again. *Daniel Deronda*

LAPIDOTH, MIRAH: A young Jewish singer and actress, who is stopped from committing suicide by Daniel Deronda, and put in the care of Mrs. Meyrick until she can make a living as a singing-teacher. The unhappy child of a shiftless actor, she escaped from him and made her way to London, hoping to find her mother, from whom she was parted at an early age. When Daniel finds her brother, Ezra, known as Mordecai, a consumptive Jew who has sacrificed everything to his vision of a united Israel, Mirah makes a home for him. She is in love with Daniel, but determined not to marry a Gentile, and thinks anyhow that he is in love with Gwendolen Harleth. When the secret of Daniel's parentage is revealed, and he is known to be the son of Jewish parents, she happily agrees to marry him, and after her brother's death they set off together for the Near East, where Daniel hopes to discover his heritage and continue the work of Mordecai and of his own grandfather, Daniel Charisi. *Daniel Deronda*

LARCHER, EDWIN: A prosperous carrier, whose business does so well that he is able to purchase a fully-furnished mansion, and sell all his previous belongings at public auction. His wife is rather shocked by 'framefuls of expensive flesh-paintings in the dining-room' of her new home, and only appeased when the subjects are discovered to be Scriptural. The Larchers' son, Caius, is in love with Rosamond Vincy, but she despises him because he cannot speak French and cannot talk about anything but the 'carrying' trade. *Middlemarch*

LASSMAN, MR.: A business man whose 'wicked recklessness' in wild speculations caused Mrs. Gascoigne and Mrs. Davilow to lose all the money left them by their father. *Daniel Deronda*

LAURE, MADAME: A French actress, with dark eyes, a Greek profile, and a lovely voice. She was appearing in a melodrama in Paris when she stabbed and killed her husband on stage. Mr. Lydgate, who was in the audience, gave what help he could, and fell in love with the apparently disconsolate widow, following her from one provincial town to another when she went on tour. She prevents the proposal which she senses is coming by telling him that she killed her husband on purpose, because he wanted to stay in Paris and she wanted to go back to her native Provence, and he was too fond of her to let her go without him. She assures Lydgate that she will not marry again, and he returns to England, convinced that he will never love anyone else. *Middlemarch*

LAWE, MISS: A hitherto-admired young woman who is eclipsed at the Arrowpoints' dinner party by Gwendolen Harleth, beside whom she appears 'broad, heavy and inanimate'. *Daniel Deronda*

LEDRU, ANNETTE: see Lyon, Annette

LEMON, MRS.: The proprietress of an excellent school 'for young ladies' at which Rosamond Vincy was educated. *Middlemarch*

LENONI, DOMINIC: *see* Dominic

LEO: A singing-master in Vienna who gives lessons to Mirah Lapidoth, and tells her father, to his annoyance, that her voice, though pure and true, is not strong enough for grand opera. *Daniel Deronda*

LETTY: The scullery-maid at Transome Court, despised by Denner the lady's maid for her red cheeks and ignorance of her own worthlessness: 'She's a poor creature . . . I know what sort of a dowdy draggletail she'll be in ten years' time.' *Felix Holt*

LEYBURN, MISS: The daughter of the local Member of Parliament. Since he hopes to take her father's place 'when public spirit and gout induce him to give way', Stephen Guest would have been wise to court her, but he preferred Lucy Deane and Maggie Tulliver. *The Mill on the Floss*

LILLO: Tessa's son by Tito. *Romola*

LILLY: A pale, neat-faced copying-clerk, in a seedy suit but with a clean shirt. He attends the philosophical discussions in the Hand and Banner, and agrees with Pash that Jews are arrogant and backward, and should intermarry with the people they live among. *Daniel Deronda*

LIMP, MR.: A meditative shoemaker, with weak eyes and a piping voice, who frequents the Tankard Inn, and tries ineffectually to argue with the landlady, Mrs. Dollop. *Middlemarch*

LINGON, ARABELLA: The wife of The Rev. John Lingon and so aunt by marriage of Harold Transome. She is not at all pleased when he announces that he is going to stand as a Radical, but is silenced by her husband's specious arguments in his favour. *Felix Holt*

LINGON, THE REV. JOHN (JACK): The Rector of Little Treby, and the brother of Mrs. Transome. A great sportsman, he regrets the recent abolition of cock-fighting, and goes everywhere with a couple of pointers, his muscular person with its red eagle face set off by a velveteen jacket and leather leggings. Known locally as Parson Jack, he feels bound to support his Radical nephew in the election, though in fact a staunch Tory. He acts bravely during the riots, riding out to confront the mob, and being finally forced to call in the troops. *Felix Holt*

LINNET, MARY: A serious young lady who becomes infatuated with Mr. Tryan, and heads the working-party which organizes his new religious lending library. Dark, with a face like a piece of putty with two Scotch pebbles stuck in it, she combines 'a love of serious and poetical reading with great skill in fancywork'. *Scenes of Clerical Life III: Janet's Repentance*

LINNET, MRS.: A widow with two daughters, living in rural surroundings on the edge of Paddiford Common. Though stout, she likes to dress in cheerful colours, and favours a rather more showy style of cap than her sober daughter Mary approves of. She is extremely affected by Mr. Tryan's ministry, and decides to make him some pocket-handkerchiefs, in lawn rather than cambric, because the local washing is so bad. She dislikes Dempster, whom she blames for the loss of her property in a lawsuit, but when she hears he has left everything to his wife unconditionally she almost forgives him. *Scenes of Clerical Life III: Janet's Repentance*

LINNET, REBECCA: Mary's younger sister, but quite unlike her in every way. Her fatness, her unsuitable finery, and her thick ankles make her a joke among the young people: but she has a delightful singing voice, and her high spirits and sharp tongue make her an asset at any party. The advent of Mr.

Tryan, with whom she too falls in love, sends her into plain grey gingham with a white collar, which makes her look like a peony in the shade, instead of in hot sun, as she did before. *Scenes of Clerical Life III: Janet's Repentance*

LINTER, LADY SARA: The former owner of the beautiful mare which is provided for Beatrice Assher to ride during her visit to Cheverel Court. *Scenes of Clerical Life II: Mr. Gilfil's Love-Story*

LIRET, MONSIEUR: A clergyman whom Dorothea Brooke much admired when she was living in Lausanne. She would listen to his lectures 'until her sister Celia's feet got cold'. *Middlemarch*

LISA, MONNA: An old peasant woman, stone deaf, who is engaged by Tito to look after Tessa and her two children. *Romola*

LIZZIE: The Jeromes' grandchild—daughter of their only daughter, whose married name is not given. Lizzie is a great favourite with her grandfather, who keeps her out in the garden long after her tea-time, much to her grandmother's annoyance. The sight of Lizzie constantly reminds Janet Dempster of her childlessness, and makes her finally resolve to adopt a little girl. *Scenes of Clerical Life III: Janet's Repentance*

LOLLO: The boy who helps the conjuror Vaiano with his tricks. He is in the hostile crowd which surrounds the French soldiers in Florence, and uses his precious new pocket knife to cut through the bonds of their prisoner Baldassarre Calvo, thus giving him a chance to escape. *Romola*

LOVEGOOD: Sir James Chettam's agent. He approves of Dorothea Brooke's plans for model cottages, and thinks they should be used. When Chettam decides to improve his estate, he thinks Lovegood not quite 'up to the mark', so replaces him by Caleb Garth. *Middlemarch*

LOWME, BOB: The handsome son of frivolous Mr. Lowme. He has 'such beautiful whiskers meeting under his chin', and amuses himself in church by making fun of old Mr. Crewe and whispering and giggling with Miss Landor. *Scenes of Clerical Life III: Janet's Repentance*

LOWME, MR.: An elderly Lothario, once wealthy, now reduced to economical sins, such as lounging at the door of Gruby the grocer, embarrassing the servant-girls who come to buy, and talking scandal with the rare passers-by. *Scenes of Clerical Life III: Janet's Repentance*

LOWME, MRS.: One of Dr. Pilgrim's patients, who, in the opinion of her friend Mrs. Phipps, is mad to let her doctor bleed and blister her, and prescribe tea and broth until she looks 'as yellow as any crowflower,' and give her lowering medicine 'till her clothes hang on her like a scarecrow's.' *Scenes of Clerical Life III: Janet's Repentance*

LUCA, FRA: The brother of Romola, originally Dino (Bernadino) de' Bardi. Reared by his father as a classical scholar so as to help him in his work, he has, to his family's surprise and dismay, become a Dominican monk, and a follower of Savonarola. Returning from a pilgrimage, he brings a letter to Tito Melema from his benefactor, Baldassarre Calvo, who has been taken prisoner by the Turks, and awaits ransom. But Tito does nothing. Although Fra Luca does not know of Romola's engagement to Tito, he sends for her when he is dying and warns her against marriage, saying he has seen the misery that will ensue if she does not remain single. At his death-bed Romola meets Savonarola for the first time. *Romola*

LUCY: A young working-class girl who was seduced by Edgar Tryan and disappeared before he could make amends. Three years later he finds her dead in the street, having taken poison. *Scenes of Clerical Life III: Janet's Repentance*

LUKE: Tulliver's head miller, a 'tall, broad-shouldered man of forty, black-eyed and black-haired, subdued by a general mealiness, like an auricula.' Always known as Luke, he nevertheless has a surname, Moggs, and a wife, who is very kind to little Maggie Tulliver while her brother is away at school. Luke has no opinion of books and thinks they are mostly full of lies. He stays on at the mill after Tulliver's death and tries to work for the new manager, Jetsome, but says he will leave if things don't get better, as Jetsome is a heavy drinker. When Tom takes Jetsome's place, Luke and his wife stay on, with their numerous children. *The Mill on the Floss*

LUKYN, DR. AND MRS.: Friends of the Jermyns. Their daughters are having lessons from Esther Lyon, before she is found to be heiress to the Transome estate, and the money they owe her is used to pay Mrs. Holt's rent while her son Felix is in prison. The name is once spelt Lukin. *Felix Holt*

LUNDY, BOB: A butcher, the cousin of Snell, landlord of the Rainbow, a jolly, smiling, red-faced man, who buys one of Mr. Lammeter's red Durham cows, and says it made 'a lovely carkiss'. Being musical, he sings in the church choir, and is distressed by the harsh voice of the new deputy parish clerk Tookey. *Silas Marner*

LUPO: A poor crazed creature who lived in Tessa's village before her marriage to Tito. She is reminded of him at times by old Baldassarre. *Romola*

LUSH, THOMAS CRANMER: The son of a vicar who stinted his wife and daughters in order to send his boy to Oxford, and make a gentleman of him. But Lush refused to go into the Church, and eventually became tutor, and then secretary, to Grandcourt, who found him useful. He has been with Grandcourt fifteen years, and knows him to be heavily in debt, when the question of his marriage first comes up. Lush would like him to marry Catherine Arrowpoint, a rich heiress, and when Grandcourt says he intends to marry Gwendolen Harleth, whom Lush dislikes and mistrusts, he arranges for her to meet Grandcourt's mistress, Lydia Glasher, and her illegitimate son. As he expects, Gwendolen breaks off her relationship with Grandcourt before he had had time to propose to her; but later, under the pressure of poverty, agrees to marry him, and asks him to get rid of Lush, which he does temporarily. But not long after their marriage he sends for Lush and forces Gwendolen to be civil to him. Lush, who is a mean-spirited fellow, with a sallow complexion and fat hands, knows she hates him, and takes pleasure in tormenting her. He makes all the arrangements for the Mediterranean trip, but is back in England when Grandcourt is drowned. However, he has the pleasure of communicating to Gwendolen the humiliating provisions of her husband's will, from which she learns for the first time that Grandcourt knew of her meeting with Lydia. *Daniel Deronda*

LYDDY: The Rev. Rufus Lyon's elderly servant, much given

to gloom and despondency over the poor spiritual state of her small world, but hardworking and kind-hearted. *Felix Holt*

LYDGATE, CAPTAIN: The third son of Sir Godwin Lydgate, and Mr. Lydgate's cousin. He comes to stay with Lydgate after the latter's marriage to Rosamond Vincy, who very much admires him and is flattered by his attentions. She also hopes that he will introduce her into high society. Lydgate dislikes him, and is very angry when he takes Rosamond riding, against his express orders, and she has a miscarriage. *Middlemarch*

LYDGATE, ROSAMOND: *see* Vincy, Rosamond

LYDGATE, SIR GODWIN: The uncle and guardian of Tertius Lydgate. He and his brother Charles are annoyed when Lydgate chooses medicine as a career in preference to the Army or the Church, and relations become strained. But after Lydgate's marriage his wife Rosamond, who has social ambitions, persuades him to take her on a visit to his uncle, and is gratified when his son and married daughter come to stay with her. When Lydgate gets involved in the scandal over Bulstrode, and is badly in need of money, Rosamond writes without telling him to his uncle, asking for help. But Sir Godwin thinks Lydgate is behind her appeal, and writes him a furious letter, saying his conduct is unmanly, and that he can do nothing for him, having six children of his own to look after. *Middlemarch*

LYDGATE, TERTIUS: A young doctor, of good family, but poor and ambitious. He studies abroad, and is full of ideas for medical reforms, which he thinks he can best carry out in a provincial hospital. He is engaged by Bulstrode to run the new infirmary he has built in Middlemarch, and settles down, intending to devote himself to his patients and his research work. He encounters a good deal of opposition, but hopes to overcome it, and in the meantime enjoys a little social life with no ties. He thinks he will never marry, as during his studies in France he had an unhappy love-affair with an opera singer, Madame Laure. But he finds himself unexpectedly caught by the beauty and deliberate wiles of Rosamond Vincy, and marries her, with disastrous results. Because he attended the death-bed of John Raffles, and later accepted a loan of £1,000 from Mr. Bulstrode, who is Rosamond's uncle by marriage, he is accused of having taken a bribe to keep silent on the relationship between Bulstrode and Raffles. Nothing is left to him but to sell up and leave Middlemarch. Giving up all his ambitions, he becomes a fashionable physician, and dies young, a disappointed man. *Middlemarch*

LYON, ANNETTE: A young Frenchwoman whom Rufus Lyon rescues from destitution, and marries. As Annette Ledru, the daughter of an officer who died fighting in Russia under Napoleon, she had married against the wishes of her family a young English prisoner-of-war, Maurice Bycliffe. When he escapes to England, she follows him. But arriving in London with her newborn baby, she learns that he is dead. She walks back to the coast, but penniless, and already mortally ill, she appeals to Lyon, who passes her on the road, for help, not for herself, but for the child. She marries him for the same reason, but dies shortly afterwards, leaving nothing but a packet of letters and a miniature of her husband which Lyon keeps for the child, Esther, until the time comes to use them. *Felix Holt*

LYON, ESTHER: The orphaned daughter of Maurice Bycliffe and Annette Ledru, who has been adopted by the Rev. Rufus Lyon after his marriage to her widowed mother. He gives her a good education, and she returns from school to look after his house and give lessons to the daughters of the local gentry. She meets and at first dislikes the young Radical, Felix Holt, but gradually falls in love with him, and when, through the papers left by her mother, she is proved to be the legal owner of the Transome estate, she renounces her inheritance and marries Felix, rather than live a life of ease as the wife of Harold Transome. *Felix Holt*

LYON, THE REV. RUFUS: A strange, fanatical little clergyman, minister of a Dissenting Chapel in Treby Magna. A widower, he lives with his adopted daughter Esther in a small house 'not as big as the parish clerk's'. He was once the admired pastor of a large congregation in a seaside town down south, but after befriending and giving shelter to a young widow, Annette Bycliffe, whom it did not occur to him to marry, he was forced to resign and move up north, finding work as a printer's reader. He does eventually persuade Annette to marry him, mainly because he offers security for her child, and after her early death he returns to his original vocation in a Midland town. When he finds, through interviews with the lawyer Jermyn, and with Maurice Christian, who knew Esther's father Maurice Bycliffe, that his adopted daughter is the legal owner of a large estate, he is very distressed, partly because he considers wealth a snare of the devil, and partly because he does not think Esther will be happy with a vast fortune and a high social position. However, she returns from her visit to Transome Court, which everyone thought would end in her marriage to the previous heir, Harold Transome, disillusioned and determined to give up the prospect of luxury, which she found, after her austere upbringing, empty and soul-destroying. Mr. Lyon is delighted at this, and furthers her marriage to the young Radical workman, Felix Holt, whom he has learned to respect and admire. *Felix Holt*

M

MACEY, MR.: A tailor, and the parish clerk of Raveloe, who has a fine voice and likes it to be heard. His memories go back a long way, and he is often appealed to by people wanting to know some detail of a past transaction, or a long-established family. When the money that was stolen from Silas Marner turns up in the drained quarry sixteen years later, Macey says that a man who could take and rear an orphan, as Silas had done, deserved his good fortune. *Silas Marner*.

MACEY, SOLOMON: A small, wiry man with long flowing white hair, the brother of the parish clerk. He does not reside in the village, but as a fine fiddler is much in demand for local festivities, and plays at the Casses' New Year's Eve ball. *Silas Marner*

MACHIAVELLI, NICCOLÒ: The famous Florentine statesman and political theorist. As a young man he is acquainted with Tito Melema, and also watches with interest the rise and fall of Savonarola. *Romola*

MACKWORTH, MR.: A friend of Daniel Deronda's, who is with him when he first sees Gwendolen Harleth, and says he does not himself admire her type of beauty. *Daniel Deronda*

MADELEY, DR.: A consultant physician from Rotherby, who is called in by Brand when Milly Barton is dying. *Scenes of Clerical Life I: The Rev. Amos Barton*
   Dr. Madeley is also called in by Pratt to confirm his diagnosis of Tryan's fatal illness. *Scenes of Clerical Life III: Janet's Repentance*

MAKEPIECE: An electioneering agent who in the opinion of Johnson is not as good as James Putty: 'Makepiece for scheming, but Putty for management.' After the election he is engaged by Harold Transome to sort out the question of expenses. These turn out to be unexpectedly heavy on account of the rioting, which is proved to have been started by some of Transome's supporters. *Felix Holt*

MALAM, JUSTICE: The local magistrate, who initiates the search for the 'pedlar, name unknown, curly black hair, foreign complexion, carrying a box of cutlery and jewellery and wearing large rings in his ears', who is believed to have stolen Silas Marner's money. *Silas Marner*

MALLINGER, HENLEIGH: The younger brother of Sir Hugo, who married an heiress called Grandcourt, and took her name with her estates. He was the father of Henleigh Grandcourt. *Daniel Deronda*

MALLINGER, LADY (LOUISA): The plump, reddish-blonde, blue-eyed wife of Sir Hugo Mallinger, who feels apologetic all the time because she has no son, only three girls, who cannot, while their cousin Henleigh Grandcourt is alive, inherit their father's property. She very seldom listens to what anyone says, as she is always thinking about her children—Amabel is due to go to a singing lesson with Mirah, or Theresa has to go to the dentist. When Daniel decides to marry Mirah, she is sorry he has got himself involved with Jews, but otherwise not interested. *Daniel Deronda*

MALLINGER, SIR FRANCIS: The father of Sir Hugo, who by an ill-advised settlement left his property to heirs male only, thus disinheriting Sir Hugo's three daughters in favour of their cousin, Henleigh Grandcourt. *Daniel Deronda*

MALLINGER, SIR HUGO: The guardian and supposed natural father of Daniel Deronda, who is in fact the son of a famous Jewish opera singer, Alcharisi, with whom Sir Hugo was at one time infatuated. He took the boy at her desire in order to bring him up as 'an English Gentleman'. In later life he married and had three daughters, his heir being his nephew Henleigh Grandcourt, whom he dislikes. He is delighted when Grandcourt is drowned at Genoa, as he is now free to settle some of his property on his wife and children. Although he very much wants Daniel to marry Grandcourt's widow after the lapse of a year or two, he becomes reconciled to his marriage to Mirah, and sends them a wonderful wedding present—complete equipment for their proposed tour of the Near and Middle East. *Daniel Deronda*

MANETTI, SIBILLA: An old woman in whose house Tessa and her children take refuge after the death of Tito. *Romola*

MARIANO, FRA: A forceful preacher who denounces Savonarola from his pulpit. *Romola*

A Dominican who has been one of Savonarola's followers from the beginning and is prepared to undergo the Ordeal by Fire in defence of his doctrines. *Romola*

MARKHAM: Sir Christopher Cheverel's bailiff. *Scenes of Clerical Life II: Mr. Gilfil's Love-Story*

MARLOWE: An elderly Methodist preacher, a linen-weaver by trade, who encourages Dinah Morris to preach after she has taken his place when he was ill. *Adam Bede*

MARNER, SILAS: A linen-weaver who lived in a small cottage by a quarry, just outside the village of Raveloe. The thud of his loom, and his reputation as a cross-grained chap of questionable powers—he could cure anyone if he had a mind to—made him an object of half-fearful fascination to the village boys. He had come to Raveloe fifteen years before, after being falsely accused of theft by a friend, William Dane, who wanted to marry Silas's betrothed, and so got Silas driven out of the town. Although he never drinks at the Rainbow, or gossips with the wheelwrights, Silas is tolerated by the community where he has settled because he is a good weaver, and the only one for many miles around. Originally a simple, trusting, impressionable creature, he has been embittered by his experiences, and become overfond of the gold pieces paid him for his work, hiding them under the floor and counting them out when he is alone at night. During his absence Dunsey Cass steals the money and disappears. Silas is in despair, and when nothing is heard of the money roams about like a lost soul, exciting the pity of the villagers, who begin to think more kindly of him and do him little services. One New Year's Eve he opens his cottage door in the vain hope, frequently indulged in, that he will see someone returning his gold, and is seized by one of his infrequent cataleptic fits; when he recovers he finds the two-year-old Eppie by the fire, and investigation reveals the body of her mother, Molly Farren, under a furze bush. Not knowing that Eppie is the daughter of Godfrey Cass, Silas adopts her, and they live happily together until Eppie marries Aaron Winthrop, whose mother Dolly Winthrop helped Silas to care for Eppie until she was old enough to manage on her own. *Silas Marner*

MARRABLES: A laboratory assistant, a florid Englishman who likes to join the Jewish group that meets at the Hand and Banner for philosophical discussions. *Daniel Deronda*

MARRIOTT, ELLEN: A pupil at Miss Townley's school, a short, plump, sandy-haired girl with a sharp tongue who is considered very witty and clever by her fellow-pupils. *Scenes of Clerical Life III: Janet's Repentance*

MARSHALL: A jeweller to whom Gwendolen Harleth hopes to sell some of her jewels after her mother has lost all her money. *Daniel Deronda*

MARTHA: The only servant the Lydgates can afford after they have run heavily into debt and have to retrench. She is not very intelligent, and by mistake shows Dorothea into the drawing-room, where she finds Rosamond and Will Ladislaw together and concludes they are in love. *Middlemarch*

One of Mrs. Tulliver's servants, who acts as nurse to Maggie when she is young. *The Mill on the Floss*

A maid at Cheverel Court, who looks after Tina Sarti when she is a child, and after her marriage to Mr. Gilfil accompanies her to Shepperton. When Tina dies, she shuts up her room and visits it only once a quarter, to clean it. She marries Mr. Gilfil's manservant, David, and together they form his entire staff. *Scenes of Clerical Life II: Mr. Gilfil's Love-Story*

MARTIN, MRS. AND SALLY: A mother and daughter who live in Butcher's Lane and are befriended by Janet Dempster, who first meets Tryan at the bedside of Sally, a deformed girl who is dying of consumption. *Scenes of Clerical Life III: Janet's Repentance*

MARUFFI, FRA SALVESTRO: The Dominican monk to whom Savonarola confides Romola after her flight from Florence. She takes an instant dislike to him, but finds him useful when she wants to plead with Savonarola for the life of her god-father, Bernardo del Nero. Fra Salvestro is finally arrested with Savonarola, and executed at the same time. *Romola*

MASKERY, WILL: A wheelwright, and except for Seth Bede the only Methodist in Hayslope. He supports Dinah Morris when she preaches on the village green, and after becoming a Methodist gives up drinking and beating his wife, an unfortunate woman who is so ugly that Lisbeth Bede says of her: 'I'd as lief look at a toad'. *Adam Bede*

MASO: Manservant to Romola and her father. He has kept in touch with Romola's brother Dino, who has left home to become a Dominican monk, Fra Luca, and when he is dying fetches Romola to see him. Maso remains with Romola after her marriage to Tito Melema, and when Tito makes arrangements to leave Florence for Milan, he stays behind to hand over the house to the new tenants. *Romola*

MASSEY, BARTLE: The Hayslope village schoolmaster, lame, irascible, sharp-tongued, but fundamentally kind-hearted. He considers himself a misogynist, and will not allow a woman inside his cottage, doing all his own work with the help of a boy. He attends Hetty's trial, bringing news of its progress to Adam, and finally going to court with him to hear the verdict. In later years he continues to befriend Adam, and attends his wedding to Dinah Morris, squiring Adam's mother in the marriage procession. *Adam Bede*

MATTEO: One of Bernardo Rucellai's menservants. *Romola*

MAWMSEY, MR.: A wealthy grocer in Middlemarch who misunderstands Lydgate's explanation as to why he does not do his own dispensing, and spreads the damaging rumour that 'the new doctor does not believe in medicines'—to which Mawmsey and his wife are much addicted. *Middlemarch*

MAZZINGHI, DOMENICO: An ardent follower of Savonarola, who plots with the King of France to depose the Pope; his letter to Charles VIII, together with one from Savonarola, is collected by Tito Melema, who arranges for their despatch secretly through Medicean agents, but also arranges for them to be intercepted by the Duke of Milan, thus providing evidence that both men are traitors to Florence. *Romola*

MEDICI, GIOVANNI DE': Son of Lorenzo the Magnificent, later Pope Leo X. He is still a boy-Cardinal when he meets Tito Melema in Florence, and takes him to Rome, to help with the establishment of a library there. *Romola*

MEDICI, PIERO DE': Son of Lorenzo the Magnificent, whom he succeeds as ruler of Florence; but owing to his arrogance and stupidity, he is driven out by the townspeople. He plots to return, and employs Tito Melema as one of his agents, not realising that Tito is also working for his enemies. *Romola*

MEDLICOTE, LORD: Donor of the land for the new hospital in Middlemarch. He is very much against the coming of the railway, and makes the contractors pay heavily for some of his land which they want. *Middlemarch*

MEDWIN: A clerk with Batt & Cowley, who was involved in Bycliffe's suit against the Durfey-Transomes. But he does not know that Bycliffe has left a daughter. *Felix Holt*

MELEMA, TITO: A young and very handsome Greek boy, who is rescued from a life of ill-treatment and poverty by a generous Italian merchant, Baldassarre Calvo. He proves to be intelligent and adaptable, and is given a good education, travelling all round the Mediterranean with his benefactor. On one of their journeys their ship is attacked by pirates and wrecked. Tito escapes, and thinks it probable that Baldassarre has been drowned, though there is a possibility that he has been captured by the Turks, and so could be ransomed. But Tito, who lands up in Florence, where he is lucky enough to find good friends, is a cold-hearted, ungrateful creature, and prefers to concentrate on his own affairs rather than try to discover Baldassarre's fate. He is momentarily disconcerted when Romola's brother, Fra Luca, brings him a letter given by Baldassarre to a pilgrim, saying he is a slave in Turkey but can be ransomed and asking Tito to arrange it. But Tito still does nothing, and as Fra Luca dies shortly afterwards, he hopes his perfidy will pass undiscovered. Although he is going to marry Romola, he makes a mock marriage with a pretty peasant girl, Tessa, under the name of Naldo, and has two children by her. Soon after, he marries Romola, and before long is in high favour with all the chief citizens of Florence. On his way to the Cathedral to attend the arrival of Charles VIII of France he is accosted by Baldassarre, now a prisoner of the French, who begs for his help. But Tito disowns him, as he does again at a dinner-party given by Bernardo Rucellai, telling the company that the man is an old servant, Jacopo di Nola, who was dismissed for theft, and therefore has a grudge against him. Baldassarre, old and ill, is thrown into prison, where Tito hopes he will die; but he does not, and is turned out into the street when an epidemic of plague attacks Florence. Tito, who is playing a double game, acting both for the Medici and for their opponents, decides that the time has come to leave Florence, deserting his wife Romola, who knows all about his perfidy and despises him for it. He intends to take Tessa and the children with him to Milan, where Duke Ludovico Sforza has promised him an official position. Caught up in a riot, he tries to escape by jumping in to the Arno and swimming to the bridge where Tessa is waiting for him with horses for the journey. Worn out with his efforts, he crawls ashore and finds Baldassarre waiting for him; too weak to defend himself, he is strangled by the old man, and his body, together with that of Baldassarre, who dies of exposure, is eventually found and taken back to Florence. *Romola*

MENGAN, MRS.: A married daughter of Sir Godwin Lydgate, who gratifies Rosamond's social ambitions by going to stay with her and Tertius Lydgate after their marriage. *Middlemarch*

MERCER, JOSEPH: An old man whom Eliza Pratt, drawn to good works under the influence of the Rev. Tryan, visits and reads to. She is rewarded by Mercer telling Mr. Tryan how much he values the Bible readings now that he can no longer get to church. *Scenes of Clerical Life III: Janet's Repentance*

MERRY, MISS (JOCOSA): The elderly, submissive, and rather sad governess of the four half-sisters of Gwendolen Harleth, who unkindly nicknames her 'Jocosa'. She takes a subdued and melancholy interest in the family's affair's, and offers her small savings when they lose all their money. *Daniel Deronda*

METHURST, LADY ALICIA: A friend of Lady Debarry's, who cites her as an example of the dangers of sudden good fortune. She 'got heart-disease from a sudden piece of luck—the death of her rich uncle, you know.' *Felix Holt*

MEUNIER, MADAME: The proprietress of the school at which Gwendolen Harleth was educated and injudiciously made much of, being put on show for the excellence of her accomplishments rather too often. *Daniel Deronda*

MEYRICK, AMY, KATE AND MAB: The daughters of Mrs. Meyrick, lively, intelligent, and well-educated, who all add to the small family income in different ways. Kate, the eldest, is an artist and illustrates books; Amy is the practical one, who runs the house, and embroiders satin cushions for a shop; Mab, the youngest, is musical, and gives lessons to small children. She is the most enthusiastic and poetical, and, like her sisters, adores Daniel Deronda, who has been a wonderful friend to their brother Hans. They all three become very fond of Mirah and would welcome her as a sister-in-law, but realise that she is in love with Daniel. *Daniel Deronda*

MEYRICK, HANS: The only son of an engraver of some distinction, who named him after Holbein. Left fatherless at ten years old, with three small sisters, he is educated at Christ's Hospital and then manages to get to Cambridge, where he shares rooms with Daniel Deronda, who proves a good friend to him. He wants to be an artist, but thinks he must get a well-paid position in order to help support his mother and sisters. Luckily his sisters soon become self-supporting, and he is able to go to Italy and study art there. On his return he finds Mirah living with his family, so takes a studio near by, uses her as a model, and falls in love with her. Being a very self-centred young man, he does not notice that Daniel too loves her, and angers him by his careless jokes about Mirah's Jewish background and her eccentric and fanatical brother. He also upsets Mirah by joking about the possibility of Daniel's marrying Gwendolen Harleth after her husband has been drowned. He does not attend Mirah's wedding. *Daniel Deronda*

MEYRICK, MRS.: A charming and accomplished woman, half Scotch, half French, who was left a widow with four young children. She has managed to send her son Hans to Cambridge, and teaches the girls herself. They live in a small house in Chelsea, poorly furnished, but neat and clean, and the girls are able to earn a little money in ladylike pursuits such as sketching, embroidery and governessing. When Daniel Deronda has saved Mirah from suicide and does not know what to do with her, he brings her to Mrs. Meyrick, who takes her in without question, and keeps her until her brother is found. Knowing that Hans has fallen in love with Mirah, Mrs. Meyrick hopes she may become a Christian and marry him, since the whole family is so fond of her. But she realises this is impossible once Mirah goes to live with her brother, who is a fanatical Jew, and is very glad when she marries Daniel. Mrs. Meyrick attends the wedding with her three daughters. *Daniel Deronda*

MICHELE, FRA: A Carthusian lay brother in the service of the Medici family. *Romola*

MIDDLETON, MR.: Mr. Gascoigne's curate when Gwendolen Harleth and her family come to live at Offendene. He is the nephew of a bishop. He admires Gwendolen very much, but she thinks him a 'stick' and makes fun of him, which nobody had dared to do before. Luckily he leaves the parish shortly after her arrival. *Daniel Deronda*

MILLER: A second-hand bookseller who knows the insides of his books as well as the outsides. Part Jewish and part German, he is one of the group that meets at the Hand and Banner for philosophical discussions. *Daniel Deronda*

MILLS, MR.: The butler at Donnithorne Chase. He is much addicted to reading the newspapers, which in the opinion of the head gardener, Craig, makes him addle-headed. *Adam Bede*

MINCHIN, DR.: A surgeon who is called in when Middlemarch patients are seriously ill, a soft-handed, pale-complexioned man, more like a clergyman than a doctor. He disapproves of Lydgate, mainly on the grounds that he is too young, and was appointed by Bulstrode, whom Minchin dislikes, to run the new infirmary. He is quite ready to believe that Lydgate —though blameless from a medical point of view—accepted a bribe from Bulstrode on the occasion of Raffles's death. *Middlemarch*

MIRAH: *see* Lapidoth, Mirah

MITCHELL: Sir Maximus Debarry's coachman, who, when all the other servants are revelling in the housekeeper's or steward's room, sits 'tippling in majestic solitude by a fire in the harness room.' *Felix Holt*

MOGGS, LUKE: *see* Luke

MOLLY: One of Mrs. Poyser's maids, a good-hearted girl, fond of the children and 'a jewel with the poultry', but plain, 'with a turn-up nose and a protuberant jaw'. *Adam Bede*

MOMPERT, DR. AND MRS.: A Bishop and his wife, who through Mr. Gascoigne offer the penniless Gwendolen Harleth the position of governess to their three daughters at a salary of £100 a year. She refuses, in favour of marriage with Henleigh Grandcourt, but afterwards thinks she would have done better to accept their offer. *Daniel Deronda*

MORDECAI: Mirah Lapidoth's brother, Ezra Cohen, always known by his second name, Mordecai. He was embarking on an excellent business career abroad when he was recalled to London to look after his mother, broken-hearted by his father's disappearance with her small daughter Mirah. Mordecai nurses her devotedly until she dies, but then becomes tubercular and finds it difficult to get work. Everyone thinks he is slightly mad, as he is an intense, visionary believer in the future of Israel as a nation. Daniel Deronda, who is searching London for him in order to reunite him with his sister, finds him and thinks he looks like the prophet Ezekiel, or 'some New Hebrew poet of medieval times'. Mordecai is living on charity with a Jewish family, also named Cohen, and dreaming of the day when he will find a kindred spirit to carry on his work of re-animating Jewish national pride through the medium of literature. He thinks Daniel has been sent to him by God, and cannot believe he is not a Jew. He allows him to arrange a lodging for himself and his sister, and in return teaches Daniel Hebrew. When Daniel returns from Genoa with the news that his parents were both Jewish, and that he can now marry Mirah, Mordecai feels that his prayers have been answered, and he dies confident that Daniel will do the work he himself was not spared to do. *Daniel Deronda*

MORGAN, MISS: Governess to the three youngest Vincy girls, rather a depressed-looking person, 'brown, dull, and re-signed'. *Middlemarch*

MORRIS, DINAH: The niece of Mrs. Poyser, who took her in when her aunt, Judith, with whom she was living, died. Under the aunt's influence Dinah had become a Methodist, and Mrs. Poyser, to her great regret, is unable to stop her leaving the farm to go and work among the brethren in a nearby manufacturing town. She also becomes a woman preacher, which upsets the Poysers, and because she feels her vocation is to minister, she refuses to marry Seth Bede. A beautiful young woman, with a pale oval face and smooth reddish hair, clear, candid eyes, full of affection, and a delight-ful voice, she is quite unconscious of the interest and affection she inspires. She is fond of her cousin Hetty Sorrel, who is also living with Mrs. Poyser, but realises that her beauty and vain, shallow nature may lead her into trouble. When she hears that Hetty is in prison, Dinah goes to her, and succeeds in breaking down her silence and getting her to confess to the murder of her child. She goes with Hetty to the gallows, and after her sentence has been changed to one of transportation, accompanies her as far as the ship. She stays with the Poysers, helping them through the difficult time which follows on Hetty's conviction, and then goes to nurse Lisbeth Bede through a grave illness. During this time she realises that she loves Adam Bede, and although she insists on returning to the town to continue her former work, she finally gives in to his pleading and they are married. *Adam Bede*

MORTON, MR.: A parishioner of St. Ogg's, who dies. The bell tolling for his funeral brings about a reconciliation between

Mr. and Mrs. Glegg after one of their frequent quarrels. *The Mill on the Floss*

MOSS: The husband of Mr. Tulliver's sister Gritty. He is very much looked down on by Mrs. Tulliver's relations, being a poor farmer, with a damp farmhouse and tumbledown barns surrounded by badly-kept land. Mr. Tulliver has lent him £300, which he is unable to pay back when it is needed. *The Mill on the Floss*

MOSS, GEORGE, LIZZY, AND WILLY: Three of the Mosses' eight children. George is useful for running errands; Lizzy is thought by her mother to resemble Maggie, though her uncle Tulliver, who dotes on his daughter, considers Lizzy her inferior in 'fire and strength'; Willy, who is twelve when Maggie goes to stay with the Mosses to escape from Stephen Guest, is very proud of being allowed to walk Stephen's beautiful mare up and down the lane. There were originally ten Moss children, but the twins died. *The Mill on the Floss*

MOSS, MRS. (GRITTY): Mr. Tulliver's sister, who is not invited to family gatherings at Dorlcote Mill because she does not get on with Mrs. Tulliver's sisters. They consider her a woman of no account, who has made a poor marriage with a man who has much ado to pay his rent. She is Maggie Tulliver's godmother, and, unlike her other aunts, thinks her both clever and beautiful. When Mr. Tulliver has a stroke, his wife forgets to let Gritty know, and hearing the news by chance she hurries over 'with her shawl and bonnet looking as if they had been hastily huddled on.' But she is very kind to the bereaved family, and makes Maggie very welcome when she takes refuge with her from the attentions of Stephen Guest. *The Mill on the Floss*

MOTT, MR.: An old gardener who decides to retire, and so gives Aaron Winthrop the chance to earn more money by taking on his work, which means that he can marry Eppie. *Silas Marner*

MUM TAFT: see Taft

MUSCAT, BROTHER: A self-important member of Rufus Lyon's congregation, who dislikes Felix Holt and believes he is responsible for the rioting on election day. *Felix Holt*

MUSCAT, MRS. MARY: Mr. Muscat's wife, a censorious woman, who blames Lyon for letting his daughter Esther spend her earnings on such fripperies as gloves, shoes, and wax candles. She dislikes Esther because she has refused young Muscat's offer of marriage, and prevents her from getting a position as governess in the Tiliot household by telling Mrs. Tiliot, her bosom friend, that the girl is badly brought up, and is encouraging the attentions of the Radical working-man, Felix Holt. *Felix Holt*

N

NALDO: *see* Melema, Tito

NANCY: One of Mrs. Poyser's maids, who takes over the dairy-work after Hetty Sorrel runs away and becomes quite good at it. *Adam Bede*
   See also Nash, Nancy

NANNI: A sallow-faced, round-shouldered Florentine tailor, who assures the crowd in the market-place that the Church will soon be purged of evil, 'and of fat cardinals', as Savonarola has promised. *Romola*

NANNY: The robust maid-of-all-work at the Bartons, who combines the functions of nurse, cook, and housemaid. She is devoted to Mrs. Barton, and it is her outspokenness which finally drives the parasitic Countess Czerlaski out of the house —too late to prevent Mrs. Barton's death from overwork and worry. *Scenes of Clerical Life I: The Rev. Amos Barton*

NARDI, JACOPO: A young Florentine who, after Savonarola's death, wrote an excellent account of him. He was with Romola at the window from which she watched Savonarola's execution. *Romola*

NASH: A bone-setter from whom Joel Dagge learned how to put back a dislocated shoulder. *Daniel Deronda*

NASH, NANCY: Charwoman to Mrs. Larcher. When Mr. Lydgate cures her of an illness wrongly diagnosed by Dr. Minchin, everyone is loud in his praises, which does not endear him to his fellow-practitioner. *Middlemarch*

NAUMANN, ADOLF: A German artist, working in Rome, who is friendly with Will Ladislaw. He is struck by Dorothea's beauty, and after tactfully using Casaubon first, as a model for St. Aquinas, he is allowed to paint her as St. Claire. *Middlemarch*

NELLO: A barber in Florence, whose shop on the main square is the recognised meeting-place of all the gossips and erudite scholars of the day. He befriends Tito Melema, who is brought to him by Bratti, and introduces him to several influential citizens who help to further his career. *Romola*

NERLI: One of the leaders of the popular party after the departure of the French, and a fervent opponent of Savonarola and the Mediceans. *Romola*

NERO, BERNARDO DEL: One of the leading citizens and scholars of Florence, a close friend of Bardo de' Bardi, and Romola's godfather. He dislikes and distrusts Tito Melema from their first meeting in Bardo's library, and foresees that he will easily gain the love of Romola. When this happens, he manages to delay their marriage for a year, but is unable to prevent Tito from selling Bardo's library after his death. He had himself intended to use his influence with Piero de' Medici to get the library accepted and maintained by the city, as Bardo had wished, but with the fall of the Medici his own position becomes untenable, and after the discovery of a plot to bring the Medici back to Florence, he and his fellow-conspirators Ridolfo and Tornabuoni are publicly executed as traitors to the state. *Romola*

NICCOLÒ, FRA: A Dominican who acts as Savonarola's secretary. *Romola*

NINNA: The daughter of Tessa and Tito Melema. *Romola*

NISBETT: The source from which Fellowes heard a titbit of scandal about Amos Barton—that he dined alone with the Countess Czerlaski while his wife was in the kitchen acting as cook. But Mr. Ely thinks Nisbett 'an apocryphal authority'. *Scenes of Clerical Life I: The Rev. Amos Barton*

NOBLE, MISS (HENRIETTA): Mrs. Farebrother's sister, a tiny, self-effacing little lady, with frills and kerchief exquisitely neat but decidedly worn and mended. She forms part of the household of her nephew, the Rev. Camden Farebrother, and is in the habit of purloining lumps of sugar and morsels of cake for the village children and old women. She becomes a great favourite with Will Ladislaw, who accompanies her on her charitable errands, and when he is anxious to have a last meeting with Dorothea, he sends Miss Noble to plead for him. She takes with her the tortoiseshell box he gave her as a parting present, to bolster up her courage, and is successful in persuading Dorothea to see him. *Middlemarch*

NOFRI: The step-father of Tessa, who beats and ill-treats her until she runs away, after the death of her mother, to live with Tito. *Romola*

NOLA, JACOPI DI: *see* Calvo, Baldassarre

NOLAN, BARUCH: A retired London hosier, who 'supplied Mr. Pitt with socks'. As a poor young man he married a Miss Pendrell of Treby Magna, and is happy to bring her back to her home town as the wife of a rich merchant and a Tory Churchman. He thinks England has been going to the dogs ever since Peel and the Old Duke turned round about the Catholics in '29, and he has a great admiration for George III: 'When he heard his ministers talking about Catholic Emancipation, he boxed their ears.' But he does not agree that trade breeds spindly Radicals. 'Plenty of sound Tories have made their fortune by trade'. He is amused when the muddle-headed farmer, Rose, says he has given one vote to the Tory candidate, and one to the Radical, and cannot convince him that both votes have been wasted. *Felix Holt*

NUTTWOOD, MR.: One of the committee who appointed the Rev. Mr. Lyon as minister of the Malthouse Yard Independent Chapel. A prosperous grocer, he objects to hymn-singing during services, particularly by those who have good voices, which he has not. Since the election-day rioting has brought disfavour on the Dissenters, who are mainly Radicals, he refuses to testify on Felix Holt's behalf when he is tried as a rioter. *Felix Holt*

NUTTWOOD, MRS.: The wife of one of the foremost dissenting

tradesmen in Treby Magna, who disapproves of the daughter of the minister, Esther Lyon, being neatly dressed and speaking French. *Felix Holt*

O

OATES, JINNY: The cobbler's daughter in Raveloe, who, being very imaginative, declares that the pedlar who is believed to have stolen Silas Marner's money not only wore earrings, as the Rev. Crackenthorp surmises (he being a foreigner), but that he had made her blood creep 'as it did at that very moment while there she stood.' *Silas Marner*

OATES, SALLY: The elderly wife of the cobbler in Raveloe. When Silas Marner took his shoes to be mended, he noticed that she was suffering from heart disease, and hearing that the doctor's remedies had done her no good at all, he gave her an infusion of digitalis, which his mother had used. This cured her, but added to Silas's already sinister reputation as a man in league with the devil. *Silas Marner*

ODDO: A dyer, who is ready with a meat-axe to attack the French when they enter Florence, and wishes Piero de' Medici would return so that he could chop his legs off. *Romola*

OLDING, JOHN: A labourer who gives evidence at Hetty Sorrel's trial, saying that he saw her walking away from the copse where she had left the baby. On his return, he saw the baby's hand sticking up through the brushwood, uncovered it, and took it to his wife; but the child was already dead. The next day he took the police to the place where he had found the body; Hetty was sitting there, and was taken into custody by the constable. *Adam Bede*

OLDINPORT, MR. AND MRS.: The family at Knebley Abbey whose escutcheons adorn the chancel of Shepperton Church. They are very good to Amos Barton, lending him £12 to settle the butcher's bill and £8 for a winter overcoat. After Mrs. Barton's death they arrange for the two elder girls, Patty and Sophy, to go to a school for clergymen's daughters. *Scenes of Clerical Life I: The Rev. Amos Barton*

OLDINPORT, MR. AND LADY FELICIA: The owners of Knebley Abbey when Mr. Gilfil was the incumbent of Shepperton Church. He always dined with them after taking the Sunday evening service at Knebley Church, and joined them out hunting, until his caustic wit caused a bad quarrel in which Oldinport came off worst, much to the delight of the tenant-farmers, who thought him a bad landlord. *Scenes of Clerical Life II: Mr. Gilfil's Love-Story*

OLD JOSHWAY: see Rann, Joshua

OLD MAXUM: A ninety-five-year-old inhabitant of Shepperton workhouse, whose real name is unknown, his nickname resulting from his sententious speech in earlier days. He is stone deaf, and sits in the front pew while Amos Barton reads and preaches, with protruding chin and munching mouth, and eyes that seem to look at emptiness. *Scenes of Clerical Life I: The Rev. Amos Barton*

OLD SLECK: A grey-haired but stalwart old miner, who thinks wistfully that it would be fun to pummel and kick a few Tories at the forthcoming election, if it could be done with impunity. But he soon gets tired of the speechifying, saying 'Let's have our pipes, then. I'm pretty well tired o' jaw.' *Felix Holt*

OLIVER: The sitting member for Middlemarch, whom Mr. Brooke hopes will be turned out, as an opponent of the Reform Bill, so that he can take his place. *Middlemarch*

OSGOOD, GILBERT: The only son of Farmer Osgood, in love with Nancy Lammeter. When she marries Godfrey Cass, he turns his attention elsewhere, and later takes over his father's farm, buying some fields for dairying from the Casses. This involves the draining of the old quarry, and leads to the discovery of the body of Dunsey Cass, drowned there sixteen years earlier, after stealing Silas Marner's gold. *Silas Marner*

OSGOOD, MR.: A well-to-do farmer, whose sister married Mr. Lammeter. He is friendly with Squire Cass, and with his family attends the Casses' New Year's Eve ball. He wonders why Dunsey Cass has not come home for Christmas, but, like everyone else, accepts the explanation that he is afraid to do so after killing Wildfire and embezzling £100. *Silas Marner*

OSGOOD, MRS.: The wife of Osgood, and aunt by marriage of Nancy Lammeter, with whom her son Gilbert is in love. Mrs. Osgood would like to see them married, even though they are first cousins, and has decided to leave Nancy all her jewellery in preference to her elder sister, Priscilla Lammeter, whom Mrs. Osgood thinks too rough in her manners. She is very good to Silas Marner, who does her weaving, and after he has been robbed sends him food and other small comforts. *Silas Marner*

OTTLEY, MR.: A farmer for whom Mrs. Poyser's maid Molly worked before coming to her. Mrs. Poyser attributes all her faults to the poor training given her by Ottley's wife. *Adam Bede*

P

PACK: A rabble-rouser who undertakes to bribe the Sproxton miners to cause trouble on election day in favour of Transome, the Radical candidate. *Felix Holt*

PAINE, MAT: Dempster's confidential clerk, who very successfully organises the demonstration against the Rev. Edgar Tryan. *Scenes of Clerical Life III: Janet's Repentance*

PARROT, BESSIE AND SELINA: Two of Mrs. Parrot's grandchildren, who share her admiration for Mr. Gilfil. Bessie is charmed by his habit of producing sugar-plums and gingerbread from his pocket, and Selina postpones her wedding for a whole month when he is laid up, rather than be married 'in a makeshift manner' by the Milby curate. *Scenes of Clerical Life II: Mr. Gilfil's Love-Story*

PARROT, MRS.: An elderly farmer's wife who has such respect for her parson, Mr. Gilfil, that whenever she sees him coming she smoothes her apron, sets her cap straight, and makes him her deepest curtsey. She also sends him a turkey every Christmas. *Scenes of Clerical Life II: Mr. Gilfil's Love-Story*

PARRY, THE REV. MR.: Amos Barton's predecessor at Shepperton, an extempore preacher who 'made the old sounding-board vibrate with his vehemence'. *Scenes of Clerical Life I: The Rev. Amos Barton*

When Parry was first appointed, Mrs. Pettifer met him at Mrs. Bond's, and was very disappointed in him. 'He may be a very good man, and a fine preacher . . . But what a difference between him and Mr. Tryan! He's a sharp-sort-of-looking man, and hasn't that feeling way with him that Mr. Tryan has.' *Scenes of Clerical Life III: Janet's Repentance*

PASH: A watch-maker, 'a small, dark, vivacious, triple-baked Jew', who attends the discussions at the Hand and Banner and upsets Mordecai by saying that the idea of Jewish nationality is dying out in Europe. *Daniel Deronda*

PASTON, THE REV. MR.: The minister who presides over the drawing of lots in chapel which declare Silas Marner guilty after he has been accused of theft by William Dane. *Silas Marner*

PATCH: The parish clerk who comes with the choir to sing carols at Dorlcote Mill on Christmas Eve. *The Mill on the Floss*

PATCH, NED: A pedlar, and drinking crony of old Tommy Trounsem's. *Felix Holt*

PATTEN, MRS.: A pretty eighty-year-old who since her husband's death has been running Cross Farm, with the help of her niece Janet, whom she dislikes, and intends, in a gently malevolent way, to disappoint of her expected legacy. Formerly a lady's maid, she adored her husband, and now adores her money, which she hates to spend. She is very ready to listen to gossip about Amos Barton, who tried to get her to subscribe to the rebuilding of the church. *Scenes of Clerical Life I: The Rev. Amos Barton*

Mrs. Patten, who had listened to Mr Gilfil's sermons for thirty years, was one of the few people in the parish to remember his young wife, 'a little pale woman, with eyes as black as soles, an' yet lookin' blank-like, as if she see'd nothing with 'em.' *Scenes of Clerical Life II: Mr. Gilfil's Love-Story*

PAZZI: A leader of the popular democratic party in Florence, opposed to both the Medici and Savonarola. *Romola*

PAZZINI, LA: A kind-hearted greengrocer's wife in Milan, where Sarti lodges with his little daughter Tina. *Scenes of Clerical Life II: Mr. Gilfil's Love-Story*

PEACOCK, MR.: The medical man whose practice Lydgate takes over after his death for the sum of £800. *Middlemarch*

PEGWELL: A corn-factor who tried to sell Bambridge a horse which was known to be a 'roarer'. Bambridge refused it, saying: 'Thank you, Peg, I don't deal in wind-instruments'— a joke which went the round of the county. *Middlemarch*

PELLEY'S BANK: A bank whose failure could have done much harm to Guest & Co. had not Tom Tulliver warned them in time. *The Mill on the Floss*

PELTON, SQUIRE: A gentleman who used to take his dogs and a long whip into his wife's room and flog them to frighten her—according to Mrs. Girdle, whose mother was Mrs. Pelton's lady's maid. *Daniel Deronda*

PENDRELL, MR.: A banker in Treby Magna, who is so alarmed by the rising tide of Methodism that he dismisses all his employees who are Dissenters and will employ only Church-men. *Felix Holt*

PENTREATH, LORD AND LADY: Elderly friends of the Mallingers, who are invited to the Abbey to meet Gwendolen as the bride of the heir, Grandcourt. Lady Pentreath, when told of Mirah by Daniel Deronda, says she will engage her to give singing lessons to her nine grand-daughters. She has a low opinion of Jews, and says of Mirah after her début in a London drawing-room: 'She is not impudent enough. She must have learned to be demure on the stage'. *Daniel Deronda*

PEPPER, MRS.: The huckster's wife at Fibb's End, one of Bob Jakin's best customers. *The Mill on the Floss*

PETTIFER, MRS.: A gentle, superior-minded widow in dowdy clothes, who is always called on by her neighbours when they are in trouble. She is fond of Janet Dempster, whom she knew as a young girl, but cannot visit her, though they live almost next door to each other, because Dempster, when drunk, turned her out of the house. When he shuts Janet out of the house in her night-clothes, she takes refuge with Mrs. Pettifer, and remains there in hiding until she has to go and nurse her dying husband. After his death she persuades Mrs. Pettifer to take up residence in a small house which Dempster has left her so that Mr. Tryan, who is seriously ill, can lodge with her and be properly nursed until he dies. *Scenes of Clerical Life III: Janet's Repentance*

PHILLIPS, SAM: A stone-cutter, who does not learn to read until he is turned twenty, and is so pleased with his new skill that he persuades Bill Downes, who works with him, to join him at night-school. *Adam Bede*

PHIPPS, ALFRED AND NED: Miss Phipps's brothers. Alfred, the elder, is blond and stumpy, likes his sister, but tries to make up for it by 'the severest attention to shirt-studs and that particular shade of brown that was best relieved by gilt buttons'. Ned behaved very badly at the confirmation service, making the other boys snigger. *Scenes of Clerical Life III: Janet's Repentance*

PHIPPS, MISS: A plain, dumpy young woman, who hopes the Countess will prove to be a wicked woman, as she herself has 'no compensating superiority in virtue to set against the other lady's manifest superiority in personal charms.' *Scenes of Clerical Life I: The Rev. Amos Barton*
Although 'finished' at a very expensive school, it was to no effect, and Miss Phipps shows her bad taste in her clothes —a crimson bonnet with a cockade of stiff feathers on the summit, or a transparent bonnet with marabou feathers. But she has a filial heart, and lights her father's pipe with a pleasant smile. *Scenes of Clerical Life III: Janet's Repentance*

PHIPPS, MRS.: The banker's wife, who is one of the first to credit the rumour that the Countess Czerlaski and Mr. Bridmain are not brother and sister. *Scenes of Clerical Life I: The Rev. Amos Barton*
Mrs. Phipps was very much against the innovations of the Rev. Edgar Tryan, and when Dunn the draper attended Tryan's lectures, she transferred her custom elsewhere. *Scenes of Clerical Life III: Janet's Repentance*

PHOEBE: A little maid engaged by the Meyricks as soon as the girls begin to earn enough to pay her. *Daniel Deronda*

Mrs. Pettifer's maid, who sleeps in the attic and does not hear Janet Dempster come in the middle of the night; next day Mrs. Pettifer sends her on holiday, so as to keep Janet's whereabouts a secret from her husband. *Scenes of Clerical Life III: Janet's Repentance*

PICKARD, THE REV. MR.: A Dissenter who considers Mr. Gilfil lacking in spiritual illumination, and prays aloud for his unfortunate parishioners. *Scenes of Clerical Life II: Mr. Gilfil's Love-Story*

PICO, GIOVANNI: An adherent of Savonarola who condemns belief in horoscopes as heresy and 'all a nonsensical dream'. *Romola*

PILGRIM, MR.: The Milby doctor, who was never so happy as when relaxing 'in one of those excellent farmhouses where the mice are sleek and the mistress sickly.' He dislikes Amos Barton—'a low-bred fellow . . . they say his father was a Dissenting shoemaker'—and is very ready to believe all the gossip about him and the Countess. *Scenes of Clerical Life I: The Rev. Amos Barton*

When Pilgrim's patients need to have leeches applied to them, he always calls in old Dame Fripp, because she knows how to make them bite. *Scenes of Clerical Life II: Mr. Gilfil's Love-Story*

Tall, heavy, rough-mannered, rather too much given to eating and drinking, and a great lover of gossip, Pilgrim is regarded askance by the Church faction in Milby because he sometimes goes to chapel, 'looking with great tolerance on all shades of religious opinion that did not include a belief in cures by miracle'. When Dempster's own doctor, Pratt, supports Tryan against Dempster, Pilgrim replaces him, and attends Dempster in his last illness. *Scenes of Clerical Life III: Janet's Repentance*

PINK, MR.: The saddler in Treby Magna, whose shop was a great place for gossip. It was there that Christian discovered who Tommy Trounsem was and where he was to be found. On election day Pink was so intimidated by the rioters that he took refuge in a cul-de-sac, stayed there all day, and never voted at all. *Felix Holt*

PINKERTON, MR.: The Tory candidate in the election, who is backed by Frank Hawley and his friends. *Middlemarch*

PIPPO: The owner of a sweet-shop in Florence from whom Tessa buys sweets for her children at Carnival time. *Romola*

PITTI, PIERO: A Florentine who is dining with Bernardo Rucellai when Baldassarre Calvo accuses Tito Melema of ingratitude in leaving him to his fate among the Turks. Tito persuades everyone that Baldassarre is mad and dangerous, and Pitti sends for two guards to arrest him. *Romola*

PITTMAN, MR.: Dempster's elderly partner, who in his younger days had amassed a good deal of money and property by rather questionable means. Later he became less affluent, because he had four daughters, long, lanky girls with cannon curls surmounted by large hats with long, drooping ostrich feathers of parrot green. *Scenes of Clerical Life III: Janet's Repentance*

PIVART, MR.: The new owner of land above Dorlcote Mill, who takes measures for irrigation which Tulliver thinks will affect his water-power. So he goes to law about it, foolishly, and loses, mainly because of the competence of Pivart's lawyer, Wakem. *The Mill on the Floss*

PLESSY, LORD: An elderly eccentric peer, who lies in bed all day playing dominoes. Mrs. Cadwallader thinks even this is preferable to Mr. Brooke's madness in standing for Parliament. *Middlemarch*

PLYMDALE, MR.: Head of 'the great Plymdale dyeing house'. He is in partnership with Bulstrode, and is just as great a villain, using dyes that rot the silk but bring in profits 'to the glory of God'. *Middlemarch*

PLYMDALE, MRS. (SELINA): Ned's mother, who is very glad when he marries Sophie Toller instead of Rosamond Vincy. She thinks Rosamond's looks and accomplishments very overrated, and when her marriage with Lydgate turns out badly Mrs. Plymdale says it serves her right. *Middlemarch*

PLYMDALE, NED: The son of Plymdale the dyer, who works in his father's business. He is in love with Rosamond Vincy, but she refuses him, mainly because he has a receding chin, red hands, cannot speak French, and can talk only of dyeing. So he marries Sophie Toller, the daughter of the local brewer, and rents a house from the Hackbutts. *Middlemarch*

POINÇON, MADAME: A Swiss lady, living in Lausanne, with whom Dorothea and Celia Brooke are sent to live, for the furthering of their education, after their mother's death. *Middlemarch*

POLITIAN (POLIZIANO), ANGELO: A famous Italian humanist and friend of Lorenzo the Magnificent. He wanted to marry Bartolommeo Scala's daughter Alessandra, but was refused in favour of Marullo. He takes his revenge by attacking the purity of Scala's Greek and Latin in his published works, and the two men become bitter enemies. Although Tito Melema is in high favour with Scala, Politian nevertheless is friendly towards him, and Tito thinks him a better classicist than most of the Florentine scholars. *Romola*

POMFRET, MRS.: Lady's maid at Donnithorne Chase. Hetty Sorrel goes to her every Thursday afternoon to learn tent-stitch, lace-mending, and cutting out, so that she too can become a lady's maid. It is on her return from these expeditions that Hetty meets Captain Donnithorne in the woods, with tragic consequences. *Adam Bede*

PONZO, FRA MENICO DA: An opponent of Savonarola, who preaches against his doctrines in the Cathedral, to the bewilderment of the congregation. *Romola*

POOLE: A client of the lawyer, Dempster, with whom he is in correspondence about a mortgage. After Dempster's death Janet is told to look for the letters in his desk, and comes across a hidden bottle of brandy. She is sorely tempted to drink it, but remembers her promise to the Rev. Tryan, and rushes out of the house, first to her husband's grave, and then to Tryan, for consolation. *Scenes of Clerical Life III: Janet's Repentance*

PORTA, BUCCIO DELLA: *see* Bartolommeo, Fra

PORTER, SIR WILLIAM AND LADY: Apocryphal friends of the Countess Czerlaski, who says she will persuade them to give poor Amos Barton a fat living which is in their gift. Actually the Countess, as Miss Bridmain, was governess to their daughters. *Scenes of Clerical Life I: The Rev. Amos Barton*

POULTER, MR.: An old Peninsular soldier turned village schoolmaster, shrunken and tremulous from too much gin, but bearing himself with martial erectness, scrupulously neat, and with a spirited air, like a superannuated charger who hears the drum. He is engaged to drill Tom when he is lodging with the Rev. Walter Stelling, and for 5s. allows him to borrow his sword for a week. Tom is showing it to Maggie when he drops it and cuts his foot badly. *The Mill on the Floss*

POWDERELL, MR.: A retired ironmonger, who is on the Board of the new hospital in Middlemarch. He is prepared to accept the new doctor, Lydgate, but he is a great believer in medicines, and when the rumour gets round that Lydgate does not believe in them, he is nonplussed. When Lydgate refuses to give Mrs. Powderell anything 'internal' for her erysipelas, her husband surreptitiously doses her with Widgeon's Purifying Pills. *Middlemarch*

POWERS, BILL: A rough, hard-drinking giant of a man who leads the beer-drinkers at the Bear and Ragged Staff in a riot against the Rev. Edgar Tryan. *Scenes of Clerical Life III: Janet's Repentance*

POYSER, CHARLOTTE (TOTTY), MARTY, AND TOMMY: The children of the Poysers at Hall Farm. Charlotte, the youngest, is a spoilt, fair-haired three-year-old, so fat that her back view looks 'like a white sucking pig'. Called after her grandmother, she was first known as Lotty, and then as Totty. *Adam Bede*

POYSER, MARTIN: Squire Donnithorne's tenant at Hall Farm, a hard-working and successful farmer, who has given a home to his niece, Hetty Sorrel, and his wife's niece, Dinah Morris. He knows and likes Adam Bede, and would like to see him married to Hetty, with whom he is in love. When Hetty disappears, Poyser thinks she has run away to become a lady's maid, and is cross, but not worried. The news of her arrest is a great blow to him, more because of the dishonour it brings on the family than for Hetty's sake. When she has been transported he decides that he must leave the farm and go where he is not known, but Adam, on behalf of the repentant Captain Donnithorne, persuades him to stay on. When Adam eventually marries Dinah, Poyser is delighted, and gives her away. *Adam Bede*

POYSER, MRS. RACHEL: The wife of Poyser of Hall Farm, a good-looking woman of about thirty-five, with a fair complexion, sandy hair, a light foot, and a pleasing shape; she usually wears an ample checkered linen apron and a plain cap and gown. She is always busy about the house and dairy, and prides herself on the excellence of her cheese and butter. A good, kind-hearted woman, who has taken in two orphan nieces, Hetty Sorrel and Dinah Morris, she has a sharp tongue and is given to speaking her mind, even to the Squire, on whose favour the renewal of her husband's lease depends. She has a poor opinion of Hetty, in spite of her good work in the dairy, and tries to check her vanity and flightiness; she deplores Dinah's Methodism and preaching, but would be very glad to keep her on the farm, as she appreciates her innate goodness and her firm handling of the three children, Totty, Tommy, and Marty. Like her husband, she dreads leaving the farm after Hetty's disgrace, and is glad to stay on and assist at the wedding of Adam and Dinah. *Adam Bede*

POYSER, OLD MARTIN: A seventy-five-year old farmer, who has made over the tenancy of the farm to his son, and spends his time sitting in the sun or in the ingle-nook. *Adam Bede*

PRATT: Mr. Casaubon's butler, who thinks Dorothea must find life with an old husband very dull, and is glad when her young cousin Will Ladislaw visits her. He eventually marries Dorothea's maid Tantripp. *Middlemarch*

PRATT, ELIZA: The twenty-two-year-old daughter of Mr. Pratt, who since the death of her mother has been under the care of her aunt, to whom she is naturally antipathetic. A handsome girl, somewhat silent, who is in danger of becoming bitter and self-centred, she improves immensely under the influence of the young curate, Edgar Tryan, with whom for a while she fancies herself in love. But when her father tells her of his illness, she is shocked into pity and true admiration of him, and works devotedly in the parish without thought of reward. *Scenes of Clerical Life III: Janet's Repentance*

PRATT, MISS: The spinster sister of Mr. Pratt; she keeps house for him and his motherless daughter Eliza. The one bluestocking in Milby, she has actually published 'a few trifles', including a poem to the curate Edgar Tryan. *Scenes of Clerical Life III: Janet's Repentance*

PRATT, RICHARD: A doctor whose working life has been spent in Milby. Left a widower with a young daughter, he is looked after by his unmarried sister. A good conversationalist and raconteur, he ascribes all illness to 'debility', and gives his patients, with whom he is very popular, port wine and quinine. He was very friendly with the Raynors, and gave

Janet away when she married Dempster, but when Dempster took to drink and quarrelled with Tryan, Pratt remonstrated with him and was ordered out of the house. So Pilgrim becomes Dempster's doctor and attends him on his deathbed. Afterwards the Pratts return to their old footing of friendship with Janet and her mother, and Pratt attends Tryan until his death in the house which Janet has lent him. *Scenes of Clerical Life III: Janet's Repentance*

PRENDERGAST, THE HONOURABLE AND REVEREND MR.: The non-resident incumbent of Milby, who appoints Mr. Crewe as his curate. When Edgar Tryan wants to give lectures on religious knowledge on Sunday evenings, to supplement the meagre sermons of old Crewe, Dempster and his friends get up an agitation about it, and succeed in having them banned. *Scenes of Clerical Life III: Janet's Repentance*

PRIOR, THE REV. MR.: An elderly man whom Fellowes calls 'the canting Prior'—'a fellow who soaked himself in spirits, and talked of the Gospel through an inflamed nose'. Fellowes is surprised Amos Barton should be on terms of intimacy with such a man. *Scenes of Clerical Life I: The Rev. Amos Barton*

PRITCHARD: The Vincy's maid, who helps to nurse Fred when he has typhoid. *Middlemarch*

PROCTOR: The local printer in Milby, a friend of Dempster's, who sets up and circulates the mock 'playbill' satirising Tryan's lectures. *Scenes of Clerical Life III: Janet's Repentance*

PROTHEROE: A medical man from Brassing, whom Lydgate calls in for important cases when the local doctors decide to boycott the new hospital. *Middlemarch*

PROWD, MR.: A watchmaker in Treby Magna, to whom Felix Holt apprentices himself after he has abandoned his medical studies. *Felix Holt*

PRYME, MR.: One of Dempster's clients, who is stirred up by Mr. Jerome, indignant on Tryan's behalf, to investigate some suspicious points in Dempster's conduct of affairs connected with the parish, with the result that Mr. Pryme and Dempster quarrel. *Scenes of Clerical Life III: Janet's Repentance*

PUCCI, GIANNOZZO: A friend of Bernardo Rucellai's, and one of the most important members of the pro-Medici party in Florence. *Romola*

PUGH, THE REV. MR.: A young curate, with neat black whiskers and a pale complexion, who performs his parochial duties in a white tie, a well-brushed hat, a perfect suit of black, and well-polished boots. *Scenes of Clerical Life I: The Rev. Amos Barton*

PUGLIA, FRA FRANCESCO DI: A Franciscan monk who, after Savonarola's excommunication, challenges him to perform a miracle by walking through fire, but is called home by his Superiors 'while the heat was simply oratorical'. *Romola*

PULLER, MR.: One of Daniel Deronda's contemporaries at Cambridge, whom he considers a much better classical scholar than he is himself. *Daniel Deronda*

PULLET, MR.: The brother-in-law of Mrs. Tulliver, a small man with twinkling eyes and thin lips, who had 'a great natural faculty for ignorance'. A gentleman farmer, he lives at Garum Firs, in a vast stuccoed and battlemented house with peacocks on the terrace, and has a great brindled mastiff as big as a lion. Tom Tulliver thinks his uncle a nincompoop and a mollycoddle because he is afraid of firearms and will never ride anything but a quiet pony. He is very proud of his wife's ill-health, is in charge of all her medicines, as prescribed by Dr. Turnbull, and sees that she takes them regularly. *The Mill on the Floss*

PULLET, MRS. (SOPHY): The elder sister of Mrs. Tulliver, and the second of the four 'Dodson girls'. A hypochondriac, she is proud of being Dr. Turnbull's most interesting patient, but nevertheless dresses in the height of fashion, with balloon sleeves and large feathered and beribboned bonnets. She has no children, and is Maggie Tulliver's godmother, paying for part of her schooling and kindly presenting her with some of her own, most unsuitable, clothes. But she has no affection for her, and is angry when she goes out as a governess rather than live with her aunt 'and do her sewing'. *The Mill on the Floss*

PUTTY, JAMES: An electioneering agent, who 'is beyond any man for saving a candidate's money—he does half the work with his tongue'. He manages the women very well, and gets them to drive their men to vote as he wishes. In the Treby Magna election he is engaged to work for Transome's opponent, Garstin. *Felix Holt*

PYM: Captain Donnithorne's valet. *Adam Bede*

Q

QUALLON, MR.: A banker, and the only man of any importance living near the Gascoignes. A generous soul, he keeps open house, and takes a liking to Gwendolen Harleth, inviting her and her mother to all his parties. When Gwendolen goes hunting for the first time, against the wishes of her uncle, he gives her the brush and escorts her home. *Daniel Deronda*

QUICKSETT: One of Daniel Deronda's contemporaries at Cambridge, who has a good chance of gaining a Fellowship. *Daniel Deronda*

QUORLEN: A Tory printer who is friendly with Christian. Together they concoct a satirical poster against Jermyn and Transome for the election, and trick old Tommy Trounsem, who has taken on the job of bill-posting, into sticking up copies of it instead of the official bills. *Felix Holt*

R

RACHEL: The Hackits' housemaid. *Scenes of Clerical Life I: The Rev. Amos Barton*

RADBOROUGH, THE DEAN OF: An eminent divine, whom the Countess Czerlaski falsely claims as a friend, promising that he will give Amos Barton a good living. *Scenes of Clerical Life I: The Rev. Amos Barton*

RADLEY: The owner of a livery-stable near Mr. Tryan's lodgings. Tryan occasionally hires a horse from him on a Sunday when he has to preach in three different places. *Scenes of Clerical Life III: Janet's Repentance*

RAFFLES, JOHN: A raffish, dissolute, florid-faced man, about whom there hangs a stale odour of travellers' rooms in commercial hotels. He married Joshua Rigg's mother, and treated her and her illegitimate son by Peter Featherstone very badly. When Rigg inherits all his father's property, Raffles tries to blackmail him, but Rigg refuses to be intimidated. He considers Raffles, whom he hates, 'a spiteful, brassy, impudent, bullying rogue', and says that if he ever sees him again, he will stop the allowance he is making to his mother, most of which finds its way into Raffles' pocket. While Raffles is visiting Rigg, he discovers the presence near by of an old acquaintance, Nicholas Bulstrode, with whom Raffles was once involved in a plot to rob a young woman of her inheritance in order that Bulstrode might marry her mother, Mrs. Dunkirk, and lay hands on the money himself. In order to get rid of Raffles, the only person who knows of this discreditable transaction, Bulstrode paid his fare to the United States. But he has drifted back again, and become a drunken wastrel, ripe for mischief. He calls on Bulstrode, now a wealthy and much-respected banker, and extorts £200 from him, with a promise of more when he wants it if only he will stay away from Middlemarch. But before he leaves, Raffles sees and recognises Will Ladislaw, the son of the woman whom Bulstrode cheated, and tells him enough of the story for Ladislaw to be able to guess the rest. When Bulstrode knows this he sends for Ladislaw, and offers him an allowance if he will keep quiet about the matter. Will indignantly refuses. Meanwhile Raffles, in one of his drunken fits, has poured out the whole story to the local horse-dealer Bambridge, whom he met at a distant horse-fair. Bambridge returns to Middlemarch and gleefully passes the story on to his cronies, from whence it spreads through the town. Raffles, robbed of the money which Bulstrode finally gave him, hoping he would drink himself to death, returns to Middlemarch in the last stages of D.T.s, and Bulstrode, pretending he is a poor relation, puts him in the care of the housekeeper at his country property, Stone Court, where he dies, having ruined not only Bulstrode's reputation, but also that of Lydgate, the doctor who attended him on his death-bed, and is said to have been bribed by Bulstrode to conceal their relationship, and even, some say, to murder the sick man, though this is disproved at the inquest. *Middlemarch*

RALPH: A manservant at Donnithorne Chase, who is sent to meet Captain Donnithorne at Liverpool on his way home from Ireland and tell him of his grandfather's death. *Adam Bede*

RAM, MR.: The Jewish owner of a secondhand bookshop in which Daniel Deronda first meets Mordecai. *Daniel Deronda*

RAMBLE, SQUIRE: A landowner who employed Daniel Knott's uncle as his bailiff. When the uncle dies, he leaves Knott enough money to be able to rent from Ramble the farm where Tina Sarti takes refuge after Captain Wybrow is found dead. *Scenes of Clerical Life II: Mr. Gilfil's Love-Story*

RANN, JOSHUA: The village shoemaker and parish clerk, known as Old Joshway. A shabby man, in rusty spectacles, he is very proud of his magnificent bass voice, and reads the services marvellously. He is also a good fiddler, and plays when Wiry Ben dances a hornpipe at Captain Donnithorne's coming-of-age celebrations. He is very upset when Will Maskery, a Methodist, calls him 'a blind Pharisee', and in revenge tries to get the parson, Irwine, to stop the Methodist Dinah Morris from preaching on the village green. *Adam Bede*

RANN, SALLY: The shoemaker's daughter, who, because he is the parish clerk, attends church regularly, and is much admired by Bessy Cranage as 'a good girl', able to find her place in the prayer book without help. *Adam Bede*

RAPPIT, MR.: The St. Ogg's hairdresser, who, 'with his well-anointed coronal locks tending wavily upward, like the simulated pyramid of flame on a monumental urn', is called in to tidy up the eleven-year-old Maggie Tulliver's hair after she has cut it off in a fit of temper. *The Mill on the Floss*

RATCLIFFE: The licensee of the Red Lion, Milby, whose brandy, in the opinion of Dempster, is British, sweet, and sooty, 'like sugared rain-water caught down the chimney.' *Scenes of Clerical Life III: Janet's Repentance*

RAYMOND, MR. AND MRS.: Relations of Lady Mallinger, who are invited to the Abbey at Christmas to meet Gwendolen as the bride of the heir Grandcourt. Mrs. Raymond sings, and Daniel Deronda, who is also at the Abbey, hopes she will take lessons from Mirah Lapidoth. *Daniel Deronda*

RAYNOR, ANNA: Mrs. Raynor's sister-in-law, who has been ill for a long time. She becomes worse shortly after Dempster's death, and Mrs. Raynor has very reluctantly to leave her widowed daughter in order to nurse Anna. *Scenes of Clerical Life III: Janet's Repentance*

RAYNOR, MRS.: The mother of Janet Dempster, who after her husband's death supported herself and her daughter by doing millinery. She gave Janet a good education in the hope that she would become a governess, but is delighted when the handsome, high-spirited girl marries a rising young lawyer, Dempster. When the marriage turns out badly, and Dempster takes to drink, she can do nothing to help, and has the added sorrow of being blamed by Janet for allowing her to marry such a man. *Scenes of Clerical Life III: Janet's Repentance*

RENFREW, MRS.: The widow of a colonel, and therefore considered suitable to meet Lady Chettam at Mr. Brooke's dinner-party. *Middlemarch*

RICHARDS, PATTY: A village girl who went into a decline and died, much envied by poor Tina because she looked so happy and didn't seem to care about her lover any more. *Scenes of Clerical Life II: Mr. Gilfil's Love-Story*

RICKETTS, DAME: A wiry old beldame who much enjoys a skirmish with her arch-enemy Molly Beale during the uproar over Tryan's lectures. *Scenes of Clerical Life III: Janet's Repentance*

RIDOLFI, GIOVAN BATTISTA: A follower of Savonarola, but strongly opposed to Valori over the death-sentence passed on the Medicean conspirators, one of whom is his brother Niccolò. He watches the execution, and later revenges himself by killing Valori during a riot. *Romola*

RIDOLFI, NICCOLÒ: A middle-aged Florentine of high rank, who is present at the dinner-party in the Rucellai Gardens when Baldassarre is repudiated by Tito Melema. He is one of the five conspirators who plot to bring back the Medici, and is arrested and executed with Romola's godfather, Bernardo del Nero. His younger brother later avenges his death. *Romola*

RIGG, JOSHUA: A middle-aged man, with a face like a frog, who turns up unexpectedly at old Peter Featherstone's funeral, and attends the reading of the will, much to the annoyance of all Featherstone's relatives. He turns out to be his illegitimate son, and inherits Stone Court, which Featherstone left him in the expectation that he would settle there and be a constant irritation to all his neighbours. But Josh, as he is called, sells it almost immediately to Featherstone's enemy, Mr. Bulstrode, and with the money buys himself a money-changer's business on a busy quay in the seaport where he was brought up. When he was a boy, Josh's mother married a handsome, drunken bully named Raffles, who ill-treated them both. He now turns up and tries to extort money from Rigg, who refuses to listen to him and sends him away with 'a sovereign and a flaskful of brandy'. *Middlemarch*

RILEY, MR.: An auctioneer and estate agent much esteemed by Tulliver, who asks his advice about the education of his son Tom. Riley himself has a houseful of daughters, and dies young of an apoplexy, leaving them all practically penniless. *The Mill on the Floss*

ROBINS, CLARA: One of Miss Townley's pupils, who was much puzzled by the fact that some clergymen were rectors and others not, until her fellow-pupil, Ellen Marriott, assured her with great confidence that it was only the *clever* clergymen who were made rectors. *Scenes of Clerical Life III: Janet's Repentance*

ROBISSON, MR.: An elderly man who in his last illness was fortified by his housekeeper, Mrs. Abel, with copious draughts of brandy. She persuades Mr. Bulstrode to let her do the same for Raffles, not knowing, as Bulstrode does, that the doctor has forbidden it, and Raffles dies. *Middlemarch*

RODNEY, JEM: A mole-catcher who once came across Silas Marner in a cataleptic trance. He often makes jests at Silas's expense, and when Silas finds his money has been stolen, he immediately suspects Jem, who, being innocent, hotly denies the accusation. *Silas Marner*

ROE, MR.: A travelling Methodist preacher, who described the rector, Mr. Irwine, as a man 'given up to the lusts of the flesh and the pride of life . . . preaching at best but a carnal and soul-benumbing morality, and trafficking in the souls of men . . .' *Adam Bede*

ROMOLA: *see* Bardi, Romola de'

ROSE, THE REV. MR.: The one-time minister at Salem Independent Chapel in Milby, whose doctrine was found to be 'a little too high, verging on antinomianism'; so he had to go. *Scenes of Clerical Life III: Janet's Repentance*

ROSE, TIMOTHY: A rather foolish gentleman farmer whose one desire is to keep out of trouble and speak everyone fair except when they are safely out of hearing. Fearing violence on election day, he swathes his more vital parts in layers of flannel, and puts on two greatcoats. Arriving at the poll, he carefully gives one vote to each candidate—one Tory, one Whig—on the grounds that the most 'an independent man can do is to try and please all'. *Felix Holt*

RUCELLAI, BERNARDO: A member of a rich Florentine family, which a hundred years ago had made a fortune from purple dye. He is a collector of precious stones, and buys from Tito Melema the intaglio of Cleopatra which he saved from the wreck. This leads him to take an interest in Tito, whom he invites to dinner. The meal is interrupted by the arrival of Baldassarre Calvo, who denounces Tito as ungrateful and a traitor to his benefactor. But Tito has no difficulty in persuading Rucellai and the other guests that Baldassarre is mad, and Rucellai sends him to prison. *Romola*

RUCELLAI, CAMILLA: A strange, hysterical woman, 'a seer of visions', strongly attracted to Savonarola, who would like to silence her, but dare not. She sends for Romola to tell her that Christ has commanded her in a vision to arrange for the death of Romola's godfather, Bernardo del Nero, who is in fact later executed for treason, and that Savonarola approves. She also tells Romola that she must betray all her godfather's secrets, for the good of the state. Romola, appalled by her obvious madness, rushes from the room and refuses to meet her again. *Romola*

RYDE, THE REV. MR.: The clergyman who succeeded Irwine. A zealous, but tactless man, who, with much that was good in his intentions, only succeeded in alienating the hearts of his parishioners. He stopped the traditional carol-singing by the choir because he said it led to too much drinking on their rounds, and was sour-tempered, haggling with the people who worked for him, and ranting in the pulpit against the Dissenters—'a sayer and not a doer of the Word'. *Adam Bede*

S

SADLER: A Middlemarch draper whom Mrs. Vincy prefers to his rival Hopkins. She buys all the linen for her daughter's trousseau from him. *Middlemarch*

SAFT, TOM: *see* Tholer, Tom

SALLY: The Garths' maidservant. *Middlemarch*

Mrs. Pullet's maid. *The Mill on the Floss*

Mrs. Hackit's maid, who is cross because her mistress *will* give the used tea-leaves to old Dame Fripp instead of to her, to sweep the floors with. *Scenes of Clerical Life II: Mr. Gilfil's Love-Story*

Servant to Mrs. Jerome, who does not trust her to wash up the best china. *Scenes of Clerical Life III: Janet's Repentance*

SALT, BEN: The sturdy five-year-old son of Sandy Jim, known as 'Timothy's Bess's Ben'. He is on the village green when Dinah is preaching, and kicks one of the Methodist women who tries to make him keep still. *Adam Bede*

SALT, BESS: The mother of Ben, known as 'Timothy's Bess' to distinguish her from her cousin, 'Chad's Bess'. She has a large family, and cannot go to Thias Bede's funeral because she is feeding the baby. *Adam Bede*

SALT, JIM: A carpenter, known as Sandy Jim, who works in

the same timber-yard as the Bede brothers. A burly, red-headed man, he is the husband of 'Timothy's Bess'. *Adam Bede*

SALT, MR.: A wool-factor in Treby Magna, a bilious man who spoke only when there was a good opportunity of contradicting someone. One of his sisters married Lawyer Jermyn's clerk Labron, and another, Mary, became the wife of Mr. Muscat, the Dissenter. *Felix Holt*

The supercargo who, having been run to earth in a cloud of tobacco-smoke in the Anchor Tavern, is commissioned to buy goods to the value of £50 on behalf of Tom Tulliver, the money being put up by his aunt and uncle Glegg, and to sell them on his next trip abroad. The profit on this venture is sufficient to enable Tom to extend his business activities and eventually build up a useful nest-egg. *The Mill on the Floss*

SALVESTRO, FRA: *see* Maruffi, Fra Salvestro

SALVIATI, MARCO: An adherent of Savonarola, who on the occasion of the abortive Trial by Fire commands three hundred armed men, drawn up in the square opposite Dolfo Spini's five hundred Companions. *Romola*

SAMPSON, MR.: The driver of the stage-coach which passed by Transome Court, who invariably told the passengers of the Durfey-Transome-Bycliffe law suits, and of old Lawyer Jermyn, who 'had had *his* pickings out of the estate'. *Felix Holt*

SAMSON, DR.: The medical attendant of Lady Assher when young. She remembers him as 'such a curious old man'. When she was ill, he said to her mother, 'What your daughter suffers from is weakness.' *Scenes of Clerical Life II: Mr. Gilfil's Love-Story*

SANDEMAN, SQUIRE: The owner of large estates at Tilston, where Mr. Jerome lived as a boy, who appointed as rector in his parish 'a terrible drinkin' fox-huntin' man; you niver see'd such a parish i' your time for wickedness'. *Scenes of Clerical Life III: Janet's Repentance*

SANDRO: Assistant to the Florentine barber Nello, a solemn-looking, dark-eyed youth who has a great admiration for Tito Melema. *Romola*

SANDY, JIM: *see* Salt, Jim

SARAH: The Cohens' maid, who minds the shop while Deronda is telling the family about Mirah and her brother Mordecai. *Daniel Deronda*

The servant-girl to whom Silas Marner, as a young man, was engaged. But she transferred her affections to his friend, William Dane, and married him after Silas had been falsely accused of theft by Dane, and had left the town. *Silas Marner*

SARGENT, THE REV. MR.: A flirtatious Oxford clergyman to whom Lord Watling gave a living in return for the help Sargent's brother, a lawyer, gave him in an unsavoury lawsuit. *Scenes of Clerical Life I: The Rev. Amos Barton*

SARTI: A poor Italian, living in Milan. He was once a successful operatic tenor, but lost his voice, and being ignorant and conceited, had no other resource but music-copying. The death of his wife and two elder children in an epidemic sent him nearly out of his mind. When he realises that he too is dying, he sends for Lady Cheverel, for whom he has been working, and asks her to take care of his remaining child, the three-year-old Caterina, known as Tina. *Scenes of Clerical Life II: Mr. Gilfil's Love-Story*

SARTI, CATERINA (TINA): The child of a poor music-copyist, known as Tina. After her father's death in Milan she is taken to England by Lady Cheverel, for whom her father had been working, and is brought up as the pet and plaything of the whole household, employed in due course in such light tasks as winding wool, reading aloud, and singing after supper. When she is eighteen, Sir Christopher Cheverel decides that she will make an admirable wife for his young ward and chaplain, Maynard Gilfil. But, unknown to anyone except Mr. Gilfil, she has been carrying on a flirtation with the Cheverels' heir, Captain Wybrow, and is determined to marry him. When she discovers that he is engaged to a most suitable young lady, Beatrice Assher, and has only been playing with her, she is furious, and decides to kill him. After a stormy scene, he agrees to meet her for the last time in a remote corner of the garden, but when she arrives there, carrying a small dagger, he is already dead of a heart attack, brought on by agitation. Overcome with remorse, Tina runs away and takes refuge with her old nurse, where Gilfil, who has been in love with her for a long time, finds her and takes her to stay with his married sister. She eventually agrees to marry him rather than go back to Cheverel Manor, but her heart is broken, and a year later she dies in childbirth. *Scenes of Clerical Life II: Mr. Gilfil's Love-Story*

SASSO, MEO DI: A courier who is bringing the good news to a starving Florence, that ships from France, laden with corn, have safely arrived at Leghorn, in spite of the Venetian and Genoese ships investing the port. However, his horse founders and Tito delivers the news to the Gonfaloniere and Priors. *Romola*

SATCHELL: Squire Donnithorne's agent, 'a selfish, tale-bearing, mischievous fellow', in Adam Bede's opinion, who has done his employer a lot of harm. *Adam Bede*

SAVONAROLA, FRA GIROLAMO: A Dominican monk who was for a time one of the most powerful men in the religious and political life of Renaissance Florence. His powerful sermons brought many men under his sway and he became the leader of the anti-Medicean party; but having aroused the hostility of Pope Alexander IV he was excommunicated, and finally condemned and executed as a heretic. Romola meets him first by the bedside of her dying brother, Fra Luca, also a Dominican, and again when she is leaving Florence to escape from the unkindness of her husband, the Greek Tito Melema. Savonarola persuades her to return home, and she is back in Florence when, through the treachery of her husband, her godfather, Bernardo del Nero, is condemned to death for plotting to restore the Medici. Romola pleads with Savonarola to intervene on Bernardo's behalf, but he refuses, and like many other Florentines she turns against him, thinking he has been led astray by personal ambition. *Romola*

SCADDON, HENRY: *see* Christian, Maurice

SCALA, ALESSANDRA: The daughter of the Florentine Secretary of State, Bartolommeo, married to the poet Marullo. She is very fond of jewellery, and buys some of the gems Tito Melema has saved from his shipwreck. *Romola*

SCALA, BARTOLOMMEO: A miller's son who, by a combination of talent and hard work, rose to a high position in Florence.

He dabbles in literature, and conducts a bitter controversy with the humanist Politian over alleged false quantities in his Greek and Latin verses. He buys some jewels from Tito, is impressed by his scholarship, and eventually employs him to write his letters. *Romola*

SCALES, MR.: House-steward and head-butler to Sir Maximus Debarry. He becomes jealous of Maurice Christian, factotum to Sir Maximus's son Philip, and plays a stupid practical joke on him which results in the discovery that Esther Lyon is the rightful owner of the Transome estate. *Felix Holt*

SFORZA, LUDOVICO: Duke of Milan. He intrigues against Savonarola, and plots with Tito Melema to intercept letters from him which can be construed as treasonable. Out of gratitude for his help, he offers Tito a position in his household, and Tito is on his way to take it up when he is strangled by Baldassarre. *Romola*

SHARP, MRS.: Lady Cheverel's lady's maid, 'of somewhat vinegary aspect and flaunting attire', who hopes to marry Bates the gardener. She was with Lady Cheverel in Milan when she decided to adopt Tina, and helps to bring the child up. After Wybrow's death, she is the first person to notice that Tina is missing. *Scenes of Clerical Life II: Mr. Gilfil's Love-Story*

SHERLOCK, THE REV. THEODORE: One of the Rev. Augustus Debarry's curates, who is deputed to take the elder man's place in the proposed debate with Rufus Lyon. Being of a nervous disposition, he takes fright at the last moment, jumps on a passing coach, and is seen no more. *Felix Holt*

SILLY CALEB: An idiot well known in Milby, who got mixed up in the demonstration against the Rev. Edgar Tryan's lectures, with a string of hooting boys at his heels. *Scenes of Clerical Life III: Janet's Repentance*

SILLY JIM: An inmate of Shepperton workhouse. *Scenes of Clerical Life I: The Rev. Amos Barton*

SIMMONS: Peter Featherstone's bailiff at Stone Court. *Middlemarch*

SIMS, MR.: The Treby Magna auctioneer, who was gossiping in Mr. Pink the saddler's shop when Christian asked about old Tommy Trounsem, and supplied him with all the details, including the fact that the old man always swore he had a right to the Transome estate. *Felix Holt*

SINKER, MR.: An 'eminent counsel' who represents 'the useful bachelor element' at Sir Hugo Mallinger's Christmas house-party. *Daniel Deronda*

SIRCOME, MR.: A miller in Treby Magna, a friend of Scales, Sir Maximus Debarry's steward, with whom he is hand-in-glove about prices and percentages of goods supplied for the Debarry household. He rather admires Jermyn, who won a law-suit for him about his mill. 'It cost a pretty penny, but he brought me through.' But even he doubts if Jermyn can get Harold Transome into Parliament as a Radical. *Felix Holt*

SITWELL, SIR JASPER AND LADY: Friends of Mr. Gilfil's, who often dined at their house, squiring Lady Sitwell into dinner with 'quaint yet graceful gallantry'. *Scenes of Clerical Life II: Mr. Gilfil's Love-Story*

SLOGAN, LORD: An unexceptionable Irish peer, 'whose estate wanted nothing but drainage and population'. He proposed marriage to the heiress Catherine Arrowpoint, but she resolutely refused him. *Daniel Deronda*

SMITH, THE REV. MR.: The former minister at Salem Independent Chapel; he had a talent for poetry, and was dismissed because he exchanged verses with the young ladies of his congregation. *Scenes of Clerical Life III: Janet's Repentance*

SNELL, JOHN: Landlord of the Rainbow Inn in Raveloe, where Eppie's wedding feast is held. *Silas Marner*

SODERINI, PAGOLANTONIO: A Florentine notability who, though not in fact greatly enamoured of Savonarola's doctrines, nevertheless votes against the death sentence passed on him. This infuriates the mob, who set out to wreck Soderini's house. Thwarted by the authorities, they wreck Tito Melema's instead. *Romola*

SORREL, HETTY: Mr. Poyser's orphaned niece, daughter of his sister by a good-for-nothing farmer. When her parents die, she is given a home by the Poysers, and grows up to be very beautiful, but vain and frivolous. Mrs. Bede, who does not want her son Adam to marry Hetty, says she is 'no more use nor the gillyflower on the wall', although, thanks to her aunt's training, she is very good at dairy-work. Her ambition is to become a lady's maid, and she has no affection for the Poysers or anyone else. She attracts the attention of Captain Donnithorne, the young heir of the local landowner from whom Poyser rents his farm, and agrees to meet him in secret. She is foolish enough to suppose that he will marry her, and has visions of a life of luxury, rudely shattered when Donnithorne, forced to it by Adam Bede, who has discovered their secret, writes to say that he is rejoining his regiment and they must not meet again. Hetty then agrees half-heartedly to marry Adam, who has been courting her for a long time, but when she discovers that she is pregnant she runs away, hoping to rejoin Donnithorne in Windsor. When she arrives there, having walked most of the way, she discovers that the regiment has moved to Ireland. Returning on her tracks, ill and almost penniless, she decides to drown herself, but cannot do it. She takes refuge in a poor cottage, where her child is born, but the next day slips out, carrying the baby, and continues her aimless progress. The child's fretful wailing so disturbs her that she finally abandons it under some brushwood in a small copse, and decides to go home and pretend it never existed, telling the Poysers that she ran away to become a lady's maid, but took fright and is glad to be back with them. However, the child's crying still haunts her, and she wanders back to the copse, where she is found and arrested by the police, who were guided to the place by a labourer who found the baby's body. Once in prison on a charge of infanticide, Hetty stubbornly refuses to answer any questions or to make any statement, until her cousin Dinah Morris, the Methodist preacher, comes to visit her. Softened by Dinah's gentle kindness, Hetty eventually confesses; she is tried and condemned to be hanged. Donnithorne, who knows nothing of her fate, but has returned from Ireland because of his grandfather's death, tries desperately to get her reprieved, but only succeeds in getting the sentence changed to transportation. She dies just as arrangements are being made about ten years later for her return to England. *Adam Bede*

SPANNING, DR.: An erudite gentleman who delights Mr. Casaubon by speaking highly, at the Archdeacon's dinner, of Casaubon's 'tractate on the Egyptian Mysteries'. *Middlemarch*

SPENCE, MR.: A clerk in the bank where Tom Tulliver's Uncle Deane is employed. *The Mill on the Floss*

SPICER, MR.: A shoe-maker and parish clerk who hears from his brother, a bell-ringer in Lowick Lane, of the execution on the Lydgates' furniture, and passes the information on to the Rev. Farebrother. *Middlemarch*

SPILKINS: The 'fungous-featured' landlord of the Cross Keys at Pollard's End, where Christian finds old Tommy Trounsem and gets from him the information he needs about the Durfey-Transome-Bycliffe case. *Felix Holt*

SPILKINS, MR.: A young gentleman who was reckless with his pocket-money, and paid a guinea at Larcher's sale for a book of five hundred riddles. *Middlemarch*

SPINI, DOLFO: A licentious Florentine, who hates Savonarola for his attempts to reform the life of the city. He gathers round him a band of young men, known as the Companions, who indulge in all the vices Savonarola is preaching against. They also represent the old aristocratic party which is against the Medici. Spini helps Tito Melema with his plot to betray Savonarola by causing letters to be intercepted on their way to France, but later thinks he has been betrayed by Tito, and eggs on the mob to wreck his house. His followers also pursue Tito himself when he is trying to leave Florence for Milan, and cause him to jump into the river, which carries him to his death. *Romola*

SPRAGUE, DR.: The senior physician of Middlemarch, who dislikes Lydgate for his arrogance, and is very ready to agree that though Lydgate may not have caused Raffles's death, he certainly profited by it to the extent of a £1,000 loan from Bulstrode, who was being blackmailed by Raffles. *Middlemarch*

SPRATT: Manager of the coal-mines at Sproxton, much disliked by the miners, who, influenced by Johnson, the Radical agent, drag him out of the Seven Stars on election day, and proceed to kick and cuff him. He is saved by Felix Holt, who first persuades the aggressors to tie Spratt to a post, and then drags them off with the promise of better sport. *Felix Holt*

SPRATT, MR.: The master of the Shepperton workhouse, a

mean-spirited, bullying creature, much disliked by the inmates, consisting of a number of old men and women and a few refractory children. *Scenes of Clerical Life I: The Rev. Amos Barton*

SPRAY, THE REV. MR.: The Independent minister at St. Ogg's, who preached political sermons which displeased some of his old-fashioned dissenting members; they thought he was 'siding with the Catholics', and would do well to leave politics alone. *The Mill on the Floss*

STANDISH, MR.. An elderly lawyer who 'had been so long concerned with the landed gentry that he had become landed himself'. He is Peter Featherstone's lawyer, and expects after the old man's funeral to be reading the last will he drew up for him. To his surprise there is a new will, recently drawn up by another lawyer. Standish was also Mr. Casaubon's lawyer, and added the codicil to his will by which Dorothea is disinherited if she marries Will Ladislaw. *Middlemarch*

STANNERY, LORD: An elderly peer, to whose title and estates Grandcourt would be heir, but for two intermediate cousins. *Daniel Deronda*

STARTIN, MRS.: The resident housekeeper at Offendene, who gets the house ready for Mrs. Davilow when she rents it. *Daniel Deronda*

STEENE, WIDOW: A poor widow in Mr. Irwine's parish, who was grateful to his sister Kate for sending her medicine for her cough. *Adam Bede*

STELLING, MRS. LOUISA: The wife of Tom Tulliver's tutor, a fair-haired, rather cool young woman who gets Tom to look after her daughter Laura while nurse is busy with the new baby, 'to make him feel at home'. Tom and Maggie both dislike her, but are grateful for the picnic lunch which she prepares for them to eat in the stage-coach on their way home when their father is ill. *The Mill on the Floss*

STELLING, THE REV. WALTER: An Oxford man whom Riley recommends as a tutor for Tom Tulliver, mainly because his wife is the daughter of an influential man, Timpson, who can put business in Riley's way in return. Because of his wife's extravagance, Stelling has got into debt, and is glad to take in

Tom, and later Philip Wakem, as resident pupils. A fair-haired man, with lightish-grey eyes, he has a sonorous bass voice and an air of defiant self-confidence inclining to brazenness. He fails to teach Tom very much, but that is mainly because Tom is not by nature academic. With the studious Philip Wakem, Stelling is much more successful. *The Mill on the Floss*

STICKNEY, THE REV. MR.: The Dissenting minister at Salem Chapel. His sermons prove a disappointment, and as he is not a very estimable person, many members of his congregation, including the wealthy and benevolent Mr. Jerome, move over to Mr. Tryan, who is not only a good preacher, but works hard. which Stickney stigmatises as 'spiritual pride'. *Scenes of Clerical Life III: Janet's Repentance*

STILFOX: An Oxford friend of Rex Gascoigne's, who lives in Southampton. Mr. Gascoigne intends to send Rex to stay with him after his unfortunate entanglement with Gwendolen Harleth, but Rex has been so much hurt in a hunting accident that he takes to his bed instead. *Daniel Deronda*

STOKES, MASTER TOM: Mr. Hackit's nephew, who said, after listening to one of Mr. Gilfil's sermons, that he could write one just as good, which he did, much to his uncle's astonishment and delight. *Scenes of Clerical Life II: Mr. Gilfil's Love-Story*

STONE, SARAH: A middle-aged widow who kept a shop in Church Lane, Stoniton, where Hetty Sorrel's illegitimate child was born. She gave evidence at Hetty's trial for infanticide. *Adam Bede*

STOPLEY, CANON: A visitor at the Arrowpoints', who expressed a wish to go to the archery meeting at Brackenshaw Park; but Catherine, who is in love with Herr Klesmer, takes the latter instead, her parents think out of kindness to a foreigner. *Daniel Deronda*

STOREY, JACOB: One of the men who attend Bartle Massey's night-school. He gets into trouble because he cannot make a Z the right way round, but, as he says, 'It was a letter you never wanted hardly'. *Adam Bede*

STOTT, MRS.: Housekeeper to one of Mrs. Tulliver's brothers, who 'took half the feathers out o' the best bed, an' packed 'em up and sent 'em away. An' it's unbeknown the linen she made away with'. *The Mill on the Floss*

STRYPE, MRS.: A poor but vociferous washerwoman whom Mr. Bulstrode championed against one Stubbs, who over-charged her for her drying-ground. *Middlemarch*

STUBBS: A workman in Middlemarch who complained of the washerwoman, Mrs. Strype, and was routed by the officious Bulstrode. *Middlemarch*

SUTTON, MRS.: A friend of Mrs. Pullet's, 'as had doubled her money over and over again, and kept it all in her own management to the last, and had her pocket with her keys in under her pillow constant.' She dies, leaving everything to her husband's nephew—'a nice sort o' man . . . for he's troubled with the asthmy and goes to bed every night at eight o'clock.' After Mrs. Sutton's death Mrs. Pullet takes her place as Dr. Turnbull's prize patient. *The Mill on the Floss*

SWINTON: Grandcourt's bailiff at Ryelands. *Daniel Deronda*

T

TACCO, MAESTRO: A quack doctor, a round-headed, round-bellied man who comes to Florence from Padua on a raw young horse, selling nostrums. *Romola*

TADDEO: One of Dolfo Spini's followers, who incites the mob to wreck Tito Melema's house, hoping to kill Tito, who is believed to have betrayed Spini. *Romola*

TAFT: A carpenter, working in the same timberyard as Adam Bede, who rebukes him for knocking off on the first stroke of six. He is known as 'Mum' because he so seldom speaks. *Adam Bede*

TAFT, BILLY: The Hayslope village idiot. Massey, the schoolmaster, says he would be quite prepared to try and teach him, if he could be made to learn. *Adam Bede*

TAFT, JACOB: The oldest inhabitant of Hayslope, and the father of Mum Taft. Known as 'Feyther' by all the village, he goes to hear Dinah Morris preach, bent nearly double, leaning on his short stick, and wearing a brown worsted night cap. But he is too deaf to hear much of what she says, and soon retires to the comfort of his inglenook. *Adam Bede*

TAFT, MRS.: An old lady in Middlemarch who is always knitting, and 'gathered her information in misleading fragments caught between the rows'. She once told Mrs. Farebrother, who was quite prepared to believe her, that Mr. Lydgate was Mr. Bulstrode's natural son. *Middlemarch*

TANTRIPP: Lady's maid to the Brooke sisters, Dorothea and Celia. She goes with Dorothea on her wedding journey to Rome, and heartily dislikes Mr. Casaubon. After his death she hopes Dorothea will marry again. It is through her gossiping to the Farebrothers' servant that Ladislaw finally hears from Rosamond—via Mrs. Farebrother and Fred Vincy—of the infamous codicil to Casaubon's will. *Middlemarch*

TARBETT, THE REV. MR.: The clergyman who preached in Shepperton Church the first Sunday after Mr. Gilfil brought home his bride. *Scenes of Clerical Life II: Mr. Gilfil's Love-Story*

TEDMAN, DAME: The owner of a little local school where Nancy Lammeter was educated. *Silas Marner*

TEGG: A shoemaker who profits from Mr. Bulstrode's calculated philanthropy, through which his son is able to be suitably apprenticed. *Middlemarch*

TESSA: A young peasant girl who gives Tito Melema a drink of milk when he is penniless, much to the annoyance of her shrewish mother and brutal step-father. Later Tito rescues her from the mountebank Vaiano, who is pestering her to help him with his act, and they fall in love. Tito, who already knows that he is going to marry Romola, cannot resist the attractions of Tessa, and goes through a form of mock marriage with her, conducted by Vaiano disguised as a bishop. Tessa thinks this is a true marriage, and is quite happy to leave home after her mother dies to live in seclusion with her two children, visited occasionally by Tito under the name of Naldo. She thinks he is away on business when he is absent from her. At one point she gives shelter to Baldassarre, who is looking for Tito in order to punish him for his ingratitude, but sends him away when Tito explains that he is mad and dangerous. When Tito decides to leave Florence for Milan, he arranges to take Tessa and the children with him, but is killed before he can reach the rendezvous. Tessa takes shelter in a cottage nearby, where she is found by Romola, who takes her and the children to live with her in the house of her cousin Monna Brigida. *Romola*

TEVEROY, MRS · The second wife of Lord Grinsell, and mother of Mrs. Beevor. *Middlemarch*

THESIGER, THE REV. EDWARD: Rector of St. Peter's, and chairman of the meeting at which Bulstrode, after the scandal about him has spread, is asked to resign from the hospital board. *Middlemarch*

THOLER, BOB: The man for whom a coffin was ordered from Thias Bede, who went off to the pub and forgot all about it; so Adam, his son, had to work all night to get it done. *Adam Bede*

THOLER, TOM: A half-wit, known as Tom Saft. He worked on Poyser's farm, where he made up for his practical deficiencies by his sudden and random remarks, which were quoted at sheep-shearing and hay-making. *Adam Bede*

THOLOWAY, BEN: One of Poyser's farm hands, a powerful thresher and useful about the place, but not entirely honest, having several times been detected carrying away corn in his pockets for his chickens, and pea and bean seeds for his garden. *Adam Bede*

THOMSON, LIZA: The Phipps' maid, who is not allowed followers. *Scenes of Clerical Life III: Janet's Repentance*

THRUPP, MR.: Mr. Landor's clerk, who tells him of the success of Dempster's petition against Tryan, and of the riotous behaviour of the mob. *Scenes of Clerical Life III: Janet's Repentance*

THURLE, MR.: A farmer who wants to rent Chase Farm after Satchell has had a stroke. But his wife is not keen on dairying, so Squire Donnithorne, to whom both farms belong, tries to get the Poysers to exchange some of their ploughland for

Chase Farm dairyland. But Mrs. Poyser, who foresees that this means more work for her, refuses, and Thurle withdraws. *Adam Bede*

TILIOT, MR.: A wine and spirit merchant in Treby Magna, who has made a fortune with Tiliot's Gin. He is very much against Dissenters, and thinks the rise of Methodism is connected with the increasing prosperity of the working-class. During the election riots he takes steps to protect the wine vaults against looting by the mob. *Felix Holt*

TILIOT, MRS.: The wine-merchant's wife, once the bosom friend of Mary Salt, now Mrs. Muscat; but since Mr. Tiliot was heard by Muscat, a chapel-goer, to refer to Dissenters as 'sneaks', relations have been strained. However, Mrs. Tiliot does confide in Mrs. Muscat that she intends to employ Esther Lyon as governess, and is persuaded not to. *Felix Holt*

TILT, MR.: One of the many sick friends of Maggie Tulliver's hypochondriacal aunt Mrs. Pullet. *The Mill on the Floss*

TIM: The ploughman and waggoner at Hall Farm, who is always at odds with Alick, the head shepherd, because he grudges the horses their due feed of corn. *Adam Bede*

TIMOTHY'S BESS: see Salt, Bess

TIMOTHY'S BESS'S BEN: *see* Salt, Ben

TIMPSON: An influential business man in Mudport, where Tulliver's friend Riley lives. One of his numerous daughters, Louisa, married the Rev. Walter Stelling, so, naturally, when Tulliver wants a tutor for Tom, Riley recommends Stelling. *The Mill on the Floss*

TINA: *see* Sarti, Caterina

TOD, JOSH: Landlord of the Holly Bush Inn at Hayslope. *Adam Bede*

TOLLER, HARRY: A successful brewer, and the brother of Thomas Toller. He dislikes Lydgate, and knows he is a heavy spender, but presumes his titled relatives 'up North' are subsidising him. *Middlemarch*

TOLLER, SOPHY: The daughter of Harry Toller; she marries Ned Plymdale, after he has been refused by Rosamond Vincy. *Middlemarch*

TOLLER, THOMAS: A Middlemarch doctor, who treats his patients by 'the lowering system'—bleeding, blistering, starving—as opposed to 'the strengthening system' of his main rival, Mr. Wrench. Both doctors agree in disliking Lydgate, and Toller, a well-bred, quietly facetious man, calls him 'the scientific phoenix'. He is quite ready to believe that Lydgate accepted a bribe from Bulstrode over the Raffles' affair, and is on the committee which forces Bulstrode's resignation from the hospital board. His wife thinks Mrs. Bulstrode should leave her husband. 'It is an encouragement to crime if such men are to be taken care of and waited on by good wives'. *Middlemarch*

TOM: Caleb Garth's assistant, who is knocked over and gets a badly sprained ankle when he and Garth go to the help of some railway surveyors who are being attacked with pitchforks by infuriated farm labourers. He goes to the nearest farm on Fred Vincy's horse, carrying the surveyors' broken instruments. *Middlemarch*

TOMLINSON, THE MISSES: The three daughters of the miller, who were 'finished' at expensive schools, where they learned to speak French very badly. They dress lavishly in ermine and feathers, which does nothing to enhance their coarse looks. *Scenes of Clerical Life III: Janet's Repentance*

TOMLINSON, MR.: A rich miller in Milby, who is against any form of education for the lower classes; night-school and lectures are only excuses for the wenches to meet their sweethearts. He much admires the drunken, bombastic Dempster, and joins him in his campaign against Mr. Tryan, saying he will instantly dismiss any of his workmen found going to Tryan's lectures. But he has to recant when his foreman, whom he cannot easily replace, defies him, and after a time he revises his opinion of Tryan, saying at least he is not a humbug, and being sincerely sorry when the young curate dies of T.B. *Scenes of Clerical Life III: Janet's Repentance*

TOMMS, JACOB: 'A young gentleman in the tailoring line', who sometimes spends an evening in the Bartons' kitchen, and to whom Nanny pours out her woes over the expense and extra work caused by the visit of the Countess Czerlaski. It is from Tomms that she hears of the scandal about the Rector and the Countess which is going round the village and indignantly denies it. *Scenes of Clerical Life I: The Rev. Amos Barton*

TOOKE, MRS.: An old washerwoman to whom Janet Dempster sometimes gives packets of snuff, her one indulgence, much to the indignation of the parsimonious Mrs. Phipps. *Scenes of Clerical Life III: Janet's Repentance*

TOOKEY, MR.: Assistant to the old tailor and parish clerk, Macey, who offends the church choir by singing out of tune. Macey allows him to make Silas a Sunday suit, cheaply, for Eppie's christening, and he sings the responses at Eppie's wedding eighteen years later. *Silas Marner*

TORNABUONI, LORENZO: One of the five Florentines betrayed by Tito Melema and Antella, and executed for plotting to bring back the Medici. *Romola*

TORRINGTON, CAPTAIN AND MRS.: Guests of Grandcourt at Diplow. Mrs. Torrington is Grandcourt's cousin, and acts as his hostess so that Gwendolen Harleth and her mother can with propriety be asked to dine. *Daniel Deronda*

TORRY, JAMES: A mill-owner in whose mill Bob Jakin put out a small fire one night, being rewarded with ten sovereigns, with which he sets up in business as a pedlar. *The Mill on the Floss*

TORRY, MISS: The daughter of James Torry, who takes Lucy Deane to see the vicar's wife about the church bazaar after dinner, thus leaving Maggie Tulliver and Stephen Guest alone together for the first time. *The Mill on the Floss*

TORRY, MRS.: The wife of James Torry. She refuses to employ Maggie, even though assured of her innocence, because one cannot have a nursery governess 'about whom such things have been said . . . and gentlemen have joked'. *The Mill on the Floss*

TORRY, YOUNG: Son of James Torry. He falls in love with Maggie Tulliver, who cannot bear him because he wears a monocle, and 'makes a hideous face'. After her disgrace he meets her in the street and bows to her 'with that air of nonchalance which he might have bestowed on a friendly barmaid.' *The Mill on the Floss*

TOTTY: *see* Poyser, Charlotte

TOWNLEY, COLONEL: An elderly gentleman who happens to be riding past Hayslope when he sees Dinah Morris preaching on the village green. He stops to listen, and is struck by the truth and simplicity of her sermon. Later, he recognises Dinah when she comes to see Hetty after her trial and as a magistrate has the authority to allow Dinah to spend the night with Hetty in the prison. *Adam Bede*

TOWNLEY, MISS: Proprietress of a school for young ladies in Milby She is very much against the Rev. Edgar Tryan's innovations in church matters, and thinks old Mr. Crewe, the curate, preaches excellent sermons. *Scenes of Clerical Life III: Janet's Repentance*

TOZER, MR.: An old gardener in Shepperton, who was very upset when Amos Barton had to leave the village for a curacy in a town. As a countryman, he has a poor opinion of town life, saying 'He hedn't much here, but he'll be wuss off theer.' *Scenes of Clerical Life I: The Rev. Amos Barton*

TRADGETT, MR.: First cousin to Arthur Donnithorne, whose mother was a Tradgett. Mrs. Irwine, who has no opinion of the Donnithornes, tells Arthur that she only became his godmother because she could see that he was 'every inch a Tradgett'. Arthur tells Adam Bede that if he dies abroad Tradgett will inherit the property and take the family name. *Adam Bede*

TRANSOME, DURFEY: A dissolute wastrel, sickly and depraved, who by his profligacy and mounting debts brings his family almost to the edge of bankruptcy. Luckily he dies in time for his younger brother, Harold, who has made a fortune in trade, to save the estate from ruin. *Felix Holt*

TRANSOME, HAROLD: The second son of Mrs. Transome and, it is believed, of her husband, the owner of Transome Court. Actually Harold is the child of the family lawyer, Jermyn, but the secret is well kept, and when he returns from abroad after his elder brother's death, everyone accepts him as the heir to the Transome estate. He has made a fortune trading in Turkey, and also married a Greek woman, now dead, who left him with a three-year-old son. Now he intends to settle down, restore the Court and its grounds, and stand for Parliament—but as a Radical, which upsets his mother and all his neighbours. He finds that during his absence his mother, who has been running the estate as best she could with a weak husband and a dissolute son to contend with, has been constantly cheated by the manoeuvres of Jermyn and, already antipathetic towards that sleek and slippery gentleman, Harold decides to take him to court for maladministration. Goaded beyond endurance, Jermyn quarrels bitterly with him, and reveals himself, in public, as Harold's father. He also reveals that there is a claimant to Harold's property in the person of Esther Lyon, and eventually her claim is substantiated. Harold hopes to avoid litigation and scandal by marrying her, so keeping the Transome property, but he fails to win her affections, and she refuses him in favour of the poor but honest Felix Holt, resigning her claim to the estate, which the Transomes retain. Harold, a clever, frank, good-natured egoist who desired only to do the best for himself, finds all his plans in disarray, and takes his parents abroad for some years, but eventually returns and settles down again at Transome Court. *Felix Holt*

TRANSOME, HARRY: The three-year-old son of Harold Transome, who comes to England with his father after the latter has become heir to the Transome property. Harry, who takes after his Greek mother in looks and temperament, creates havoc in the staid English household, biting his grandmother, teasing the dogs, tyrannising over his grandfather, who adores him, and being partially tamed by Esther Lyon, to whom he takes a fancy when she comes on a visit. *Felix Holt*

TRANSOME, JOHN JUSTUS: The owner of a large estate in the Midlands which in 1727 he entailed upon his son Thomas and his heirs male, on condition that should the male line die out, the estate would go to another branch of the family, the Bycliffes. This was the foundation of Esther Bycliffe's claim to the Transome property. *Felix Holt*

TRANSOME, MR.: A weak, elderly man with a receding chin and light, watery eyes, whose uneven gait and feeble gestures give evidence of a slight stroke. He is very afraid of his wife, and when she comes near him he shrinks from her 'like a timid animal looked at in a cage where flight is impossible'. He vaguely suspects that he is not the father of her second son, Harold, but has always accepted him. When Harold returns from Turkey with a three-year-old boy, Mr. Transome becomes the child's willing slave, finding in his company some happiness at last. He is barely conscious of the upheaval caused by the arrival of Esther Lyon, though he would be glad enough to accept her as a daughter-in-law, and knows nothing of her claim upon his estate, and her subsequent rejection of it. *Felix Holt*

TRANSOME, MRS.: Wife of the owner of Transome Court. As 'the beautiful Miss Lingon' she had been a spoilt, imperious, high-spirited creature, who married Mr. Transome, not for love, but because she thought him a weak man whom she could rule. By him she had a sickly, depraved son, Durfey, whom she hated, and, after a passionate but short-lived affair with the young lawyer Jermyn, a second son, Harold, on whom she concentrated all her hopes for the future. When Harold left home to seek his fortune abroad, she took over the management of the estate, drained of ready money by Durfey's debts, and by the machinations of Jermyn, who took advantage of the situation to further his own interests. To her great joy, Durfey eventually dies and Harold becomes heir to the property. She is disappointed when he comes home a widower with a three-year-old child and decides to stand for Parliament as a Radical, but even more distressed to find that he has outgrown his boyish affection for her and will allow her no say in the future management of his affairs. Lonely and idle, cut off from her Tory friends in view of the forthcoming election, she has the added grief of watching the growing hostility between Harold and Jermyn, which is brought to a head when Harold, unaware of their relationship, decides to take Jermyn to court on a charge of maladministration. This goads Jermyn into disclosing his parentage to Harold, which has the effect of alienating Harold still further from his mother, though he does not openly reproach her. When Esther Lyon's claim to the Transome estate is established, Mrs. Transome's one hope is that Harold will marry this charming, sympathetic girl, who brings a little sunshine into her sad life. But Esther prefers to return to her adoptive father, Rufus Lyon, and marry Felix Holt. Mrs. Transome, after spending some years abroad, comes back to Transome Court to die, pitied by her neighbours, and conscious always that her early lapse has been paid for by a lifetime of loneliness and self-reproach. *Felix Holt*

TRANSOME, THOMAS: The son of John Justus Transome, and heir to his estate which, being a profligate and spendthrift, he sold, without his father's permission, to a lawyer-cousin, Durfey. The Durfeys were to keep the estate as long as there existed a direct male heir to Thomas. But if this line died out, the estate would then revert to another branch of the family, the Bycliffes. Thus, when old Tommy Trounsem, the last male descendant of Thomas, was killed in the election-day rioting, Esther, the only child of Maurice Bycliffe, became entitled to claim the Transome estate. *Felix Holt*

TRANTER, GIL: A young man who once had a fight with Adam Bede, and was laid up for a fortnight afterwards; this made Adam decide never again to fight 'for fun', but only to punish a scoundrel. *Adam Bede*

TRAUNTER, DEB: A prostitute in Milby, well-known as cohabiting with the churchwarden Budd. She turned up to join the demonstration against Mr. Tryan 'in a pink flounced gown and floating ribbons', flanked by two men in sealskin caps and fustian. *Scenes of Clerical Life III: Janet's Repentance*

TRAWLEY: A fellow student of Lydgate's in Paris. He had high ideals, but these came to nothing and he ended up with a lucrative practice in a German spa, where he married one of his wealthy patients, much to Lydgate's disgust. *Middlemarch*

TRECCA, MONNA: 'Dame Greengrocer', an old woman who had a vegetable stall in the Old Market in Florence. *Romola*

TRENT: The farmer for whom Mrs. Poyser's dairymaid Betty worked before going to the Poysers. All Betty's faults are attributed by Mrs. Poyser to the shortcomings of her former employers. *Adam Bede*

TRITON, LORD: An amiable gentleman 'who will be a marquis one day'. Mrs. Cadwallader thinks he would make a good second husband for Dorothea; he is full of plans for making people happy, in a soft-headed sort of way, which would suit her, and she would look the part of 'Her Ladyship' so well. *Middlemarch*

TROUNSEM, TOMMY: A drunken old poacher who is discovered by Jermyn somewhere 'up North', and proves to be the last male descendant of the Transomes, after whose death the estate held by the Durfey-Transomes will revert to the Bycliffes. Jermyn uses old Tommy to bar the claim of Maurice Bycliffe, and then leaves him hanging around Treby Magna for twenty years, supporting himself by doing odd jobs, and spending most of his time in alehouses, boasting of his claim to the Transome estate. When he is trampled to death in the election-day riots, Maurice Bycliffe's daughter Esther, who is living in Treby Magna as the adopted child of the Rev. Rufus Lyon, is found and succeeds to her father's claim, *Felix Holt*

TROWER, MR.: A client of the lawyer Dempster, who breaks up a pleasant meeting at the Red Lion in Milby by sending for Dempster in a hurry, because he is ill and wants to make his will. *Scenes of Clerical Life III: Janet's Repentance*

TRUBERRY, MR.: A Member of Parliament who changed sides on the question of the Reform Bill because his wife was sure this would bring him a peerage, thus enabling her to take precedence of her younger sister, who had married a baronet. *Middlemarch*

TRUFFORD, LORD: A local landowner with whom the Bishop dines after the confirmation. *Scenes of Clerical Life III: Janet's Repentance*

TRUMBULL, BORTHROP: A Middlemarch dealer in land and cattle. He is second cousin to Peter Featherstone, and did business for him. He decides, if Featherstone leaves a substantial legacy to Mary Garth, who is nursing him, to marry her, as he thinks she would make a good wife. In the event, he remains a bachelor, and considers Featherstone's legacy to himself—a gold-headed cane—an insult. When he contracts pneumonia, Lydgate persuades him to try a revolutionary new treatment, which consists of 'doing nothing'. He recovers, which adds greatly to Lydgate's reputation. Trumbull officiates at the sale of Larcher's effects, and would have successfully let Lydgate's expensive house to Ned Plymdale had not Rosamond countermanded his orders. *Middlemarch*

TRYAN, THE REV. EDGAR: A young man of good family, who

was intended for the diplomatic service, but entered the Church by way of expiating what he thinks of as a mortal sin. He casually seduced a young working-class girl, Lucy, and returning after a vacation to see her again, with some idea of making amends, found she had disappeared. Three years later he found her dead in the street, having taken poison. She had fallen into the clutches of an evil woman and become a prostitute. Overcome with remorse, Tryan takes holy orders, and spends his time helping others, preaching, lecturing, reading and expounding the Scriptures in poor cottages, and comforting those in trouble. Appointed curate at a remote chapel-of-ease on Paddiford Common, where he lives in uncomfortable lodgings, sharing the privations of his parishioners, he is very unpopular with certain elements in the town, mainly non-churchgoers led by the dissolute lawyer Dempster, who does all he can to thwart and harass the young curate, helped at first by his young wife Janet. But after meeting Tryan several times in poor homes, and by the bedside of dying cottagers, Janet recognises his goodness and sincerity, and when she is herself in trouble she sends for him. He helps her to overcome her incipient drunkenness, and supports her through the sad trial of nursing her husband during the fatal illness caused by a fall from his gig. Just as most of the people in Milby have begun, like Janet, to appreciate his true worth, he is stricken with T.B., and dies in a house lent him by Janet, who realises too late that she is in love with him. *Scenes of Clerical Life III: Janet's Repentance*

TUCKER: A constable in Treby Magna, who in helping to save Spratt from the mob on election day is knocked down, and later dies of his injuries. Felix Holt, who was trying to protect him from the anger of the rioters by disarming him, is accused of his murder, and sent to prison, but later released. *Felix Holt*

TUCKER, THE REV. MR.: Mr. Casaubon's curate, who distresses Dorothea by telling her that all Casaubon's parishioners are sober, hard-working, virtuous, and well-fed; the women are mostly engaged in straw-plaiting, therefore there are no looms, no Dissenters, and no vice. So there will be nothing for her to do. *Middlemarch*

TUDGE, JOB: A small, ragged boy, with round blue eyes and

red, curly hair, who lives with his grandfather, an old stone-
breaker, and is suffering from malnutrition and T.B. He is
befriended by Mrs. Holt, and is a great comfort to her when
Felix is in prison. He attends Esther's wedding in 'an entirely
new suit with brass buttons'. *Felix Holt*

TULLIVER, MAGGIE: The daughter of the mill-owner Tulliver,
who admires her quick brain and unusual character, and
spoils her, to the annoyance of her mother and brother Tom.
She is given very little education, and runs wild, reading
whatever she can lay hands on, and envying her brother his
schooling. She is passionately attached to him, and suffers
agonies when Tom goes off on his own affairs without her.
With her dark, rough hair and untidy ways, she is the despair
of her mother and aunts, and the great need of loving and
being loved, which is the driving force behind all her actions,
finds no outlet until she falls in love with Philip Wakem, the
crippled son of her father's bitterest enemy. When misfortune
falls on the Tulliver family, Maggie has no sympathy for her
fretful and self-centred mother, but only for her father, lying
helpless after a stroke brought on by the news of his bankruptcy. After his stroke Maggie finds herself at loggerheads
with her brother, who makes her promise not to see Philip
Wakem again, since he intends to carry on his father's feud
with old Wakem. But she meets Philip while staying with her
uncle Deane, whose daughter Lucy is on the point of becoming engaged to a very attractive young man, Stephen
Guest. Unfortunately Maggie and Stephen find themselves
mutually attracted, and although they both try to fight it,
they are not proof against the magnetism that draws them
together. While they are out on the river, Stephen, yielding
to a mad impulse, rows so far that they cannot get home that
night. He begs Maggie to go away with him, and in a moment
of weakness she follows him on to the deck of a trading
steamer which takes them to Mudport, where Maggie, suddenly aware of her folly, decides to return home. After a
bitter, passionate scene with Stephen, who cannot shake her
resolution, they part and she goes back to the mill, spending
a night at an inn on the way. But she has not allowed for
the reactions of a censorious world. Her brother refuses to
take her in, and with her mother she takes lodgings with the
Jakins; her family, with the exception of Mrs. Glegg, turn
against her, and Lucy is inconsolable at the defection of her

lover. In spite of a letter from Stephen proving Maggie to be guilty of nothing worse than recklessness and ill-judgement, few people are prepared to believe in her innocence, or to give her work; and when Dr. Kenn does try to employ her as a nursery-governess to his motherless children, he is forced by public opinion to dismiss her. Lucy, when she has recovered from the shock of Stephen's defection, visits Maggie and assures her of her forgiveness and continued affection, but even she cannot champion her cousin openly, and Maggie is preparing to go far away as a governess, to a place where she is unknown, when the river rises in flood. She takes one of Jakin's boats and goes to the mill to see if her brother needs help, drawn to him by memories of their happy life there as children. They are together in the boat when it is overturned by floating wreckage and they are both drowned. *The Mill on the Floss*

TULLIVER, MR.: The owner of Dorlcote Mill, whose Christian name is either Edward or Jeremy, or perhaps both. A self-made man, with little education, he married 'one of the Dodson girls', Bessy, and is the father of Tom and Maggie. Although Maggie has the brains, Tulliver decides that Tom shall be educated and go into business. Everyone thinks the Tullivers are well off, but in fact the mill is mortgaged, as Tulliver has a bad habit of going to law with his neighbours, and losing, mainly owing to the astuteness of his opponents' lawyer, Wakem. He finally goes bankrupt, and when he learns that the mortgage on his mill has passed to Wakem, whom he considers his worst enemy, he has a stroke. He recovers enough to run the mill as a hired manager, but becomes sullen and miserly, and by dint of hard saving, and some money made by Tom, whose education has been cut short in favour of a job, he pays off his creditors. But meeting Wakem one day, all his grievances come to the fore, and he knocks the lawyer off his horse and thrashes him; the effort kills him. *The Mill on the Floss*

TULLIVER, MRS. (BESSY): A blonde, comely woman, the youngest of four sisters, and always worried by what they or their husbands will think of her family. She is very anxious about little things, and neglects the big ones. Though 'the flower of her family for beauty and amiability', she is slow-witted, and in later life becomes peevish. She is no help to her husband in his troubles, and never understands that he will always do the opposite of what she suggests. She is far more concerned at the loss of her household goods than she is over her husband's illness, and does not realise what a sacrifice he makes when he accepts, for her sake, to become manager of the mill which was once his own, 'so that she will not be uprooted'. Yet when her daughter Maggie is in trouble she is courageous enough to defy her son Tom, who was always her favourite, and go and live with Maggie. *The Mill on the Floss*

TULLIVER, RALPH: A far-off Tulliver ancestor, who is held responsible, by Maggie's aunts, for her faults. He was 'a wonderfully clever fellow who ruined himself'. Quite unlike the family of Mrs. Tulliver, the Dodsons, who *never* ruined themselves! *The Mill on the Floss*

TULLIVER, TOM: The son of Tulliver the mill-owner, a pleasant, uncomplicated, rather slow-witted youngster, very conscious of his superiority to his sister Maggie, who is 'only a girl'. He is sent by his father to a private tutor, and learns nothing, being more inclined to fishing and other country pursuits than to the study of dead languages. When his father is ruined, Tom returns home, and with great difficulty gets a job. The change from his easy, idle way of life embitters him, and intensifies his habit of thinking himself always right and those who differ from him wrong. This colours his attitude to Maggie, who offends him by falling in love with Philip Wakem, the son of his father's bitterest enemy. It shows even more when, after he has, by great efforts, got back his father's mill, Maggie comes to him for shelter after her foolish, though innocent, elopement with Stephen Guest. He refuses to allow her inside his house, and considers no punishment too great for the sorrow she has caused her cousin Lucy Deane, with whom he is in love, and the shame she has brought upon her family. Yet in the end, when she comes to rescue him from the flood in one of Bob Jakin's little pleasure boats, he remembers their old happy relationship, and goes with her, ready to forgive her everything. But they are both overwhelmed by floating wreckage and drowned. *The Mill on the Floss*

TURNBULL, DR.: The medical practitioner who attends Tulliver after his stroke, and ministers to the hypochondriacal Mrs. Pullet and all her family. He had been very intimate with the Tullivers, but when his wife and daughter met Maggie in the street after her elopement, 'they both looked at her strangely and turned a little aside without speaking.' *The Mill on the Floss*

TURVEY: Sir Hugo Mallinger's valet. *Daniel Deronda*

TYKE, THE REV. WALTER: Mr. Bulstrode's nomination for the post of chaplain at the new infirmary. But nobody else likes him, and he only gets the post—and the salary which is for the first time attached to it—£40 a year—by Bulstrode's casting vote. After Casaubon's death Dorothea is urged by her uncle to appoint Tyke to the vacant living, but luckily she takes the advice of Lydgate and chooses the charming and popular Mr. Farebrother. Tyke is upset by this, and also by the disgrace of Bulstrode, not without reason, since, as Mrs. Hackbutt says: 'The Bulstrodes have half kept the Tyke family for many years.' *Middlemarch*

V

VAIANO, MAESTRO: A mountebank who is amusing the holiday crowds in Florence on Midsummer Day, and tries to make Tessa help him. But she is frightened, and is rescued by Tito Melema. At the fair later in the year Vaiano, dressed up as a burlesque bishop, pretends to marry young couples from the country who are out to enjoy themselves. Tito, in a reckless mood, induces Tessa to go through the ceremony with him, but she thinks it is real, and always considers herself his wife. The barber Nello uses Vaiano and his monkey to help him play a trick on the quack doctor Tacco. *Romola*

VALORI, FRANCESCO: An authoritative and powerful Florentine, who becomes a convinced follower of Savonarola. Bernardo del Nero, who is later condemned to death by Valori for plotting to restore the Medici, does not believe in his conversion, but says he 'christens private grudges by the name of public zeal'. Valori makes use of Tito Melema, who later betrays him, and is murdered by the younger Ridolfi and Tornabuoni, whose brothers were executed with Bernardo del Nero. *Romola*

VANDERNOODT, MR.: One of the visitors at Leubronn, who sees and admires Gwendolen Harleth in the Casino. He meets Sir Hugo Mallinger, who likes him enough to ask him to the Abbey at Christmas, where Gwendolen makes her first appearance as the bride of Sir Hugo's heir, Grandcourt. An industrious gleaner of personal details, he knows all about Grandcourt's liaison with Lydia Glasher, and tells Daniel Deronda about it. *Daniel Deronda*

VESPUCCI, GIOVANNI: A wealthy Florentine who has commissioned a picture of Oedipus and Antigone at Colonos from the painter Piero di Cosimo, for which Romola and her father reluctantly agree to pose. *Romola*

VESPUCCI, GUIDANTONIO: One of the Florentines who sign the 1494 treaty with Charles VIII of France. In place of the Medici, he favours a Council elected by the members of leading families, no shopkeepers or working men being allowed to vote. Most of those already in power agree with him. *Romola*

VIGO, MRS.: A former reader and secretary to royal personages, whom the Dowager Lady Chettam recommends to the widowed Dorothea as a suitable companion and chaperone. *Middlemarch*

VINCY, BOB: The second son of Walter Vincy, who works in his father's warehouse, and gives no trouble. *Middlemarch*

VINCY, FRED: Walter Vincy's eldest son, who has been sent to Oxford and is intended for the Church. Idle, handsome, and self-assured, he is in high favour with his crabby old uncle, Peter Featherstone, and confidently expects to inherit most of the old man's property; therefore he need not bother about his future. He is in love with Mary Garth, a niece of Featherstone's on her mother's side, but she rejects him, saying she will only marry a man who, like her father, can earn his own living. Nor will she marry him if he becomes a clergyman, as she considers him totally unfit for such a life. Fred is staying in his uncle's country house, recovering from a bad attack of typhoid, when the old man dies and leaves him nothing. Mary, who refused to burn his latest will when Featherstone asked her to do so shortly before his death, thus depriving Fred of the £10,000 left him in an earlier will, tries to console him, and when he has worked faithfully as her father's assistant in land valuation and management for over a year, agrees to marry him. Fred, whose good qualities have come to the fore under adversity, is made manager of Stone Court and farms it well, and he and Mary settle down happily. *Middlemarch*

VINCY, MRS. (LUCY): The wife of Walter Vincy. She is considered to have made a good marriage, as she was only an innkeeper's daughter, and looks 'just like a handsome, good-humoured landlady, accustomed to the capricious orders of gentlemen'—much to the sorrow of her eldest daughter Rosamond. She is proud of her handsome family—six children in all—but reserves her deepest affection for her eldest son, Fred, whom she spoils, and is sorry when he marries Mary Garth, whom she does not consider his equal in looks or social standing. *Middlemarch*

VINCY, ROSAMOND: The eldest daughter of the Vincys, extremely handsome, flirtatious, a blonde beauty with a swan neck. She intends to make a splendid marriage, and rejects all the young men of her immediate circle in favour of the young doctor, Lydgate, whom she knows to have aristocratic relations, and believes to be wealthy. In spite of Lydgate's determination not to marry until he has established his position in the town, where he has met with some strong opposition to his medical reforms, he is beguiled into an engagement, thinking Rosamond will prove a gentle, affectionate, and undemanding wife. The marriage is a failure from the start. Disappointed in her hopes of social advancement through Lydgate's titled relations, with whom he is not on good terms, Rosamond revenges herself by spending money freely, plunging her husband into debt, and by treating him with contempt and coldness. She also amuses herself by flirting with Will Ladislaw, and has visions of leaving her husband to lead an exciting life with Ladislaw in London until she discovers that he is in love with the recently-widowed Dorothea. In an impulse of generosity, she lets Dorothea know this, and renounces any claim on his affections. In the midst of these preoccupations the scandal about her husband and Bulstrode falls like a thunderbolt. The Lydgates are forced to leave Middlemarch, and Lydgate becomes a fashionable physician, dying young. Left a beautiful widow with four young children, Rosamond marries an elderly and very wealthy physician, and considers her subsequent life of ease a just reward for the trials she had to undergo in her first marriage. *Middlemarch*

VINCY, WALTER: A prosperous tradesman and mayor of Middlemarch, who has ambitions for the advancement of his family, hoping his eldest son Fred will go into the Church and his eldest daughter Rosamond will make a brilliant marriage. Both disappoint him. Fred, idle, always in debt, and living in expectation of a large legacy from an old uncle which does not materialise, eventually becomes assistant to the land agent and valuer, Caleb Garth, and Rosamond makes an unhappy marriage with the new doctor, Lydgate. When the scandal about the local banker Bulstrode becomes generally known, Vincy is left with the unpleasant task of breaking the news of it to his sister, Bulstrode's wife. *Middlemarch*

VULCANY, MRS.: An old lady who forms part of the 'genteel society' which revolves round the Rev. and Mrs. Gascoigne. She does not like their niece Gwendolen Harleth, saying she is too fond of the gentlemen, but does not realise it is their homage she likes, not themselves personally. *Daniel Deronda*

W

WACE, MR.: Brewer of the celebrated Treby beer, and owner of the pigs which make their home in the ruins of the old castle. A jolly, red-faced man, he is a staunch Tory, and though he agrees there must be Whigs, to form an opposition, he would never vote for one. When rioting breaks out on election day, Wace suggests sending for the military to protect his brewery and Tiliot's wine vaults, which will otherwise be looted. In spite of Felix Holt being a Radical, Wace says that his marriage to Esther Lyon makes him feel as if he 'believed more in everything that's good'. *Felix Holt*

WAGSTAFF, MRS.: A poor cottager at Paddiford Common, in whose house Edgar Tryan takes lodgings, where he is very uncomfortable, and is fed on 'hard carrots and watery potatoes'. Everyone who has Tryan's welfare at heart wants him to leave Mrs. Wagstaff's 'dingy house and dubious cooking', but he refuses to do so until a new tenant, the exciseman, is found for her. *Scenes of Clerical Life III: Janet's Repentance*

WAKEFIELD, JIM: A farmer who worked on Sunday the same as any other day, and came to no good. Poyser, who had predicted his downfall, saw him reduced to selling oranges in the marketplace. *Adam Bede*

WAKEM, LAWYER (JOHN): A tallish man with an aquiline nose and abundant, iron-grey hair; a widower with one crippled son, he has prospered, and has a fine house at Tofton and the best stock of port wine in the neighbourhood. Mr Tulliver considers Wakem his mortal enemy, as every time he goes to law, Wakem represents his opponents, and Tulliver loses. The tension between them reaches such a point that an argument over farming causes Tulliver (now bankrupt and forced to work for Wakem as manager of the mill he once owned) to attack the lawyer and horse-whip him. Wakem is upset when his son Philip falls in love with Maggie Tulliver, but agrees to countenance the marriage after he has met and approved of Maggie. Consequently he is thunderstruck when she runs off, as he thinks, with her cousin Lucy's fiancé, Stephen Guest. *The Mill on the Floss*

WAKEM, PHILIP: The only child of the lawyer, Wakem, hunchbacked as the result of an accident in childhood. He goes to the same tutor as Tom Tulliver, and meets Maggie, whom he first admires and then falls in love with, in spite of the fact that his father and Maggie's father are mortal enemies. 'A pale, puny fellow . . . with brown hair round his face curled and waved at the ends like a girl's . . . who can't run or play at anything', he excites Tom Tulliver's scorn, though even he has to admire Philip's undoubted gifts as an artist. Philip is angry when, after Mr. Tulliver's bankruptcy and stroke, Tom forces Maggie to promise not to communicate with him. But after a separation, during which Philip goes abroad and tries to forget his love for her, they meet again, and Philip is able to help Tom achieve his great ambition of returning to Dorlcote Mill by getting his father, who now owns it, to sell it to Guest & Co. who install Tom as manager. He should have gone with Maggie, Stephen Guest and Lucy Deane on a river picnic, but he is ill, and Lucy is prevented from going at the last moment. So, to Philip's despair, Stephen and Maggie go off together, and although Maggie returns almost at once, Philip goes abroad and does not meet her again. *The Mill on the Floss*

WALSH, THE REV. MR.: The young curate who comes to help Edgar Tryan when he is too ill to work. He conducts Tryan's funeral service about six months after his arrival. *Scenes of Clerical Life III: Janet's Repentance*

WARREN, MR.: Sir Christopher Cheverel's valet. *Scenes of Clerical Life II: Mr. Gilfil's Love-Story*

WATLING, LORD: An eccentric peer, who has a model farm on which he spends all his money. He has a fancy for all-black cattle, and sends his drunken old Scotch bailiff back to Scotland every year with a pocketful of money, to buy them. *Scenes of Clerical Life I: The Rev. Amos Barton*

WAULE, MRS. (JANE): One of Peter Featherstone's sisters, a widow who speaks in a low, muffled tone, as of a voice heard through cottonwool, and always dresses in black crepe. Although she is quite well off, she expects to inherit some of her brother's money, and tries to make mischief between him and his favourite nephew, Fred Vincy. She has a son, John, and three girls, Rebecca, Joanna and Elizabeth, whom Featherstone won't have near him, preferring the company of his first wife's niece, Mary Garth. When Jane finds that Featherstone has not left her anything, she decides to sell some of her land to the railway contractors, but is worried about the effect the trains will have on her cattle. *Middlemarch*

WEBB: A medical man from Crabley whom Lydgate calls in when all the local doctors decide to boycott the new hospital. *Middlemarch*

WEST, MR.: The factor whom Poyser has gone to see about wool, and so misses the visit of Irwine and Captain Donnithorne at which Donnithorne first has a chance to talk to Hetty Sorrel. *Adam Bede*

WIENER, MR.: The jeweller in Leubronn to whom Gwendolen Harleth, having lost all her money at roulette, sells her turquoise necklace to provide funds for her journey home. Daniel Deronda buys it back and returns it to her anonymously. *Daniel Deronda*

WILLIAMSON, SARAH: A Methodist woman preacher in Leeds who is a friend of Dinah Morris. *Adam Bede*

WILLOUGHBY, MISS: Rosamond Vincy's schoolfriend, with whom she several times goes to stay. Mrs. Vincy is hopeful that Rosamond will meet an aristocratic gentleman there whom she can marry, as the family is highly connected. *Middlemarch*

WIMPLE, THE REV. MR.: The vicar of Shuttleton, to whom the Rev. Augustus Debarry takes exception, thinking him typical of the new 'Evangelicals, with their extempore incoherence and their pipe-smoking piety . . . without his gown and bands, anybody would take him for a grocer in mourning.' *Felix Holt*

WINSHIP: The auctioneer who conducts the sale of the household effects at Dorlcote Mill after Tulliver's bankruptcy. *The Mill on the Floss*

WINTHROP, AARON: The son of Ben the wheelwright. His mother helps Silas Marner to take care of Eppie when she is a baby, and the two children grow up together. Aaron becomes a gardener, and when old Moss retires is able to get enough work to justify him proposing to Eppie, with whom he has always been in love. They are married the following spring. *Silas Marner*

WINTHROP, BEN: The Raveloe wheelwright, a jolly, convivial person, who leads the choir on Sundays, and is delighted when his small son Aaron turns out to have a beautiful voice, 'singing a tune straight off, like a throstle'. *Silas Marner*

WINTHROP, DOLLY: The wheelwright's wife, a 'comfortable, good-looking, fresh-complexioned woman', always the first to be sent for in cases of accident or illness in the village. She helps Silas Marner to look after the baby Eppie, giving him her son Aaron's baby clothes, and making sure he and Eppie have enough to eat and a clean house. She even persuades Silas to have Eppie christened, and is her godmother. She is delighted when Aaron and Eppie get married. *Silas Marner*

WIRY BEN: *see* Cranage, Ben

WOODCOCK, MR. AND MRS.: A Shepperton couple who are introduced to the Countess Czerlaski and her brother. The husband, who has a weakness for a pretty face, is much taken with the Countess and makes his wife call on her; but the wife, a plain woman with no fortune, does not like or trust the Countess, and refuses to continue the acquaintance. *Scenes of Clerical Life I: The Rev. Amos Barton*

WOODS: The butcher who supplies the Bartons with meat. They owe him £12, which Amos Barton borrows from Mr. Oldinport. *Scenes of Clerical Life I: The Rev. Amos Barton*

WOOLL, MRS.: An elderly lady in St. Ogg's, whom Maggie Tulliver's aunt Mrs. Glegg despises, 'because she wore her lace before it was paid for.' *The Mill on the Floss*

WRENCH, MR.: An irascible little medic, normally abstemious, but inclined to drink a little too much at parties. He does not like the new doctor, Lydgate, which makes it doubly hard that when he has failed to diagnose Fred Vincy's typhoid, it is Lydgate who treats and cures him. Wrench has a lymphatic wife, who makes a mummy of herself indoors in a large shawl, and they live with their six children, in soiled pinafores, 'in an untidy, grubby house, with black-handled knives, and willow pattern china'. Rosamond, Lydgate's wife, despises them, and Lydgate himself thinks that he would not like to live as Wrench does. Both the Wrenchs are pleased when Lydgate gets implicated in the Bulstrode scandal and has to leave the town. *Middlemarch*

WRIGHT: Mr. Brooke's head stableman. *Middlemarch*

WRIGHT, JACOB: A Dissenter who ran a night-school for working men, mainly youngsters, in Tilston, where Mr. Jerome got his scanty education and his introduction to Methodism. He greatly admired Wright: 'he was a good man, was Jacob'. *Scenes of Clerical Life III: Janet's Repentance*

WYBROW, CAPTAIN ANTHONY: The nephew and heir of Sir Christopher Cheverel. Handsome, but without charm, tending to accept homage from women rather than offer it, he has a weak heart, and his uncle is anxious for him to marry young and have a son. He therefore chooses as a suitable bride for him the daughter of one of his old flames, the elegant and rather haughty Beatrice Assher, and invites her to visit him, with her mother, at Cheverel Court. Anthony is quite ready to fall in with his uncle's wishes, even though he has no particular affection for Beatrice. He has, however, been carrying on a sustained flirtation for some time with Tina, an Italian girl whom Lady Cheverel brought back as a small child from Milan. She has taken the flirtation very seriously and is sure Anthony means to marry her, until he tells her himself that he is engaged to Beatrice. He agrees unwillingly to meet Tina for the last time in the shrubbery, and she goes to the rendez-vous equipped with a dagger, intending to kill him. But when she arrives she finds him dead of a heart-attack, brought on by the agitation of a scene with Beatrice, who is jealous of Tina, and the prospect of having to make a final break with his past. *Scenes of Clerical Life II: Mr. Gilfil's Love-Story*

WYLDE, COUNSELLOR: A man much esteemed by Tulliver, who engages him on his side during the law-suit with Pivart over water rights, which Tulliver unfortunately loses. *The Mill on the Floss*

WYVERN, LORD: A local landowner who is the standard by which everything in the neighbourhood is measured. When Mr. Nolan wishes to impress his hearers with the wealth of his friend Calibut, he says: 'He has a larger rent-roll than Lord Wyvern'. *Felix Holt*

Y

YODDRELL: A farmer near Frick, where the new railway line is to run. Caleb Garth leaves his horse at Yoddrell's when he goes to value some land nearby, and sends his injured assistant Tom back to Yoddrell's on Fred Vincy's horse after they have routed the haymakers who were attacking the railway surveyors with pitchforks. *Middlemarch*

Z

ZACHARY· The pew opener at the Rev. Rufus Lyon's chapel. Lyon employs him to do odd jobs. *Felix Holt*

The small son of the old pew opener. When Lyddy boils the eggs too hard, Esther Lyon suggests giving them to 'little Zachary' to play football with. *Felix Holt*

Animals

BLACKBIRD: Daniel Knott's horse, on which he comes to bring news of Tina Sarti to Cheverel Manor. *Scenes of Clerical Life II: Mr. Gilfil's Love-Story*

BLUCHER: The Bulstrodes' dog. When Raffles is pestering Mrs. Bulstrode, Blucher breaks his chain and frightens him away. *Middlemarch*

BROWNIE: 'An active-minded but probably shallow mongrel' belonging to the Garths. *Middlemarch*

CORYDON: A chestnut horse which Chettam wants to lend to Dorothea Brooke, but she refuses. *Middlemarch*

CRITERION: A beautiful horse belonging to Grandcourt which he lends to Gwendolen Harleth. *Daniel Deronda*

DIAMOND: A dapple-grey horse which Fred Vincy hopes to sell at a profit, but it kicks the groom and lames itself before the sale is completed. *Middlemarch*

DOBBIN: Mr. Lammeter's horse, on which he rides to the Casses' New Year's Eve ball with his daughter Nancy riding pillion behind him. *Silas Marner*

FAG: The Dagleys' sheepdog. *Middlemarch*

FETCH: A liver-coloured spaniel bitch belonging to Grandcourt. *Daniel Deronda*

FIDO: Miss Lydia Donnithorne's fat pug. *Adam Bede*

FLEET: Squire Cass's deerhound. *Silas Marner*

FLUFF: A tiny Maltese dog, with a silver collar and a bell, belonging to Grandcourt. *Daniel Deronda*

FLY: A small black-and-tan terrier belonging to Mrs Farebrother. *Middlemarch*

GIANNETTA: A mule belonging to Tessa's mother, which carries the milk to market. At their first meeting, Tessa gives Tito Melema a drink of milk from the mule's wooden milk-pannier, and the only thing she regrets leaving when she runs away from home to live with Tito is 'the little mule'. *Romola*

GROWLER: The Hall Farm yard dog. *Adam Bede*

GYP: Adam Bede's grey, tailless sheepdog. *Adam Bede*

HAFIZ: A Persian cat belonging to the Meyrick family. *Daniel Deronda*

JET: A little King Charles spaniel belonging to the Countess Czerlaski. *Scenes of Clerical Life I: The Rev. Amos Barton*

JUNO: The Rev. Mr. Irwine's brown setter, who has two pups. *Adam Bede*

KITTY: Mr. Gilfil's black mare, on which he gallops from Cheverel Manor to Callam to find Tina Sarti. *Scenes of Clerical Life II: Mr. Gilfil's Love-Story*

LOLO: Lucy Deane's dog, who dies and is replaced by Minny. *The Mill on the Floss*

MEG: Captain Donnithorne's mare, who was kicked and lamed by one of the carriage horses. *Adam Bede*

MINNY: A King Charles spaniel given to Lucy Deane by Tom Tulliver when she lost Lolo. *The Mill on the Floss*

MISCHIEF: A staghound belonging to Dolfo Spini. *Romola*

MONK: A Great St. Bernard belonging to Dorothea and Celia Brooke. *Middlemarch*

MORO: A black King Charles puppy belonging to the Transome family. *Felix Holt*

MUMPS: A bull terrier of brindled coat and defiant aspect which belongs to the packman Bob Jakin. *The Mill on the Floss*

NIMROD: A black retriever belonging to old Mr. Transome. *Felix Holt*

OLD BROWN: A sober horse that drew Mr. Poyser's cart, with all the family in it, to the celebrations for Captain Donnithorne's coming-of-age. *Adam Bede*

PONTO: Mr. Gilfil's old brown setter. *Scenes of Clerical Life II: Mr. Gilfil's Love-Story*

PRIMROSE: The Rev. Henry Gascoigne's elderly nag, of sober years and ecclesiastical habits, which Rex Gascoigne borrowed without permission to go hunting with Gwendolen Harleth. *Daniel Deronda*

PUFF: A Blenheim spaniel, fat and elderly, which belongs to Mrs. Transome. *Felix Holt*

PUG: Mrs. Irwine's lapdog. *Adam Bede*

RATTLER: The horse usually ridden by Captain Donnithorne's man Pym, which Donnithorne rides because his own horse, Meg, is lame. *Adam Bede*

RUPERT: Sir Christopher Cheverel's bloodhound. *Scenes of Clerical Life II: Mr. Gilfil's Love-Story*

SALLY: A shorthorn cow which Mr. Poyser sells to Chowne. *Adam Bede*

SINBAD: Lucy Deane's chestnut horse. *The Mill on the Floss*

SNAP: Eppie's brown terrier. *Silas Marner*

SNUFF: A brown spaniel belonging to Godfrey Cass. *Silas Marner*

SPECKLE: Mr. Lammeter's old grey horse. *Silas Marner*

TANCRED: Stephen Guest's bay horse, on which he rides out to Aunt Moss's farm for a painful interview with Maggie Tulliver. *The Mill on the Floss*

TORTOISE: The Garths' cat. *Middlemarch*

TRIP: the Poysers' black-and-tan terrier. *Adam Bede*

TROT: A tiny spaniel, the inseparable stable companion of Captain Donnithorne's mare Meg. *Adam Bede*

VIXEN: A brown-and-tan bitch belonging to Bartle Massey. He saved her from drowning, and was very annoyed when she had puppies on a Sunday, which prevented him from attending Thias Bede's funeral. *Adam Bede*

WILDFIRE: Godfrey Cass's hunter, fatally injured in a fall while being ridden by Godfrey's brother Dunsey. *Silas Marner*

YAP: A white-and-brown terrier belonging to Maggie Tulliver. *The Mill on the Floss*

YARICO: A black horse on which Grandcourt rides to Offendene to propose to Gwendolen Harleth. *Daniel Deronda*

The Characters—Book by Book

Adam Bede

	Book	Chapter
Alick	I	6
Allen, Sister	I	3
Bacon, Miss	I	15
Baker, Will	2	21
Bale, Kester	6	53
Barnes, John	4	30
Bede, Adam	I	1
Bede, Lisbeth	I	4
Bede, Seth	I	1
Bede, Thias (Matthias)	I	4
Best, Mrs.	I	7
Bethell	4	32
Betty	I	6
Bridget	I	5
Brimstone	2	21
Britton, Luke	I	5
Burge, Jonathan	I	1
Burge, Mary	I	1
Bygate, Mr.	5	44
Carroll	I	5
Casson, Mr.	I	2
Chad's Bess (*see,* Cranage, Bessy)		
Chester	2	18
Chowne, Mr.	2	18
Choyce	I	6
Craig, Mr.	I	9
Cranage, Ben	I	1
Cranage, Bessy	I	2
Cranage, Chad	I	2
Dacey, Lady	I	5
Dalton	I	12
David	6	53
Dingall, Mr. and Mrs.	2	18
Dolly	I	1

	Book	Chapter
Donnithorne, Captain Arthur	I	2
Donnithorne, Lydia	I	9
Donnithorne, Squire	I	2
Downes, Bill	2	21
Dummilow, Job	I	5
Gawaine, Mr.	I	12
Gedge, Mr.	2	17
Goby, Mr.	I	6
Godwin	I	5
Hazelow, Tom	2	21
Holdsworth, Michael	2	18
Irwine, The Rev. Adolphus	I	5
Irwine, Anne	I	5
Irwine, Kate	I	5
Irwine, Mrs.	I	5
James	I	15
John	I	12
Judith	I	6
Kitty	I	6
Knowles	4	32
Marlowe	I	8
Maskery, Will	I	1
Massey, Bartle	I	5
Mills, Mr.	3	23
Molly	I	6
Morris, Dinah	I	2
Mum Taft (*see* Taft)		
Nancy	I	6
Old, Joshway (*see* Rann, Joshua)		
Olding, John	5	43
Ottley, Mr.	I	6
Phillips, Sam	2	21
Pomfret, Mrs.	I	7

Adam Bede (cont.)

	Book	Chapter		Book	Chapter
Poyser, Charlotte (Totty), Marty, and Tommy	1	6, 15	Taft	1	1
			Taft, Billy	2	21
			Taft, Jacob	1	2
Poyser, Martin	1	14	Tholer, Bob	1	4
Poyser, Old Martin	1	14	Tholer, Tom	6	53
Poyser, Mrs. Rachel	1	6	Tholoway, Ben	6	53
Pym	1	12	Thurle, Mr.	4	32
Ralph	5	40	Tim	2	20
Rann, Joshua	1	2	Timothy's Bess (see Salt, Bess)		
Rann, Sally	1	2			
Roe, Mr.	1	5	Timothy's Bess's Ben (see Salt, Ben)		
Ryde, The Rev. Mr.	2	17			
Saft, Tom (see Tholer, Tom			Tod, Josh	1	1
			Totty (see Poyser, Charlotte)		
Salt, Ben	1	2	Townley, Colonel	1	2
Salt, Bess	1	2	Tradgett, Mr.	1	5
Salt, Jim	1	1	Tranter, Gil	1	16
Sandy Jim (see Salt, Jim)			Trent	1	6
Satchell	1	5	Wakefield, Jim	2	18
Sorrel, Hetty	1	3	West, Mr.	1	6
Steene, Widow	1	5	Williamson, Sarah	5	40
Stone, Sarah	5	43	Wiry Ben (see Cranage, Ben)		
Storey, Jacob	2	21			

Daniel Deronda

	Book	Chapter		Book	Chapter
Adam, Mrs.	8	63	Brewitt	8	58
Alcharisi (see Halm-Eberstein, The Princess Leonora)			Buchan	6	42
			Bugle	1	3
			Bult, Mr.	3	22
Angus	7	54	Charisi, Daniel	7	51
Arrowpoint, Catherine	1	5	Charisi, Ephraim	7	51
			Clintock, Young	1	5
Arrowpoint, Mr.	1	5	Cohen, Addy	4	33
Arrowpoint, Mrs.	1	5	Cohen, Adelaide Rebekah	4	33
Banks, Mr.	2	16			
Bazley	3	21	Cohen, Eugenie Esther	4	33
Blough, Lord	5	35	Cohen, Ezra	4	33
Brackenshaw, Lady Beatrice and Lady Maria	1	7	Cohen, Ezra Mordecai (see Mordecai)		
			Cohen, Jacob Alexander	4	33
Brackenshaw, Lord and Lady	7	10	Cohen, Mrs.	4	33
Brecon, Young	2	16	Cohen, Sara	2	17
Brendall, Harry	3	22			

Daniel Deronda (cont.)

	Book	Chapter		Book	Chapter
Cragstone, Lady	4	28	Jarrett	1	6
Crane	5	35	Jeffries	3	21
Croop	6	42	Jenning	1	5
Cushat, Mr.			Jocosa (*see* Merry,		
and Mrs.	2	12	Miss)		
Dagge, Joel	1	7	Jodson, Mr.	6	44
Dagge, Sally	1	7	Kalonymos, Joseph	4	32
Davilow, Alice,			Klesmer, Herr Julius	1	5
Bertha, Fanny			Langen, The Baron		
and Isabel	1	3	and Baroness von	1	1
Davilow, Mrs.			Lapidoth	3	20
(Fanny)	1	2	Lapidoth, Mirah	2	17
Deronda, Daniel	1	1	Lassman, Mr.	1	2
Fenn, Juliet	1	10	Lawe, Miss	1	5
Fenn, Mr.	5	35	Leo	3	20
Fitzadam,			Lilly	6	42
Mr. and Mrs.	5	35	Lush, Thomas		
Fraser, Mr.	2	16	Cranmer	2	11
French, Mrs.	2	16	Mackworth	1	1
Gadsby, Mrs.	1	7	Mallinger, Sir Francis	2	15
Gascoigne, Anna	1	3	Mallinger, Henleigh	2	16
Gascoigne, Edwy,			Mallinger, Lady		
Lotta, and			(Louisa)	2	15
Warham	1	3	Mallinger, Sir Hugo	2	15
Gascoigne, The Rev.			Marrables	6	42
Henry	1	3	Marshall	3	21
Gascoigne, Mrs.			Merry, Miss (Jocosa)	1	3
(Nancy)	1	3	Meunier, Madame	1	3
Gascoigne, Rex	1	6	Meyrick, Amy, Kate,		
Gibbs	7	54	and Mab	2	16
Gideon	6	42	Meyrick, Hans	2	16
Girdle, Mrs.	4	31	Meyrick, Mrs.	2	16
Glasher, Henleigh			Middleton, Mr.	1	3
(*see under,* Glasher,			Miller	6	42
Mrs. Lydia)	2	13	Mirah (*see* Lapidoth,		
Glasher, Mrs. Lydia	2	13	Mirah)		
Gogoff, Mr. and Mrs.	2	12	Mompert, Dr.		
Goodwin	6	42	and Mrs.	3	21
Grandcourt, Henleigh			Mordecai	4	33
Mallinger	1	9	Nash	1	7
Graves, Miss	3	21	Pash	6	42
Halm-Eberstein, The			Pelton, Squire	4	31
Princess Leonora	7	50	Pentreath, Lord and		
Harleth, Gwendolen	1	1	Lady	5	35
Haynes, Mr.	1	2	Phoebe	2	18
Hollis, Lady Flora	2	13	Puller, Mr.	2	16
Hudson	4	31	Quallon, Mr.	1	5
Hutchins	3	25	Quicksett	2	16

Daniel Deronda (cont.)

	Book	Chapter		Book	Chapter
Ram, Mr.	4	33	Stopley, Canon	1	10
Raymond, Mr.			Swinton	4	28
and Mrs.	5	35	Torrington, Captain		
Sarah	6	46	and Mrs.	2	13
Sinker, Mr.	5	35	Turvey	2	16
Slogan, Lord	1	9	Vandernoodt, Mr.	1	1
Stannery, Lord	4	28	Vulcany, Mrs.	1	5
Startin, Mrs.	1	3	Wiener, Mr.	1	2
Stilfox	1	7			

Felix Holt, the Radical

	Chapter		Chapter
Banks, Mr.	1	Hickes, Mrs. (see Denner)	
Batt & Cowley	21	Holt, Felix	3
Bodkin, Brother	5	Holt, Mr.	4
Brent	7	Holt, Mrs. (Mary)	3
Brindle, Mike (Michael		Jabez	1
Brincey)	11	Jermyn, Louisa	5
Button, Peggy	11	Jermyn, Matthew	2
Bycliffe, Maurice Christian	7	Johnson, John	11
Calibut, Mr.	20	Joyce	20
Cherry, Mrs.	12	Kemp, Brother	19
Christian, Maurice	7	Kitty	1
Chubb, Mr. (William)	11	Labron, Lawyer	2
Clement, Sir James	2	Lambert	18
Crow, Mr.	31	Ledru, Annette (see Lyon,	
Crowder, Mr.	7	Annette)	
Cuff, Jacob	31	Lenoni, Dominic (see Dominic)	
Debarry, The Rev. Augustus	3	Letty	39
Debarry, Harriet and Selina	7	Lingon, Arabella	2
Debarry, Sir Maximus	7	Lingon, The Rev. John	1
Debarry, Philip	12	Lukyn, Dr. and Mrs.	4
Denner	1	Lyddy	4
Dibbs	20	Lyon, Annette	6
Dominic	1	Lyon, Esther	5
Dow	28	Lyon, The Rev. Rufus	3
Dredge	11	Makepiece	17
Durfey	Introduction	Medwin	21
Dymock and Halliwell	35	Methurst, Lady Alicia	7
Filmore, Mr.	7	Mitchell	7
Filmore, Mr.	23	Muscat, Mr.	4
Garstin, Peter	2	Muscat, Mrs. Mary	5
Gills	11	Nolan, Baruch	20
Goffe, Mr.	8	Nuttwood, Mr.	3
Gottlib, Mr.	20	Nuttwood, Mrs.	6
Hawkins	17	Old Sleck	11
Hickes	1	Pack	11

Felix Holt, the Radical (cont.)

	Chapter			Chapter
Patch, Ned	28	Tiliot, Mr.		3
Pendrell, Mr.	5	Tiliot, Mrs.		24
Pink, Mr.	28	Transome, Durfey		1
Prowd, Mr.	4	Transome, Harold		1
Putty, James	17	Transome, Harry		1
Quorlen	24	Transome, John Justus		29
Rose, Timothy	20	Transome, Mr.		1
Salt, Mr.	20	Transome, Mrs.		1
Sampson, Mr.	Introduction	Transome, Thomas		29
Scaddon, Henry (*see* Christian, Maurice)		Trounsem, Tommy		20
Scales, Mr.	7	Tucker		33
Sherlock, The Rev. Theodore	23	Tudge, Job		22
Sims, Mr.	28	Wace, Mr.		3
Sircome, Mr.	7	Wimple, The Rev. Mr.		23
Spilkins	28	Wyvern, Lord		2
Spratt, Mr.	11	Zachary		15
		Zachary, Little		26

Middlemarch

	Book	Chapter		Book	Chapter
Abel	7	69	Carter, Mrs.	1	6
Abel, Mrs.	7	69	Casaubon, Dorothea (*see* Brooke, Dorothea)		
Bagster	4	38			
Ballard, Mrs.	4	40	Casaubon, The Rev. Edward	1	1
Bambridge, Mr.	3	23			
Bass, Trapping	8	84	Chettam, Lady	1	10
Beck, Mrs.	3	25	Chettam, Sir James	1	1
Beevor, Mrs.	6	55	Chichely, Mr.	1	10
Bowyer, Mr.	2	16	Clemmens	4	35
Bretton, Mrs.	4	36	Clintup, Mr.	6	60
Briggs	8	84	Cooper, Timothy	6	56
Brooke, Arthur	1	1	Crabbe, Mr.	7	71
Brooke, Celia (Kitty)	1	1	Cranch, Mrs. (Martha)	3	32
Brooke, Dorothea (Dodo)	1	1	Crowse, Mr.	2	14
Bulstrode, Ellen and Kate	3	26	Dagley, Mr.	4	39
			Dibbitts	4	45
Bulstrode, Mrs. (Harriet)	2	13	Dill, Mr.	7	71
			Dollop, Mrs.	5	45
Bulstrode, Nicholas	1	10	Dover, Mr.	6	58
Bunch	1	4	Downes, Kit	4	39
Bunney, Master	8	80	Duncan, Archie	6	60
Cadwallader, Elinor	1	1	Dunkirk, Sarah	5	53
Cadwallader, The Rev. Humphrey	1	6	Farebrother, The Rev. Camden	2	13
Callum	6	56			
Carp, Dr.	3	29	Farebrother, Mrs.	2	17

Middlemarch (cont.)

	Book	Chapter		Book	Chapter
Farebrother, Winifred	2	17	Laure, Madame	2	15
Featherstone, Jonah	1	11	Lemon, Mrs.	1	11
Featherstone, Peter	1	12	Limp, Mr.	7	71
Featherstone, Samuel (*see* Featherstone, Solomon)			Liret, Monsieur	1	2
			Lovegood	1	3
			Lydgate, Captain	6	58
Featherstone, Solomon	1	12	Lydgate, Sir Godwin	4	36
Fitchett, Mrs.	1	6	Lydgate, Rosamond (*see* Vincy, Rosamond)		
Flavell	4	39	Lydgate, Tertius	1	10
Fletcher	7	71	Martha	8	77
Ford, Hiram	6	56	Mawmsey, Mr.	5	45
Freke, The Rev. Mr.	1	8	Medlicote, Lord	2	13
Gambit, Mr.	5	45	Mengan, Mrs.	6	58
Garratt	5	50	Minchin, Dr.	2	15
Garth, Alfred	3	24	Morgan, Miss	1	11
Garth, Ben	3	24	Nash, Nancy	5	45
Garth, Caleb	3	23	Naumann, Adolf	2	19
Garth, Christy	4	40	Noble, Miss (Henrietta)	2	17
Garth, Jim	4	40	Oliver	4	38
Garth, Letty	3	24	Peacock, Mr.	1	11
Garth, Mary	1	11	Pegwell	3	23
Garth, Mrs. Susan	3	23	Pinkerton, Mr.	1	6
Giles	4	38	Plessy, Lord	4	38
Goby, Mrs.	5	45	Plymdale, Mr.	1	11
Griffin, Mr. and Mrs.	2	17	Plymdale, Mrs. (Selina)	3	21
Grinsell, Lord	6	55	Plymdale, Ned	3	27
Hackbutt, Mr. and Mrs.	2	18	Poinçon, Madame	1	1
Harfager, Clara	6	62	Powderell, Mr.	2	18
Hawley, Arabella	4	36	Pratt	4	37
Hawley, Frank	2	18	Pritchard	1	11
Hicks, Dr.	1	10	Protheroe	5	45
Hopkins	4	36	Raffles, John	4	41
Horrock, Mr.	3	23	Renfrew, Mrs.	1	10
Job	3	24	Rigg, Joshua	4	35
John	1	3	Robisson, Mr.	7	70
Johnson	4	39	Sadler	4	36
Jonas	1	5	Sally	3	24
Jonas, Mr.	7	71	Simmons	2	14
Joseph	6	60	Spanning, Dr.	4	37
Keck	4	38	Spicer, Mr.	7	70
Kell, Mrs.	6	62	Spilkins, Mr.	6	60
Kibble	4	36	Sprague, Dr.	2	15
Ladislaw, Julia	1	9	Standish, Mr.	1	10
Ladislaw, Will	1	9	Strype, Mrs.	2	16
Larcher, Edwin	2	18			

Middlemarch (cont.)

	Book	Chapter		Book	Chapter
Stubbs	2	16	Tucker, The Rev. Mr.	1	9
Taft, Mrs.	3	26	Tyke, The Rev.		
Tantripp	1	4	Walter	2	13
Tegg	2	16	Vigo, Mrs.	6	54
Teveroy, Mrs.	6	55	Vincy, Bob	1	11
Thesiger, The Rev.			Vincy, Fred	1	11
Edward	2	18	Vincy, Mrs. (Lucy)	1	11
Toller, Harry	7	63	Vincy, Rosamond	1	11
Toller, Sophy	7	64	Vincy, Walter	1	11
Toller, Thomas	2	15	Waule, Mrs. (Jane)	1	12
Tom	6	56	Webb	5	45
Trawley, Mr.	2	17	Willoughby, Miss	4	36
Triton, Lord	6	54	Wrench, Mr.	1	11
Truberry, Mr.	8	84	Wright	1	6
Trumbull, Borthrop	3	32	Yoddrell	6	56

The Mill on the Floss

	Book	Chapter		Book	Chapter
Abbott, Cousin	1	7	Gore, Lawyer	2	2
Alice	7	4	Gray, Mrs.	1	9
Askern, Mr.	2	6	Guest, The Misses	6	2
Ben	3	9	Guest, Stephen	6	1
Bincome	2	2	Gypsies	1	11
Brumby, Dick	3	6	Harry	1	4
Brumley	2	2	Haxey, Job	3	2
Bucks, Mrs.	5	2	Hyndmarsh, Mr.	3	7
Carr, Mr.	3	3	Jacobs	1	3
Crake, Sir John	2	3	Jakin, Bob	1	6
Darleigh, Squire	3	7	Jakin, Mrs.	1	6
Deane, Lucy	1	7	Jakin, Prissy	6	4
Deane, Mr.	1	7	Jetsome	6	5
Deane, Mrs. (Susan)	1	7	Kenn, Dr.	5	9
Dickison, Mr.	1	8	Kezia	1	6
Dix	1	3	Kirke, Miss	7	4
Dodson	1	6	Leyburn, Miss	6	1
Dolly	1	12	Luke	1	4
Fawks, Bill	3	6	Martha	1	7
Firniss, Miss	2	7	Moggs, Luke		
Furley	3	1	(see Luke)		
Gadsby	1	3	Moggs, Mrs. (see		
Garnett	1	7	under Luke)		
Gell	6	5	Morton, Mr.	1	12
Gibbs, John	1	2	Moss	1	8
Glegg, Mr.	1	7	Moss, George, Lizzy,		
Glegg, Mrs. (Jane)	1	7	and Willy	1	8
Goodrich, Mr.	2	4	Moss, Mrs. (Gritty)	1	8

The Mill on the Floss (cont.)

	Book	Chapter
Patch	2	2
Pelley's Bank	6	5
Pepper, Mrs.	5	2
Pivart, Mr.	2	2
Poulter, Mr.	2	4
Pullet, Mr.	1	7
Pullet, Mrs. (Sophy)	1	7
Rappit, Mr.	1	9
Riley, Mr.	1	3
Sally	1	9
Salt	5	2
Spence, Mr.	3	5
Spray, The Rev. Mr.	1	12
Stelling, Laura (*see under* Stelling, Mrs. Louisa)	2	1
Stelling, Mrs. Louisa	1	3
Stelling, The Rev. Walter	1	3
Stott, Mrs.	1	3

	Book	Chapter
Sutton, Mrs.	1	7
Tilt, Mr.	6	12
Timpson	1	3
Torry, James	3	5
Torry, Miss	6	6
Torry, Mrs.	7	4
Torry, Young	6	6
Tulliver, Maggie	1	1
Tulliver, Mr.	1	2
Tulliver, Mrs. (Bessy)	1	2
Tulliver, Ralph	4	1
Tulliver, Tom	1	2
Turnbull, Dr.	3	1
Wakem, Lawyer (John)	3	7
Wakem, Philip	2	3
Winship	3	7
Wooll, Mrs.	1	7
Wylde, Counsellor	2	1

Romola

	Book	Chapter
Acciajoli, Dianora	1	12
Alexander VI, Pope	1	14
Antella, Lamberto dell'	3	56
Antonio, Luca	1	12
Baccio	3	49
Bardi, Bardo de'	1	5
Bardi, Dino de' (*see* Luca, Fra)		
Bardi, Romola de'	1	5
Barone, Ser Francesco di Ser (*see* Ceccone, Ser)		
Bartolommeo, Fra	2	25
Benedetto	3	68
Benevieni, Girolamo	2	25
Berta, Monna	1	12
Boni	3	51
Bonsi, Domenico	2	29
Braccio, Ser	1	20
Bratti (*see* Ferravecchi, Bratti)		

	Book	Chapter
Brigida, Monna	1	12
Calcondila, Demetrio	1	6
Calvo, Baldassarre	1	9
Cambini, Andrea	3	59
Caparra, Niccolò	1	1
Capponi, Piero	2	25
Cecca	1	8
Cecco	3	42
Ceccone, Ser (Ser Francesco di Ser Barone)	3	45
Cei, Francesco	1	8
Cennini, Bernardo	1	4
Cennini, Domenico	1	4
Cennini, Pietro	1	8
Charles VIII of France	2	21
Cioni, Ser	1	1
Corsini, Luca	2	21
Cosimo, Piero di	1	4
Credi, Lorenzo di	3	49
Crinito, Pietro	1	3

Romola (cont.)

	Book	Chapter		Book	Chapter
Cristoforo, Fra	1	12	Nola, Jacopo di (see Calvo, Baldassarre)		
Cronaca	1	8			
Domenico, Fra	1	12	Oddo	2	22
Dovizi, Bernardo	1	13	Pazzi	2	39
Dovizi, Piero	1	13	Pico, Giovanni	1	16
Fantoni, Gian	3	43	Pippo	3	50
Ferravecchi, Bratti	1	1	Pitti, Piero	2	39
Gaddi, Francesco	2	26	Politian (Poliziano),		
Ghita, Monna	1	2	Angelo	1	3
Girolamo, Fra (see Savonarola, Fra Girolamo)			Ponzo, Fra Menico da	1	1
			Porta, Buccio della (see Bartolommeo, Fra)		
Giuliano, Fra	3	65			
Goro	1	1	Pucci, Giannozzo	2	39
Guccio	1	1	Puglia, Fra		
Guicciardini, Piero	3	58	Francesco di	3	63
Jacopo	3	68	Ridolfi, Giovan		
Landino, Christoforo	1	13	Battista	3	58
Lillo	2	33	Ridolfi, Niccolò	2	39
Lisa, Monna	2	33	Romola (see Bardi, Romola de')		
Lollo	1	22			
Luca, Fra	1	8	Rucellai, Bernardo	2	38
Lupo	2	34	Rucellai, Camilla	3	52
Machiavelli, Niccolò	1	3	Salvestro, Fra (see Maruffi, Fra Salvestro)		
Manetti, Sibilla	3	70			
Mariano, Fra	1	12	Salviati, Marco	3	65
Mariano, Fra	3	64	Sandro	1	3
Maruffi, Fra Salvestro	2	41	Sasso, Meo di	3	43
Maso	1	5	Savonarola, Fra		
Matteo	2	39	Girolamo	1	15
Mazzinghi,			Scala, Alessandra	1	7
Domenico	3	64	Scala, Bartolommeo	1	7
Medici, Giovanni de'	1	13	Sforza, Ludovico	2	21
Medici, Piero de'	1	3	Soderini,		
Melema, Tito	1	1	Pagolantonio	2	25
Michele, Fra	3	45	Spini, Dolfo	2	25
Naldo (see Melema, Tito)			Tacco, Maestro	1	16
			Taddeo	3	66
Nanni	1	1	Tessa	1	2
Nardi, Jacopo	3	72	Tornabuoni, Lorenzo	2	22
Nello	1	1	Trecca, Monna	1	1
Nerli	2	39	Vaiano, Maestro	1	10
Nero, Bernardo del	1	6	Valori, Francesco	1	12
Niccolò, Fra	3	64	Vespucci, Giovanni	1	18
Ninna	3	50	Vespucci,		
Nofri	1	10	Guidantonio	2	29

Scenes of Clerical Life I: The Sad Fortunes of the Rev. Amos Barton

	Chapter		Chapter
Alice	3	Gilfil, The Rev. Maynard	1
Bagshawe, The Rev. Mr.	6	Hackit, Mr. and Mrs.	1
Baird, The Rev. Mr.	6	Higgins, Mary (*see* Fodge, Poll)	1
Barton, The Rev. Amos	1	Hood, Jem	1
Barton, Chubby, Patty, and Sophy	2	Jackson, Miss	5
		John	3
Barton, Dickey, Fred, and Walter	2	Johns, The Rev. Mr.	2
Barton, Mrs. Milly	1	Landor, Mrs.	4
Betty	1	Madeley, Dr.	8
Blarney, Lord	3	Nanny	2
Bond, Miss	5	Nisbett	6
Bond, Mr.	5	Oldinport, Mr. and Mrs.	1
Bond, Mrs.	2	Old Maxum	2
Brand, Mr.	5	Parry, The Rev. Mr.	1
Brick, Mrs.	2	Patten, Mrs.	1
Bridmain, Edmund	2	Phipps, Miss	4
Carpe, The Rev. Mr.	6	Phipps, Mrs.	4
Cleves, The Rev. Martin	6	Pilgrim, Mr.	1
Cramp, Mrs.	10	Porter, Sir William and Lady	3
Czerlaski, The Countess (Caroline)	2	Prior, The Rev. Mr.	6
		Pugh, The Rev. Mr.	6
Dolby	6	Rachel	8
Duke, The Rev. Archibald	6	Radborough, The Deane of	3
Ely, Parson	1	Sargent, The Rev. Mr.	6
Farquhar, Arabella and Julia	2	Silly Jim	2
Farquhar, Mr. and Mrs.	2	Spratt, Mr.	2
Fellowes, The Rev. Mr.	6	Tomms, Jacob	7
Fitchett, Mr.	2	Tozer, Mr.	10
Fodge, Poll (Mary Higgins)	2	Watling, Lord	6
Furness, The Rev. Mr.	6	Woodcock, Mr. and Mrs.	3
Gibbs, Miss (Janet)	1	Woods	2

Scenes of Clerical Life II: Mr. Gilfil's Love-Story

	Chapter		Chapter
Albani, Maestro	3	Cheverel, Sir Christopher	2
Assher, Beatrice	5	Crichley, The Rev. Mr.	12
Assher, Lady	5	David	1
Assher, Sir John	5	Dorcas	4
Bates, Mr.	2	Ford	21
Becky	19	Francesco	2
Bellamy, Mr. and Mrs.	2	Fripp, Dame	1
Bond, Tommy	1	Gilfil, The Rev. Maynard	1
Brooks	7	Griffin	5
Cheverel, Lady (Henrietta)	2	Hackit, Mr. and Mrs.	1

Scenes of Clerical Life II: Mr. Gilfil's Love-Story (cont.)

	Chapter		Chapter
Hart, Dr.	16	Pazzini, La	3
Hartopp, Mrs. Bessie	2	Pickard, The Rev. Mr.	1
Heron, The Rev. Arthur	20	Pilgrim, Mr.	1
Hester	7	Ramble, Squire	19
Hibbert, Miss	5	Richards, Patty	11
Higgins, Mrs.	1	Sally	1
Jennings, Mrs.	1	Samson, Dr.	11
Knott, Daniel	4	Sarti,	3
Linter, Lady Sara	5	Sarti, Caterina (Tina)	1
Markham, Mr.	2	Sharp, Mrs.	2
Martha	1	Sitwell, Sir Jasper and Lady	1
Oldinport, Mr. and Lady		Stokes, Master Tom	2
Felicia	1	Tarbett, The Rev. Mr.	1
Parrot, Bessie and Selina	1	Tina (see Sarti, Caterina)	
Parrot, Mrs.	1	Warren, Mr.	2
Patten, Mrs.	1	Wybrow, Captain Anthony	2

Scenes of Clerical Life III: Janet's Repentance

	Chapter		Chapter
Ann	14	Landor, Benjamin	2
Armstrong, Mr.	7	Landor, Eustace	2
Beale, Molly	4	Landor, Miss	2
Betty	5	Landor, Mr.	2
Brady	17	Linnet, Mary	3
Brinley, Mrs.	13	Linnet, Mrs.	3
Budd, Mr.	1	Linnet, Rebecca	3
Butts, Sally	26	Lizzie	8
Byles, Luke	1	Lowme, Bob	2
Cook, Phib	4	Lowme, Mr.	2
Crewe, Mr. and Mrs.	2	Lowme, Mrs.	2
Dawes	17	Lucy	18
Dempster, Janet	3	Madeley, Dr.	27
Dempster, Mrs.	5	Marriott, Ellen	5
Dempster, Robert	1	Martin, Mrs. and Sally	3
Dunn, Mary	5	Mercer, Joseph	3
Gardner, Maria	5	Paine, Mat	4
Gruby, Mr.	1	Parry, The Rev. Mr.	11
Hardy, Jim	26	Pettifer, Mrs.	3
Horner, The Rev. Mr.	2	Phipps, Alfred and Ned	2, 6
Jerome, Mr. (Thomas)	2	Phipps, Miss	2
Jerome, Mrs. (Susan)	8	Phipps, Mrs.	2
Job	21	Phoebe	15
Kitty	17	Pilgrim, Mr.	1
Lakins, The	23	Pittman, Mr.	2
Lamb, Jonathan	5	Poole	25

Scenes of Clerical Life III: Janet's Repentance (cont.)

	Chapter		Chapter
Powers, Bill	4	Silly Caleb	4
Pratt, Eliza	3	Smith, The Rev. Mr.	2
Pratt, Miss	3	Stickney, The Rev. Mr.	2
Pratt, Mr. Richard	2	Thomson, Liza	21
Prendergast, The Honourable		Thrupp, Mr.	3
and Reverend Mr.	5	Tomlinson, The Misses	2
Proctor	7	Tomlinson, Mr.	1
Pryme,Mr.	13	Tooke, Mrs.	13
Radley	11	Townley, Miss	5
Ratcliffe	6	Traunter, Deb	1
Raynor, Anna	25	Trower, Mr.	1
Raynor, Mrs.	3	Trufford, Lord	0
Ricketts, Dame	4	Tryan, The Rev. Edgar	2
Robins, Clara	5	Wagstaff, Mrs.	3
Rose, The Rev. Mr.	2	Walsh, The Rev. Mr.	27
Sally	8	Wright, Jacob	8
Sandeman, Squire	8		

Silas Marner

	Part	Chapter		Part	Chapter
Blick, Dr.	1	11	Kimble, Mrs.	1	10
Bryce	1	3	Ladbrook, Mrs. and		
Cass, Bob	1	11	Miss	1	11
Cass, Dunstan			Lammeter, Mr.	1	6
(Dunsey)	1	3	Lammeter, Nancy	1	3
Cass, Godfrey	1	3	Lammeter, Priscilla	1	5
Cass, Squire	1	3	Lundy, Bob	1	6
Cliff, Mr.	1	6	Macey, Mr.	1	1
Coulter, Ann	1	2	Macey, Solomon	1	11
Cox	1	3	Malam, Justice	1	7
Crackenthorpe, The			Marner, Silas	1	1
Rev. Mr.	1	6, 11	Mott, Mr.	2	16
Cromlech, Lord	1	4	Oates, Jinny	1	8
Dane, William	1	1	Oates, Sally	1	1
Dowlas, Mr.	1	6	Osgood, Gilbert	1	11
Drumlow, The			Osgood, Mr.	1	3
Rev. Mr.	1	6	Osgood, Mrs.	1	2
Eppie (Hephzibah)	1	12	Paston, The Rev. Mr.	1	1
Farren, Molly	1	3	Rodney, Jem	1	1
Fawkes, Bessie	2	16	Sarah	1	1
Fowler	1	3	Snell, John	1	6
Gunn, The Misses	1	11	Tedman, Dame	1	11
Jay, Betty	1	3	Tookey, Mr.	1	6
Jortin	1	4	Winthrop, Aaron	1	6
Keating	1	3	Winthrop, Ben	1	6
Kench	1	7	Winthrop, Dolly	1	10
Kimble, Dr.	1	2			